BUSINESS CORPORATIONS AND THE BLACK MAN

Chandler Publications in
The Applications of Management

Waino Suojanen, *Editor*

BUSINESS CORPORATIONS AND THE BLACK MAN

An Analysis of Social Conflict: The Kodak-FIGHT Controversy

S. PRAKASH SETHI

University of California, Berkeley

With a Foreword by

JAMES FARMER

Assistant Secretary of Health, Education, and Welfare

And an Introduction by

Dow Votaw

University of California, Berkeley

CHANDLER PUBLISHING COMPANY
An Intext Publisher · Scranton, Pennsylvania 18515

To

My Mother

Contents

Foreword

By James Farmer

The extraordinary, if not bizarre, events in Rochester in 1966 and 1967 assume new significance in Dr. Sethi's conceptual framework. What was viewed merely as a militant black organization's confrontation with an industrial giant, becomes an instructive lesson in the nature of systemic changes now taking place in American society at a dizzying pace.

It is a different ballgame now and the rules are new, and this book brings skillful analysis to bear in defining the game and comprehending the rules. What happens to paternalism when the child grows up? What happens to the formulae which have traditionally governed race relations in the nation when the factors in each equation have been shattered and reassembled in a constantly shifting pattern? What happens, as Langston Hughes asked, "to a dream deferred? Does it dry up like a raisin in the sun . . . or does it explode?" The explosions which have rocked the land since 1964 have merely posed the questions, not answered them. The answers will lie in the responsiveness of America's power equations to the demands of the powerless for shared power—politically, economically, institutionally. Such responsiveness can only follow—it will not precede—the kind of understanding which Dr. Sethi helps us achieve.

In earlier generations the nation reeled under the pummeling of the working class, as its members demanded to help fashion the decisions governing their lives. Their demands, too, were "nonnegotiable"—as a first step in negotiation; and they were demands, not requests. The nation's corporate power was shocked beyond belief at this encroachment upon its "management prerogatives." It absorbed the assault, accommodated the demands, and enlarged the parameters of democracy. Now, new "outsiders" are hammering on the door to the conference room. Blacks, Puerto Ricans, Mexican-Americans, students demand a seat at the decision-making table. They are the consumers of the goods and services. Formerly a "field of exploitation" for American industry, to use Dr. Sethi's words, they now insist upon being eyeball-to-eyeball equals, partners in improving the quality of life, their own life.

I hope that American business will hear the message of these pages in time to prevent Langston Hughes' question from becoming die-hard prophecy. The strong institution, like the strong man, is not of iron, but of rubber.

United States Department of Health, Education, and Welfare
Washington, D.C.

Introduction

By Dow Votaw

Many corporation executives will not read this book. Some of them may come, sooner or later, to regret the omission. When Franklin Delano Roosevelt Florence, representing the Rochester social-action group FIGHT, appeared in the executive offices of Eastman Kodak at 10 A.M. on September 2, 1966, and said: "I want to see the top man," he began to administer, albeit inadvertently, a series of lessons which Kodak, and others who took the time to observe the proceedings, would probably never forget. A company which rested confidently, secure in the belief that its record of responsible public and private service would protect it from social conflict, was to become, within a few months, the target of unprecedented hatred, vitriol, and accusations, not just in Rochester, but in the nation as a whole. As one of Kodak's executives said, "It is inconceivable that it could happen to us."

The theme of Professor Sethi's book is that most of the unhappy consequences which followed Minister Florence's visit could have been avoided. Although certain lessons on how *not* to respond to social conflict can be learned from the Kodak experience, Sethi does not stop there. The real value of *Business Corporations and the Black Man* is found, not in a simple exposition of the "Kodak-FIGHT case," but in Sethi's development of a theoretical framework against which the Rochester episode, and others in the future, can be tested and in his construction of basic guidelines for corporate responses to social conflict. Although the literature is by now voluminous, the study of social institutions, and especially of social conflict, is still essentially in its infancy. It will take many more case studies than Kodak and many more theorems than Sethi's to provide society with reliable methods of achieving understanding of its institutions and efficient tools for dealing with its conflicts, but a start has to be made. In the relatively narrow area of the confrontation between corporations, on the one hand, and the aspirations of racial minorities, on the other, Sethi has made a valuable beginning.

Sethi sees Kodak's basic error in the company's traditional responses to challenges which were not of a traditional sort. Kodak tried an "industrial relations" response to a challenge which had little, if anything, to do with wages, conditions of employment, or even bargaining rights—an error compounded by the fact that Kodak, as a nonunion firm, had rather specialized industrial-relations policies and strategies in the first place. Kodak tried a "public relations" response to an indictment which the company did not really understand and which was not, in essence, a public-relations issue. The results were major blunders by a company which, for good reason, had always taken pride in its successful efforts to maintain a good public image. Eastman Kodak also attempted a legal response to a nonlegal challenge and managed only to destroy communication with the challenging group.

Perhaps an even more basic error on the part of Kodak and its officers was in losing touch with the realities of what was going on in the minority community. For example, an organization which had its radar tuned in accurately to the society in which that organization worked would have known that the meaning of the term "radical" had changed, that self-identified "radicals" are not necessarily far left, new left, or Communist, and would not have got "uptight" over a word that really was not very threatening. Feeling threatened, however, it is not surprising that Kodak fell back on traditional responses to challenge. Overreactions and outright blunders were sure to follow and did.

The collision between Kodak and FIGHT was not an isolated episode. It reached dramatic levels of intensity and attracted national attention as a result of the way events developed and not because the issues were unique. Had Kodak responded a little differently to FIGHT's demands, had the unfortunate Mr. Mulder not received confused instructions and signed, as a consequence, the agreement of December 20, 1966, had Kodak listened to what Minister Florence was trying to say, instead of hastily, arbitrarily, and irrevocably repudiating the agreement, the course of history probably would have been very different. The surface issues changed during the conflict, unquestionably, but more as a result of Kodak's own conduct than anything else.

Episodes with the same potential for drama, and for damage to company and community alike, are taking place in many parts of the country, and it is reasonable to expect that their incidence will increase during the next decade. The struggle of the black minority for recognition, identity, and equality has not reached its peak; the Mexican-American people of California, Texas, and the Southwest have only just begun to manifest their deep unrest; and the arena of social conflict is not limited alone to the aspirations of racial minorities. The corporation which does not know this or does not let the knowledge affect its decisions, conduct, and attitudes is marching down the same trail that Eastman Kodak took. The corporation which believes that it is above the fray or that social conflict is not within its sphere of interest or that a reputation for good deeds and public service will protect it from attack need only glance at Rochester to learn the price that can be exacted for such complacency. The corporation which thinks it will have the support of the community at large and get a "fair shake" from the news media had better take a look at Kodak's experience in 1966 and 1967. Sethi devotes two chapters to the special roles played by the church and the news media in the Rochester events and to the ways in which these two institutions became protagonists in the drama.

A word might be added here for those executives of large corporations who are wondering why the corporations are now often becoming the targets of social unrest and why the corporations are usually not very successful in their responses to these challenges. The Kodak-FIGHT affair provides a magnificent collection of answers. One does not have to read Berle, or Hacker, or Mason to know that the modern corporation has come to play one of the dominant roles in our society and in our local communities. Kodak prided itself on the many ways it used its power and influence in Rochester to support museums, symphony orchestras, colleges and universities, and training programs for the unemployed. It would be surprising, I think, in a time of social unrest and conflict, if such institutions were not important targets for attack. There is little reason these days for

attacking "His Majesty's Government" while holding immune from attack
"His Majesty." Because much social unrest stems from economic origins,
involvement in the conflict of society's chief economic institutions seems
only natural. Sethi suggests also that there is an increasing tendency today
toward recognizing the interactions among the various subsystems in the
whole social system and away from attempts to improve subsystems without taking into account the whole system. The corporation, then, is important and very visible as a social institution, and the causal relationships
between it and social phenomena in general are becoming better understood by everyone.

Why have corporate responses to these new social challenges been so
often unsuccessful? We live in a social environment which is changing
rapidly, and these changes have already had an impact on social attitudes,
concepts, values, and motivations. The great corporations, in many cases,
have not kept pace. Though not always perceived as such, the great corporations themselves have been the major instruments of change in our society for almost three-quarters of a century, a truly revolutionary force.
Largely as a result of these revolutionary changes, other powerful forces of
change are now at work, and the corporations, once the prime movers, are
now becoming also the moved. One of Sethi's underlying premises is that
Kodak was not aware of many of the changes that were taking place and,
as a result, responded to challenge in ways which were no longer appropriate or effective and without understanding the meaning of the challenge.
Corporate structures, strategies, procedures, and attitudes were not appropriate for the day, producing blunders and misunderstandings on all sides,
and virtually destroyed communication with the sources of the challenge.
Sethi warns that it will not be enough simply for the senior executives to
become more aware of the new demands of a changing social environment
and of the new rules and constraints by which social conflicts are worked
out. The awareness must pervade the whole organization. Old structures
and procedures must be held amenable to change. Only in this way can
unsuccessful responses to social conflict be replaced by conduct which is
better calculated to resolve the problems at issue.

The Kodak experience tells us also that "the top man" may have to
play a different sort of role from that to which he has become accustomed. The situation in Rochester deteriorated very rapidly after the senior executives of the company retreated behind their facade of experts and
underlings. Communication broke down; the scope of company representatives' authority became a major issue; the need for consultation with
superiors, and the consequent delays and contradictions, led Minister Florence and the FIGHT sympathizers to conclude that they were getting the
runaround. The prestige and security of "the top man" from FIGHT were
threatened when he was forced to talk with subordinates from Kodak, and
the resulting humiliation and loss of standing did everything except enhance the chances of meaningful discussions between the parties. Presidents and board chairmen may frequently have to enter the arena themselves and expect to stay until the issues are settled and agreement
reached.

Prakash Sethi has done a great deal more than write a "business-school
case." He has provided the theoretical foundations on which the "case"

can take on meaning and has used the meaning to construct guidelines for policy and procedure. Even without the Kodak-FIGHT case, the foundations and guidelines make this book interesting and worthwhile reading for corporate officers, students, and the general public. It places on a sound and rational basis a phenomenon with which all Americans are going to become more familiar.

University of California
Berkeley, California

Preface

This book developed out of my studies on the role of business corporations in a changing social system. Business corporations today find themselves confronted by new groups, especially those representing minorities, who question the social value of the economic services the corporations perform, whose demands defy long-accepted criteria of economic efficiency, and, more important, whose strategies and tactics seem to violate all the rules of the game.

Much as business corporations might wish it to be otherwise, these confrontations are likely to increase, both in number and intensity, in the future. Unless we develop a conceptual framework within which these confrontations can be analyzed and some method found to deal with them constructively, there is a very real danger that such conflicts will lead to mutual hatred and permanent distrust between various elements of American society. More important, the result might be a net economic and social loss for society that no one wants but that no one might be able to control if the situation is allowed to drift.

The case of Eastman Kodak and its confrontation with a local minority group called FIGHT (Freedom, Integration, God, Honor—Today) was especially suited for this study not only in terms of the nature of the conflict but also in terms of the environment which gave rise to it and to some extent conditioned the outlook and determined the strategies followed by the different parties. This case appears to be but the first major incident of its kind. It involved a major corporation that, according to currently acceptable criteria of performance, is economically successful and socially responsible. It also involved the major religious denominations in issues which were hitherto considered outside the purview of traditional church activities. The conflict thus offers an opportunity to study the implications of this new role for both church and society. It also provides an example for the study and evaluation of the strategies used by militant minority groups to achieve their professed goals. Finally, it gives evidence for the study of the behavior of a community under pressure for change both from within and without and of the role of the various news media not only in reporting the conflict but in shaping its course and direction.

Depending on the viewpoint of the reader, this book may appear to be a criticism of either Kodak or FIGHT. Criticism it is, but it is also protest: a protest against the stubbornness of business in its refusal to see these conflicts as anything but the actions of a misguided minority; a protest against some of the actions of minority groups which, following an initial success, become obsessed with militant tactics without taking into account the cost—alienation of supporting groups both black and white, increased resiliency on the part of the corporations, and overreaction by the forces of law and order—and thereby escalate the conflict to the point where tactics become an end in themselves and, therefore, self-defeating. Honest criticism, to some extent, is always personal, and to be useful must be constructive. This book is therefore also an expression of hope in that it is a search for positive alternatives to conflict.

I owe an intellectual debt of gratitude to Professor Ivar E. Berg, Jr., of Columbia University, who first exposed me to the problems in the area of corporate social behavior and who, by his dedication and sense of commitment, aroused my interest and a desire to pursue this field of inquiry. For reading and commenting on the manuscript, thanks are due Professors Edwin Epstein and Ray Miles, University of California, Berkeley; Professors Lee Preston and Myron Fottler, State University of New York, Buffalo; and Professor John Logan, University of South Carolina. I am grateful to Kenneth Howard and Charles Fitzgibbon of the Eastman Kodak Company, Rochester, for giving me access to company data and for providing information on company policies and strategies. Thanks are also due Michael Hawkins, who helped in the research for the book.

Acknowledgments are due to the Institute of Business and Economic Research at Berkeley for partial financing of the project, and to the School of Business Administration, University of California at Berkeley, for typing and clerical assistance in the preparation of the manuscript.

S. Prakash Sethi

Berkeley, California
January 15, 1969

Business Corporations and the Black Man

CHAPTER 1

A Theory of Social Systems
and the Role of Business

There are moments in history when nations and societies must radically alter their institutions if they are to survive. New conditions, new needs, newly conscious and articulate groups call for new kinds of responses and responsiveness from the institutions that make society run. — James M. Gavin, Chairman, Arthur D. Little, Inc.

The dissent visible in the American social system during the past decade has now attained crisis proportions. Groups of all sizes and all persuasions march and picket both the "Establishment" and one another on every conceivable issue. To a large extent, this dissension has to do with significant changes that have taken place in the institutional arrangement of American society. One analyst [120] * has said:

These are changes in allegiance to institutions, in the location of social functions, in the relationship of men and the norms of culture, and above all, in the source and diffusion of political power.

The irony of the situation, however, lies in the fact that while its economic institutions have provided the nation with goods and services of unprecedented magnitude, the business corporation, which is the most dominant of economic institutions and a uniquely American phenomenon, has come under increasing attack by all segments of society. Instead of earning the nation's gratitude, business corporations have been accused of polluting our air and waters and turning vast areas of natural beauty into wastelands. In their desire to generate ever increasing profits, business corporations are said to have produced goods and services of dubious social value, manufactured shoddy and even potentially dangerous goods for public consumption, and constantly attempted to thwart public investigation through effective lobbying and mass propaganda.[1] Further, to suppress public criticism of their actions, business corporations have also been charged with using coercive tactics to intimidate dissenting individuals, both within and without the corporation, and to curtail such constitutionally guaranteed individual rights as freedom of speech and freedom of association.[2]

Corporations in a Changing Social Milieu

The criticism has not been confined to professional muckrakers or misguided sociologists; it has been equally vocal from various respected economists and other members of the Establishment. These critics have raised issues that are of wide concern to society. They suspect the corporations of usurping the rights of other social institutions which satisfy the noneconomic needs of society. They voice concern about a value system, presumably fostered by business institutions, in which private needs are given priority over communal needs and in which the gap between the haves and have-nots continually widens.[3]

*Citations are given in full in the References section at the end of the book.

1

Business institutions are not without their defenders, however. Business can still present an impressive lineup of supporters, with impeccable credentials, who can offer weighty arguments favoring the business system and justifying the conduct and behavior of business institutions. If anything, these scholars criticize those who seek changes in the goals pursued by business as meddlers who will make the social system inefficient, slow the rate of progress, lower the standard of living, and even threaten individual freedom—economic, political, and social. These supporters of the business system—a system in which the allocation of resources is determined in the marketplace by the forces of supply and demand and in which every individual and firm pursues those activities which, within the confines of the law, generate maximum profit—link economic freedom with social and political freedom, and chide those corporate executives who seek to temper their quest for profits with other social goals.[4]

Notwithstanding the economic contributions to society made by the business system or the eloquent defense of the market mechanism by its proponents, criticism of business and especially of large corporations has been widespread and intense. Since business institutions cannot survive in a vacuum, they have been increasingly concerned about the public antagonism to their social role and legitimacy. Their initial reaction was to attribute this antagonism to misunderstanding and ignorance, which could be cured by a mass public-education campaign. This strategy, followed during the 1940's and 1950's, still has a substantial number of adherents in the business community. However, as William Whyte noted in his book *Is Anybody Listening?* [175], this billion-dollar attempt "to sell business to America" was a miserable failure. The campaign was based on the mistaken belief that the American people need convincing of the virtues of free enterprise. Little thought was given to the possibility that the corporations also might need to reconsider their role in society.

Of late, an important debate has developed among corporate managements as well as in the public at large about the social role of the large corporation. The issue encompasses a variety of problems, ranging from what the terms "public interest" and "social responsibility" really mean, to matters of an operational nature, such as the criteria of accountability, measurement, and determination of priorities for different choices—all of which are seemingly in the (by some definition) public interest. Although the key problems of this debate are by no means resolved, there is a definite trend toward recognition of the legitimacy of some social claims on the profits of the corporation, in addition to the claims of stockholders.

The corporations have come a long way from their original self-concept as economic institutions that exist solely to maximize profits for the private benefit of the owners. The separation of ownership from control, the large and floating nature of stockholders (and their ineffectiveness in controlling management), the ever increasing size of large corporations and the corresponding breadth of economic and social impact of their decisions, the professionalization of management—these factors have all combined to speed up change in the concept of the corporation.

Followers of the classical liberal tradition tend to be chagrined by this trend. These scholars do not doubt the good faith of the proponents of social responsibility, but they consider the latter misguided and their arguments self-defeating. If corporate managers were to be socially responsible, these theorists contend, they would also have to be both more powerful and more open to abuse. To require social responsibility would remove the criterion of economic performance without substituting any definite or precise new criteria. In any case, this argument runs, corporate managers are not appointed for their competence in determining what is socially desirable but for their ability to produce and distribute goods efficiently. Providing more and better goods desired by the community is a legitimate social goal which the corporations have fulfilled. Indeed, any distraction from that function would be detrimental to the long-term interests of society, for no social services can be provided unless the national economy is strong.

Corporate managements face a dilemma for which neither their training nor their background provide a guide. In the normal functioning of business, today's reality is far different from yesterday's theory. The concentration of industrial resources in fewer and fewer hands is a fact of life—and has often been spurred by competitive pressures generated within the American economy. Thus, while corporations pay lip service to the myth of a free market economy, they continually face the possibility of violating antitrust laws because of their continuous effort to gain better control of the market forces. The dichotomy between the myth of a free market economy and the reality of the concentration of economic resources and corporate power was best summarized by Galbraith [51] when he wryly pointed out that the corporations which the State Department shows to its foreign visitors as model employers and showcases of American efficiency and enterprise are very often the same corporations whose officers are visited by lawyers from the Justice Department.

Even though the concept of social responsibility has come to be increasingly accepted by the corporations, there remains a major disagreement between the public and the corporations about the nature and scope of that social responsibility. The corporations insist on the purely voluntary nature of their involvement with social problems and resort to such terms as "corporate conscience" or "corporate statesmanship" to describe the restrictive and nonobligatory nature of their actions. According to Votaw and Sethi [167],

There is scepticism on both sides as to the conviction and sincerity with which the views of the other side are held. The wide acceptance among the corporations of some sort of social responsibility, for example, has been attributed to status anxiety, expediency and the decline of corporate legitimacy, rather than to an accurate perception of a social role. The implication is usually present in these attacks that the men of corporate business may have been thinking, but neither greatly nor about the right functions. It is hardly necessary to point out that the corporations have responded in kind.

That the conflict between business institutions and society exists cannot be denied. What is not clear, however, is to what extent this conflict has been caused by a change in social conditions and to what extent it could be attributed to deliberate actions taken by the corporations.

The purpose of this book is twofold. First, I intend to develop a theoretical framework within which the relation of the business corporation to other social institutions, both existing and emerging, can be examined in terms of social goals and value systems. I aim to show the process by which the value system of a society changes, necessitating an alteration in the value systems of the constituent institutions within the society, a readjustment in the distribution of power and role assignments among various institutions, a new ordering of priorities, and a new set of rules by which interinstitution as well as intrainstitution conflicts can be resolved. Second, by means of a case study, I intend to provide some insight into the workings of this theory and into the inapplicability of those operational strategies followed by business institutions which do not take into account the changed nature of the social system. The paramount concern is to provide a conceptual framework within which a corporation can evaluate its existing goals and strategies of action and also develop guidelines for future policies.

The study is not intended as an evaluation or criticism of the policies followed by the firm and other parties in the case. Nor is it intended to be a comparison with the activities of other corporations in similar situations. Social systems comprise a large number of institutions, each of which is involved in an infinitely large and varying number of actions. To say that one action determines or even reflects the underlying trend in the system would be naive and misleading. What I aim to show is the extent to which environmental factors, both external and internal, could propel various parties in directions which they might not have pursued had they analyzed their proposed strategies within the framework of a social system where all elements of society are intricately linked together and are affected by one another's actions.

Social Systems: A Theoretical Framework

The role of business corporations cannot be studied in isolation either on temporal or spatial dimensions, divorced from its environment and other social institutions. A social system is a complex arrangement of individuals who organize themselves into various institutions—subsystems in the main system—to perform various activities and to pursue commonly accepted goals. A well-functioning social system must do the following:

1. Crystallize the goals of the total system and its subsystems and provide for a systematic procedure by which these goals can be changed over time.

2. Create a system or order of rules by which interaction between the units in a subsystem and between various subsystems in the total system is regulated.

3. Ensure a congruity between the total system's goals and those of its subsystems.

4. Develop criteria and procedures by which individual members or institutions can change their allegiance away from existing subsystems and form new subsystems with different goals.

A social system, however, is not merely the sum total of its subsystems; it is much larger and has a life of its own. The technological orientation of today's society has increased the degree of interdependence between various subsystems. Society is therefore not a mere expression of economic self-interest of individuals or of a particular subsystem, but is held together by a system of mutual though varying delegation of interconnected and interdependent social obligations. Social well-being can exist only insofar as each unit performs its functions and receives proportionate benefits. As Churchman [24] pointed out,

[W]e seem forced to conclude that anyone who actually believes in the possibility of improving systems is faced with the problem of understanding the properties of the whole system, and that he cannot concentrate merely on one sector. The problem of system improvement is the problem of the "ethics of the whole system."

If a philosophy of society is to be effective, it must be as dynamic and realistic as the forces it must control. American society is in rapid motion; it is being rocked by new ambitions and haunted by new terrors. The present is so different from the past that both success and failure have lost their original meanings. Of all the established institutions, religion and business have come under the most searching scrutiny as to their role in society. The isolation of economic aims as a specialized object of concentration and systematic effort, and the escalation of economic criteria into an independent and authoritative standard of social expediency, though acceptable under yesterday's conditions, no longer seem relevant to the members of an affluent society.

What, then, can corporations do to anticipate changes in the social environment and to bring their actions into congruence with the expectations of society? To understand the role of business corporations and the expectations society has of business, let us again turn to social theory and see how social goals are determined and how social tasks are allocated.

The social goals or value sets of a society at any given time represent the consensus of its individual members and constituent units as to their expectations, aspirations, and modes of behavior. According to Chamberlain [20],

The value set also establishes the norms which govern economic strategy. The internal distribution of power; the accepted avenues of social change; the ways in which interpersonal competition is expressed; sentiments which determine the roles and rights of the young, the elderly, women, minority groups; . . . these and other persisting guides to conduct growing out of a society's values will delimit the manner in which specific objectives are sought.

However, it must be clearly understood that any single criterion-economic or otherwise—cannot determine a society's value set, which must be satisfactory to all its constituent units and produce an optimally integrated system. Wherever a society exists, there exists a system of obligation and rights. A social system incessantly creates these reciprocal relations between every man and all other men.

Thus, it would be fallacious to argue that a society can produce a unique hierarchy of social choices—alternative uses of its resources—by some criterion of economic efficiency. By doing so, the society might maximize its economic resources without maximizing all of the satisfactions desired by its members. As Bell [10] has pointed out,

In the "real" world, the problem of social priorities, of what social utilities are to be maximized, of what communal enterprises are to be furthered, will be settled in the political arena by "political" criteria—i.e., the relative weights and pressures of different interest groups balanced against some vague sense of the national need and the public interest. But it is precisely at this point that the problem becomes most irksome. For increasingly, one of the "issues" of a Great Society—which can be defined as a society that seeks to become conscious of its goals—is this relationship between "rationality" and "politics." The Great Society aims to rise above "mere" politics toward some kind of rational political behavior—but rigorous theoretical analysis leads us back to "mere" politics.

Establishing Goals for the Total System

Political rationality, defined as the rationality of the decision-making structure to produce results which are socially acceptable, is therefore the only kind of rationality applicable to total systems.[5] Economic rationality is secondary to other, subjective criteria, such as desire, personal gratification, and group equality, in that these criteria provide goals for calculation while technical and economic rationalities furnish the actual calculation process. [33]

The value set of a social system is affected by three sets of considerations: past history, futuristic orientation, and dissatisfaction of individuals and institutions with the status quo.[6] We inherit from our past not only physical possessions, traditions, and values, but also a system of structuring data and analyzing new phenomena. The evolution of ideas and the quality of civilization depend not so much on the transmission of physical possessions or natural endowments as on the complex structure of habits, knowledge, and beliefs. History provides us with the raw material from which we construct generalizations which are essential to prediction. The evolved set of rules and regulations brings about a stability in social relations. The past, however, does not regulate behavior; it merely conditions it. Chamberlain [20] has written:

Present behavior depends not only on where one has been but also on where he proposes to go. . . . It would then seem that behavior is not predictable solely by reference to observed regularities arising from the past but must also rely on present purpose, which may not be predictable from the past.

An ongoing social system has a purpose, which gives its value set a futuristic orientation causing existing value sets to be continuously examined. In a highly technological society, internal changes within the system when combined with its futuristic orientation cause changes in the environment. These changes are often so abrupt and different that even the most recent experiences are rendered invalid. The increased interdependence of subsystems, which is inevitable in a technologically oriented society, makes it necessary that the social system *plan* for changes in its value set if its purpose and future goals are to be realized. However, as Bell [9] pointed out,

The irony is that the more planning there is in a society, the more there are open group conflicts. Planning sets up a specific locus of decision, which becomes a visible point at which pressures can be applied. Communal coordination—the effort to create a social choice out of a discordance of individual personal preferences—necessarily sharpens value conflicts.

Subsystems within a Social System

A social system consists of various subsystems which differ in relative size, in basic function, in the satisfactions they generate for their members, in the influence they exercise over the lives of individuals they touch, and in the powers they exert against each other and over the community. [169] The subsystems within a total system have their own value sets which are largely self-defined to give specific expression to those needs of their members which can be satisfied only in narrower space, time, communal, and personality dimensions.

Individual members of a social system have a large number of different social needs which they can satisfy only through forming a variety of combinations with other members of the system. That there are different needs gives rise to a large number of subsystems within the total system, with each individual belonging to more than one subsystem. Thus, one may find an association corresponding to every possible human interest. A community is constantly arranging and rearranging itself into associations —permanent and transient. Moreover, since individual needs change over time, it is important that there be adequate provision in the social system to allow individuals to form new institutions (subsystems) and to change their allegiance from existing institutions. Such a social system can be identified as pluralistic, flexible, and stratified.

The underlying assumption is that the existence of a large number of subsystems is a necessary prerequisite for the freedom of individual members of society. However, these subsystems, over a period of time, develop a life and momentum of their own which may not only result in greater conflict between the goals of a subsystem and those of the total system, but also alienate a system from its *raison d'être*, namely, fulfilling the needs of its members. While subsystems may protect individuals from totalitarianism and even against the possibility of ascent to power by one subsystem, they do not safeguard an individual from the excesses of the institution to which he belongs. To do so would be to restrict the power of the institution and, therefore, would be contrary to its own interests. Large corporations and large unions may counteract each other's power in determining the economic aspects of an individual's life; organized church and secular educational institutions may balance each other in their influence on the development of human thought; and organized political parties may offer individuals alternative political ideologies by which they can govern themselves. However, as McConnell [102] has pointed out,

[The various subsystems] do not protect the members of any of these groups when they are threatened by their own organizations. To provide such protection, countervailing organizations would have to exist *inside* the associations or, alternatively, they would have to be very nearly parallel or rival associations between which members might move without being deprived of the benefits that go with association membership.

To an extent, the divergence between the goals of a subsystem and those of the over-all system on the one hand, and between those of its members on the other hand, is to be expected. Nevertheless, the divergence between the goals of the subsystem and those of the over-all system can never be total, or a subsystem would be swiftly liquidated. Because each subsystem has a functional role to perform, there is guaranteed a large measure of meshing in the objectives of the subsystem with those of the total system. Although the objectives of subsystems are self-defined and more closely oriented toward their members, subsystems do not follow the dictates of either the total system or their membership in quiet subservience. Consequently, subsystems operate in a complex bargaining relationship situation, as opposed to a monolithic chain of command, where conflicting objectives and needs are constantly negotiated, reappraised, and adjusted to assure maximum achievement of the objectives of the subsystem without injury to the performance of the total system.

Conflicts between and within Subsystems

A dynamic social system and its subsystems are constantly under pressure to change. The need for change results from the reaction of individuals to new circumstances and their consequent efforts to comprehend these circumstances, make them meaningful, and build them into new values and new systems of allegiance. As Nisbet [120] has pointed out,

It is thus a matter of conflict *within* a social system-family, or community, or church—and more significantly, a matter of frequent conflict *among* institutions. For, since each institution is a pattern of functions and meanings in the lives of individuals, and hence demanding of individual loyalties, the change in one institution—the loss or addition of functions and meanings that are vital—most frequently react upon the structure of some other institution and thus awaken conflicting responses in the mind of the individual . . . .

These pressures are of three kinds. One, they may result from an abrupt or even violent occurrence outside the system, forcing the system to change its over-all objectives and thereby setting up a chain reaction for readjustment within the system. Two, the futuristic orientation of the system may lead it to change its current objectives, necessitating alterations in the relationship among its subsystems and the distribution of social power among them. Three, as Tannenbaum [163] believes, all major social institutions, in their own inner logic, tend to be all-embracing—laying claim to the entire man and showing an impelling tendency to assume all responsibility for the governance of society. Conflicts arise when there is pressure for a shift in the balance of power from one dominant institution to another. These conflicts are not confined to the struggle for power between various subsystems, but extend to similar struggles among different units within a subsystem. As has been mentioned earlier, one manner by which an individual can escape the tyranny of an existing institution is to form a parallel institution, which should be possible because of the voluntary nature of these institutions. However, in real life, established institutions have shown an intolerance for rival organizations. The history of church, labor, business, political, and other voluntary organizations is replete with accounts of bitter conflicts, often mutually destructive, when attempts were made to create parallel organizations.[7] The appeal is made to a notion of unity against some external enemy, with little or no regard for the needs and aspirations of the dissident members who should have an equal right to regroup into organizations which more closely fulfill their needs.

This emphasis on unity results in a deepening rift between an institution and its members. If individual members find it difficult to form rival associations, the next alternative open to them is to change the institution from within. However, even here the individual comes up against obstacles which are equally insurmountable. No association can be efficiently run directly by the membership; some kind of leadership must be initially created to make an organization function. However, once created, the leadership controls the organization not only by its superior competence and knowledge but also through the use of such devices as office records, inside information, and organization funds to perpetuate its control and name its heirs. Consequently, leaders come to acquire a different outlook and different interests and to assume a different status from their followers. As McConnell [102] pointed out,

Organizations become conservative; leaders tend to identify their own interests with those of the organization and seek to preserve the foundations of their own position, thus laying the foundation for conflict between leaders and led. The identity that is commonly assumed to exist among the interests of all within the organization is therefore false. And in contests between leaders and led, the former have virtually all the advantages.

Three imperfections in the existing system and the interrelationships among the subsystems may cause disruptions in the total system. These inefficiencies or imperfections may arise because of time lag between expectations and performance or because of occasional dissatisfaction of the members with the distribution of power and rewards as lasting compromises are being made between the subsystems and the over-all system, among the subsystems themselves, and within each subsystem. As such, these interruptions are temporary and do not call for substantial change in the value sets of the various subsystems. Adjustments, when needed, are of a marginal nature.

The over-all system develops a whole body of regulations by which it sets limits to the free play of self-interest by the existing subsystems and the forces which oppose them in order to provide for a smooth and nondisruptive adjustment process. This body of regulation can be called the "legal rationality" of the total system by which disputes between various subsystems are adjudicated. These regulations may remain unformulated and traditional, as in a primitive community ruled by "unwritten law," but usually the most essential of these relationships of right and obligation are set out in clear formulas, as political laws, and protected by a central authority endowed with communal power. [101] In Chamberlain's [20] words:

Changes occurring in population composition, tastes and technology may briefly upset the tendency to systematization, but to the extent possible they are assimilated into familiar behavioral patterns and the process of consolidation into regularities rolls on.

However, it must be borne in mind that a successful working of legal rationality implies an acceptance, whether deliberate or unconscious, of the objectives (and their premises) of the total system by the members of the system.

Some inefficiencies in the system may, however, be of a more permanent nature and may modify the conditions under which the evolutionary process of adjustment in the social system takes place. The current institutions may collude with each other and use the regulatory process—whose sole purpose was to smooth out the temporary interruptions in the system —to freeze the existing relationships. Schwartz [157] maintains that the large-size units in a social organization are prone to substitute compulsion for persuasion and to emphasize discipline rather than liberty. The long-established institutions become more interested in maintaining the stability of the present order. Custom, law, and bureaucratic regulation are used to force deviant elements into expected behavior patterns; those elements which do not fit into the system are labeled as destructive and, therefore, undesirable.

This stability, however, perpetuates the dissatisfactions among the individual members in the subsystems as the avenues of change and freedom to develop new subsystems are no longer open to them. The total system is no longer flexible. Although it displays all the trappings of a stratified system, it becomes in fact a monolithic system incapable of responding to the needs of one or more segments of its membership. The ensuing struggle between the haves and the have-nots, under these circumstances, could be quite violent, causing permanent and irreparable damage to the fabric of the over-all system with an outcome no one could have predicted or may have wanted.

The state's role in the total system is somewhat unique. First, as one of the subsystems, the state vies for its share of social power to achieve those objectives which its constituent members demand. Second, as manager of the over-all system, the state administers that set of rules and regulations designed to settle temporary disputes between different subsystems and smooth over temporary disruptions in the system within the existing value set of the society. The third and perhaps most important role of the state often consists in speeding or slowing the rate of change that would occur if existing relationships among the subsystems were allowed to stand within the framework of current social objectives. For it is this rate which would determine whether the dispossessed and the deprived could adjust themselves to changed conditions, and avail themselves of new opportunities, without seriously damaging their substance, human and economic, physical and moral.

Business as a Subsystem

Business institutions have had a preferred position in Western civilization since the advent of the market economy. This status has been especially true in American society, where the need for continuous business expansion is taken for granted and the catchword for politics is the encouragement of private enterprise. In a system where the prime concern of the total system is to provide for the basic physical needs of its members, the enhanced position of business is quite understandable. Economic objectives under such conditions assume a high priority which must be achieved even at the cost of other social objectives. Since economic objectives can be attained only by business, it makes sense to allow the latter maximum latitude to exercise initiative and discretion in performing its function, namely, producing goods and services. However, as Chamberlain [20] pointed out, this high degree of autonomy permits business to treat society itself—the system of which it is a part—as a field of exploitation for its own ends. It is as though a department or plant of a company were free to exploit any opportunities it could find within the company.

In a sense, this single-minded preoccupation of business to achieve its goals aggressively has brought about the conflict situation that we face today. First, the abundance of goods and services produced by business institutions has had its costs in the form of a deteriorating physical and social environment. Second, an affluent society is no longer willing to assign economic objectives the same high priority as before affluence. Pollution of air and water and discrimination against minorities are but the most obvious and pressing examples of physical and social decay, none of which is solely the making of either large corporations or even business as a whole. Local communities, including some of the biggest ones, contribute more to pollution by burning garbage and dumping untreated or partially treated refuse in rivers. Individuals discriminate against minorities in personal contact and in housing. School districts and private institutions discriminate in education. Corporate behavior, ironically enough, often constitutes "good citizenship," adhering to local custom and abiding by local law.

Why is it, then, that business institutions, especially large corporations, are being held accountable for social ills for which everyone is to blame? The answer is a complex one. Hitherto, economic values have been predominant in American society, and business corporations have constantly tried to encourage this identification. Social ills are therefore associated with economic goals and economic institutions. Furthermore, business institutions have been slow to recognize changes in the environment and in social objectives, with the result that they have either ignored these environmental changes or resisted them, with consequent injury to both the business institutions and the social system.

The long delay in correcting the social ills caused by almost unrestricted exploitation of our physical and human resources has introduced an element of extreme emergency in the social equation that has made impossible an evolutionary process of adaptation to a new situation. Business institutions, by and large, still do not recognize that changes in the role of subsystems within the over-all system depend on public decision as to whether social objectives are better served by further limiting or by increasing the subsystem's discretion. The insistence of business on being judged *only* by the traditional criterion of economic performance and by none other is typified in the following quotation from the *Harvard Business Review* [64]:

If we all understood the basic ground rules of private enterprise a little better, we would realize that the large corporation is not a rain god, and that no amount of prayer or incantation will unleash its power. The spectacle of otherwise sophisticated people going on bended knee to companies and pleading with them to have the kind of conscience and moral sensibilities only rarely found in individuals is nothing less than laughable.

In a fast-changing environment, business goals can be achieved only if business changes its course. To be able to do so, business institutions must first become sensitive to these shifts in external environmental conditions that have made the past a less effective guide to the future. Unfortunately, such sensitivity has generally not been characteristic of business. In narrating the behavior of various large corporations under severe stress, Smith [162] observed, "Unhappily, corporate difficulties are more often the result of inaction in the face of a dangerous change than of being the hapless victim of circumstances." While corporations are not insensitive to social needs in the sense that managements do not set policies that will work obvious hardship on those affected, they are often insensitive in failing to detect the real issues at stake or to foresee the results of their acts. [159] The problem lies with the naive and self-delusory assumption by business that the only changes which need be made in its behavior are "rational" (that is, economic and technological), whose effect on the social system is gradual and therefore predictable.. However, the phenomena which are the subject of observation have themselves changed radically over time, thus requiring new objectives as well as different rationalizations for existing objectives. These radical changes comprise, among other things, those minority groups which have been deprived of their share of economic gains or of an opportunity to develop their own subsystems to bargain for economic gains with other subsystems in order to alter the over-all social goal. Second, society at large, concerned about the pollution and waste of its natural resources, is no longer impressed by business's economic contributions or its achievements in efficiency in production—regardless of costs in human welfare. Economists like Galbraith question the logic whereby the production of electric toothbrushes supposedly adds to our national vigor while the provision of low-income housing is considered beyond the nation's pocketbook. Similarly, many scholars question whether it is not time for some economic efficiency to be sacrificed, if necessary, in order to preserve our natural human resources and promote a qualitatively richer life.

Corporate actions affect the lives of millions of people far beyond the narrow scope of the economic aspects of their lives. Therefore, the question of control of corporate resources and the legitimacy of this control raises serious questions of a political nature. Ostensibly, corporate managements derive their power from the stockholders. However, studies by Berle, Means, and others have proved beyond doubt that there is a separation between the ownership and the control of corporations and that management by and large is self-perpetuating. The extent of self-discretion and its impact on all the members of the over-all system make it imperative that corporations be subjected to some form of social control other than the nonexistent control by stockholders or the invisible hand of the market mechanism.

Any appreciation of the goals of the over-all system by the business subsystem must allow for the fact that unless industry is to be paralyzed by recurrent revolts on the part of individuals in other subsystems, it must satisfy criteria which are not narrowly economic. A reasonable view of its possible modifications must recognize that subsystem objectives must always be subject to the control of some larger body of interests. Unless business changes its goals and cooperates with the total system in curbing, instead of promoting, the nation's appetite for material goods, it cannot expect to stop the deprived minorities from demanding those goods. When these minorities find that they cannot succeed either in changing the social goals or in acquiring the wherewithal which signifies success in terms of these goals, they resort to the only avenue available to them, namely, the defiance of those rules and regulations of the social structure which prevent their acquisition of economic goods. In the final analysis, it is not the economic goods that the minorities desire but the social success which these goods represent. As Polanyi [133] has pointed out,

The outstanding discovery of recent historical and anthropological research is that man's economy, as a rule, is submerged in his social relationships. He does not act so as to safeguard his individual interest in the possession of material goods; he acts so as to safeguard his social standing, his social claims, his social assets. He values material goods only in so far as they serve this end. Neither the process of production nor that of distribution is linked to specific economic interests attached to the possession of goods; but every single step in that process is geared to a number of social interests which eventually ensure that the required step be taken.

The process of adjusting or adapting to a changing external environment is likely to be different for different units of the business subsystem. According to Chamberlain [20],

[Each firm] has its own history which necessarily differs in some respects from the history of other firms, leaving it with a set of conditions which renders it both more or less vulnerable and more or less favorably situated with respect to the environmental circumstances with which it must cope.

The Case of Eastman Kodak

The case study that is closely analyzed in this book to see the relevance of our theory of social systems to real-life situations concerns an episode during 1966-1968 involving the Eastman Kodak Company, a major corporation located in Rochester, New York, and a local minority group called FIGHT (Freedom, Integration, God, Honor—Today). In September 1966, FIGHT asked Kodak to hire and train 600 minority-group members—to be selected and referred to Kodak by FIGHT—over an 18-month period. Kodak management refused to accede to these demands on grounds of economic considerations, management's prerogatives, and nonexclusion of other minority groups active in the community. The ensuing struggle, which eventually involved the entire community, also received national attention because of its possible impact on other business corporations, other minority groups, and other communities.

Although the Eastman-FIGHT confrontation is an isolated incident and, if studied by itself, may be of little value in offering any guidelines for future action, it cannot be perfunctorily dismissed. The incident represents a pattern for what may occur repeatedly in different cities beset with essentially similar issues. Here is a city with a good growth rate in new jobs and an affluent corporation with an enlightened management and an enviable record of helping the minorities and the communities where it has its plants and offices. Yet Rochester was not immune from the kind of controversy over minority rights that bitterly divides all social groups within a community.

To what extent can the lessons of Rochester be applied to other areas and similar incidents? To answer this question, we must first put it in the context of a theoretical framework that enables us to analyze the actions of various parties so as to bring out both the underlying reasons for the conflict and the individual and social motivations that give rise to different and often self-defeating behavior patterns. Just as a theoretical formulation without empirical validity is little more than an academic exercise, no amount of data or case histories can offer useful generalizations unless viewed within a conceptual framework where the logical connections between various elements of a system have been carefully thought out beforehand. Such a theoretical framework has been presented in the preceding sections for an analysis of the case study that follows.

Doubtless, to some extent each incident is unique. Both Kodak and FIGHT were victims of their own traditions, organizational frameworks, personal prejudices, and of the social environment within which they operated. However, with the help of theory, we can isolate those features of an incident which are nothing but outer manifestations of basic underlying causes. These underlying causes are of a more general nature and represent elements and conditions that affect and are affected by more than one subsystem in a society. Furthermore, theory helps in determining the parameters within which a problem can be usefully analyzed and the limits within which generalizations developed earlier can be effectively applied. Studied in this light, the case offers an opportunity to analyze the following elements of our theory of the social system:

1. The case offers an excellent example of an external environment in turmoil where not only the value set of the total system is in a state of change but also there is pressure for reexamination of the goals of other subsystems. Consequently, there is uncertainty about objectives and hesitation about deciding on a right course of action. There is no longer any surety as to the balance of power and conventional relationshps among various subsystems. We suddenly find nonbusiness institutions, for example, churches, news media, and other community organs, taking positions on questions which were considered outside their purview. The corporation finds itself accused of performing its economic function "callously" (read: efficiently), for which it was praised before. Suddenly, the rules of the game seem to be changing and there seems no clear-cut guide as to what the corporation is supposed to do and, more importantly, as to who is supposed to decide about the new goals of the system as well as the rules by which intrasystem relationships are to be regulated.

2. The case also offers an occasion to study the role of two institutions, in addition to Kodak and FIGHT, which are not ordinarily considered as part of economic disputes. These institutions are the church and the news media. The parts played by these institutions were instrumental in vitally changing the character of the Kodak-FIGHT controversy. Their involvement raises questions which are important not only for business corporations and minority groups but also for the members of the church, the users of the news media, and society at large. No analysis of the case would be complete without putting these two institutions into the same conceptual framework along with Kodak and FIGHT.

3. The case also throws light on the problems created by various individuals both inside and outside a given institution who wish to develop new associations. It throws light on the need for different allegiances, for a rearrangement of current relationships, and for a redistribution of social power. The case also affords an opportunity to develop an understanding of how new associations are formed, nurtured in their embryonic stage, and matured in a pluralistic and stratified social system. It also brings to the surface the nature of stresses imposed on the system when new institu-

tions attack the inflexibility and rigidity that have existed in the system due to the desire of established institutions to maintain the status quo and to hold onto their share of social power.

4. Similarly, we can study the actions of a major, well-established unit of a subsystem, that is, business, which suddenly finds itself in a hostile situation that is not entirely of its own making. We study the response patterns of such an institution to other institutions and subsystems and see the extent to which this institution plans its actions and responses and to what extent its posture is dictated by external circumstances and social expectations, real or imagined, as to its role in the social system.

5. Finally, the case study offers an opportunity to analyze the performance of the corporation's decision-making structure under severe stress of the kind which it is not geared to face. We will try to understand the cause of the breakdown in communication, both internal and external, and the decision-making structure of the corporation when faced with unusual situations and the consequences that follow from such a breakdown.

The ultimate objective is to develop some guidelines which might assist the various parties in foreseeing similar problems in the future and preventing their occurrence or at least minimizing their impact. An understanding of the causes of disruption in the social system and an appreciation of the possibilities of various alternatives are likely to make the process of transition and adjustment smoother and less violent, to the benefit of all concerned. The case study is not intended to suggest the faults of various parties. Nor will it automatically suggest any self-evident and definitive solutions to be followed in similar incidents. If it is successful in stimulating a dialogue and a search for new alternatives, it will have served a useful purpose.

Footnotes for Chapter 1

1. Baker [6], Harrington [59], *New York Times* [54], *Newsweek* [124], Packard [127, 128].

2. Kuhn and Berg [94], *Newsweek* [106], *Wall Street Journal* [143].

3. See, for example, Bell [9, 10], Galbraith [52], Heilbroner [63], and Reagan [139].

4. See for example, Friedman [50], Hayek [62], Henderson [64], and Rostow [151].

5. For the reader who is interested in various concepts of rationality, an excellent treatise is offered in Paul Diesing's book *Reason in Society* [33].

6. The discussion in this section, as well as in the next, is based in part on Chamberlain's book *Enterprise and Environment* [20].

7. As late as October 1968, Walter Reuther's United Auto Workers and Teamsters Union created a new organization called Alliance for Labor Action (ALA) to launch programs for social action by labor. Although the AFL-CIO had no objection to the objectives of the ALA, it nevertheless warned its affiliated unions that any association with the ALA would constitute a violation of the AFL-CIO charter and might mean suspension from the Federation.

CHAPTER 2

The Rochester Incident: Background and Crisis

It is beneficial for businessmen to indulge in introspection and, in the words of Robert Burns, "see ourselves as others see us." It seems ironically fitting that the line should be from Burns' poem, "To a Louse," because that is precisely how some people do see businessmen . . . . – George R. Vila, chairman and president, Uniroyal Inc.

Rochester, N.Y., April 22, 1967 (AP) – A screamy, bloody riot shattered this proud city's self-confidence three years ago. Now racial unrest is bubbling again in Rochester. And again Rochester is asking, why here?

"Somewhere," says a member of the County Human Relations Commission, "something went awry."

His dismay reflects the irony that underlies the current turmoil, an ugly dispute laced with poisonous telephone calls, mutual threats, even a suicide.

The fact is, Rochester's woe stems from Rochester's weal. There has been a great influx of poor, mostly untrained Negroes lured by jobs and opportunities in greater abundance in Rochester than in the nation as a whole.

An even more bitter irony is that the new troubles seem to spring from apparently sincere efforts to erase the causes that led to the 1964 eruption.

In a sense, the Negro problems of Rochester are different than those of other cities in the nation. Unlike other cities, job opportunities in Rochester have increased at a higher rate than in the nation as a whole. [99]

The City of Rochester

Rochester's unemployment rate of 1.8 per cent in 1966 was the lowest of the 39 major industrial areas in the United States. More than 10,000 jobs were unfilled. Indeed, Rochester companies had had to expand their recruiting programs to New York and Washington, D.C., to sponsor Manpower and Training Development Act programs in their plants, and to develop their own programs. [18]

According to the 1960 census, Rochester was the 38th-largest city in the country. *The World Almanac* for 1968 [179] described New York State's third-largest city as a

world leader in the manufacture of precision goods and a major U.S. cultural center. Located on Lake Ontario, it leads the world in the manufacture of photographic film and cameras, optical goods, dental equipment and thermometers.

Rochester's largest employers are Eastman Kodak (41,000), Xerox Corporation (9,000), and Bausch and Lomb (4,600). Also in Rochester are Taylor Instruments, Fanny Farmer, R. T. French Company, Graflex, Stromberg-Carlson, Bond Clothes, Neisner Department Stores, and Hickey-Freeman.

As reported by *America* [156], in a public-relations ad in the *New York Times* (February 5, 1967), Rochester said of itself,

[We are] a community of more than 700,000 people with the highest percentage of skilled, technical and professional employees of any major U.S. metropolitan area: more engineers than any one of 23 states: the highest median family income of any city in the state, sixth highest in the nation . . . 67 percent of the residents owning their own houses.

16

While the population in the suburbs of Rochester had increased during the period 1960-1967, the population in the city of Rochester had declined from a total of 332,488 in 1950 to an estimated 296,000 in 1967, according to a special census made by the city.

For the Negro, it would seem that things had never looked better. Employment of whites in the county had increased by 11 percent since 1960 but employment of non-whites had gone up 43 percent—more than four times the national average. [18]

The city housed some of the most enlightened corporations in the nation, including Kodak, Xerox, and Bausch and Lomb, with enviable records in labor relations and social-welfare policies. Why is it, then, that such a proud and socially conscious city had to face the humiliation of race riots and that all its efforts toward alleviating the misery of its poor seemed to bear little fruit? Paradoxically, it is precisely this progressive setting which contributed to the problems of the city. Rochester, like other industrialized Northern cities such as New York and Chicago with good job opportunities and liberal health, welfare, and unemployment provisions, acts as a magnet for poor blacks from the South. These Southern regions are, in fact, exporting their problems to the Northern cities which are struggling—thus far unsuccessfully—to cure national ills with local resources. According to Cloward and Piven [27], in June 1951, the Aid to Families with Dependent Children (AFDC) averaged only $14 per person per month in the Southern region. All of the other regions had payment levels almost twice as high: $27 per person per month in the West, $25 in the North Central region, and $27 in the Northeast. Between 1951 and 1966 payment levels rose but still averaged at least 50 per cent higher outside of the South. At the extremes, Mississippi paid less than $8 per person per month, while New York paid $48. Another sharp contrast appears to be in the rate of acceptance in different states of those who apply for assistance. In 1960, the Southern region granted assistance to 48 per cent of those who applied. Elsewhere the rates were appreciably higher: 57 per cent in the Western and North Central regions; 63 per cent in the Northeast. At the extremes, Texas admitted only 34 per cent, while Massachusetts admitted 80 per cent. Stated another way, a family migrating from Texas to Massachusetts improved its chances of getting on welfare almost threefold.

Discrimination of the type mentioned above, when coupled with political and social intimidation, has caused a large-scale migration of the poor from the South to the North and has created problems of massive proportions for the Northern cities. Rochester has been no exception. Even though black employment has increased since 1960, increased black population has wiped out any gains. According to *A Study of the Unemployed* (Rochester Bureau of Municipal Research, January 1967), black employment increased 43 per cent since 1960 as compared to an increase of 46 per cent in the black work force (15,250 to 22,268). The city's black population in 1966 was estimated at 41,000. Three-fourths of the black force is not native to Rochester. Although the 10,000 job openings exceed black unemployment of 2,000 (5,000 is the total Rochester unemployment), a high-school education is prerequisite for 60 per cent of these and a college degree for 15 per cent. Of the 2,000 black unemployed, 54 per cent have less than a ninth-grade education. [156] Up to a point, the city was able to absorb the newcomers successfully; if there were difficulties, they were not conspicuous. Later, however, the increases in employment rates and job opportunities were more than outrun by the increase in population. Because the new jobs are disproportionately of a technical nature, the people most in need of employment were those least qualified for the openings.

There has also been a substantial increase in the Puerto Rican population in Rochester in recent years—to about 12,000 people. Puerto Rican leaders have begun to form their own antipoverty organization to seek government funds for job training, housing, education, and the like separately from other minority organizations, such as the NAACP and the Urban League, whose aims are more closely allied with the black people.

The mass migration not only alters the geography of black welfare eligibility, but also changes the ecology of political power in the Northern cities. Sensing the possibilities for use of its voting power, the black community organizes itself to gain political leverage which results in further welfare and other measures. At the same time, however, the financial problems of already overburdened cities are aggravated by the influx of more poor to the cities and the exodus to the suburbs of the white middle class, thereby eroding the cities' tax base.

Rochester's blacks and other minorities did not fare worse than those of other Northern cities or the national averages. According to the 1960 census, the median income of all families in Rochester in 1959 was $7,177, while the median nonwhite family income was $4,335. At that time families with incomes of under $3,000 a year represented 31.3 per cent of the nonwhite population. There has been some indication of improvement in these statistics; however, in the absence of any firm data, it is not possible to go beyond the conjecture stage.

Even if the improvements were more dramatic and tangible, there is no evidence that the riots or the civil discontent would have been prevented. Recent riots in Washington, D.C., Newark, New Jersey, and Baltimore, Maryland, have shown that the discontent has been most vocal among those blacks who were job holders and that a large number of looters were not those who were either unemployed or on welfare rolls. Various sociologists have tried to explain this phenomenon. For example, Pettigrew [131] has maintained that it is not absolute deprivation but relative deprivation which is the source of dissatisfaction:

One of the principles we seem to have demonstrated in the last twenty years in social science is what we call the theory of relative deprivation. When we talk about social motivation, we are not talking of hunger, thirst, or the other basic psychological drives, but what an individual has, not in absolute terms, but in relation to what he aspires to. It refers to what he realistically and rightfully expects to attain.

. . . [The black's] aspiration levels have risen very rapidly. In fact, his progress of the last twenty years has caused his aspiration levels to go up much faster than his actual gains, even though in some cases these have been dramatic.

Thus after twenty years of progress, particularly in certain areas, the Negro is nevertheless considerably more frustrated today than he was at the beginning of this period of change because, while his absolute standard has been going up, his aspiration level has been rising much faster. His relative deprivation, the difference between what he has and what he expects to have, and what he thinks is his right to have, is now probably greater than at any other time in American history.

Rochester, in 1966, was suffering from all the malaise of a city in the doldrums. The vigor of its industry, the high level of income, and the high rate of employment for the majority of its work force on the one side were matched by the recurrent and persistent problems of its poor. The city's antipoverty and civil-rights programs were not bringing any significant change in the lives of the poor. Public-housing units numbered 450, with only 1,400 more in the planning stage. One school-board member said that school segregation was "more severe than ever." [18] A few organizations, mainly the NAACP and the Urban League, spoke for the poor and the underemployed, but according to an article in the *New Republic*, "the other civil rights organizations don't amount to much. An NAACP rally last year [1966] drew eight people." [144]

Reporting for the *New York Times* [78] on June 20, 1966, John Kifner quoted a minister on the state of the city. Reverend Herbert D. White, a young clergyman who headed the Board for Urban Ministry of the Rochester Area Council of Churches, said:

This is a city with five settlement houses, whose Community Chest Drive always goes over the top, and which prides itself on having every available service. And it's a city which has gone on line—against a lot of opposition—to have an open enrollment plan in the school and a police review board. But one thing that is crucial here is the high degree of affluence in this community. If you are poor in this town, you really know you are poor.

The city is almost a boom town, but not for the black man. The affluence of the whites is everywhere. On the one hand, everything is there for the asking and yet, on the other hand, for the poor, so far away as to be almost unobtainable. For the black, it was a living dream, never to see the daylight, a mirage never to become a reality. At the time FIGHT came into existence, there were no blacks on the city council, the board of education, or the planning commission. There were 602 whites in the fire department and 2 blacks; 490 whites in the police force and 25 blacks. [145]

The Birth and Growth of FIGHT

The city's first riots during July 23-26, 1964, made it clear that something needed to be done if the town was to avoid similar occurrences in the future. However, there was disagreement over the course of action to be taken. The local authorities and civic leaders were hurt. The city, proud of its public and private welfare, felt that the riots indicated a condemnation of its policies and a repudiation of its efforts. The civic leaders were nevertheless not yet ready to try anything radically different or innovative.

The local clergy held a different view and provided a stimulus for a new kind of social environment between the town's people, clergy, business, and minority groups. What was needed, the clergy felt, was an awakening of consciousness among the blacks, together with a viable black organization to provide a dialogue between the minorities and the rest of the community. The initial efforts came haltingly and proceeded along conventional lines. The Rochester Ministers' Conference, an association of black ministers, invited a team from Dr. Martin Luther King's Southern Christian Leadership Conference to visit the black community of Rochester. However, the standard King approach of the team did not stir much enthusiasm among the angry and frustrated men of the community. As an alternative, the team suggested that the Rochester Ministers' Conference seek assistance from Saul Alinsky's Chicago-based Industrial Areas Foundation. [105]

The black churchmen turned for help to the interdenominational Board for Urban Ministry, a semiautonomous offshoot of the Rochester Area Council of Churches. In this effort, they found the board a willing ally. The Board for Urban Ministry believed that the basic cause of the black's discontent was the "lack of a potent organization to raise his hopes and needs" [99] and felt that Alinsky's foundation might be able to direct some of the hatred blacks felt toward whites into a democratic organization that would give them a constructive voice in community affairs. [144] After investigating Alinsky's efforts elsewhere, the Board for Urban Ministry, with the blessing of the board of directors of the Rochester Area Council of Churches, decided to invite Alinsky and set about the task of raising the necessary $100,000 for a two-year contract ($90,000 for expenses and $10,000 for salary). In the weeks that followed, ample support came from the local, regional, and national church bodies as well as from white liberals, and by December 1964 all the necessary funds had been raised. Alinsky went to work.

Much of Alinsky's fame is based on TWO (The Woodlawn Organization), a powerful group now in its tenth year of operation in the slums around the University of Chicago. The Industrial Areas Foundation also has projects in Detroit and Kansas City. Alinsky's name is anathema to the Establishment in these cities, bringing cries of protest from the white community's political officials, businessmen, and newspapers. He was dismissed as a consultant to the federal antipoverty program's demonstration training project for community organizers at Syracuse University, and the project was finally abandoned. [78] Alinsky's *modus operandi* has been to seek out "natural leaders" who, with his help, build a "people's organization" whose goal is self-determination, relying "solely on the force of organized numerical strength with no quarter asked or given." [99] Alinsky's methods have always been controversial; critics say they leave deep scars of division in a community, others see them as the only hope for the have-nots. Alinsky [99] has said,

People don't get opportunity or freedom or equality or dignity as a gift or as an act of charity, they only get these things in the act of taking them through their own efforts. . . .The haves never do anything unless forced.

IAF organizers came to Rochester in early 1965; three months later, in April, 134 black organizations had banded together to form FIGHT (Freedom, Integration, God, Honor–Today). It was no easy task. According to one source [145],

[Alinsky's] rough tactics will be blamed if there is another riot. Alinsky says Rochester, more than most Northern cities, "reeks of antiquated paternalism. . . . It is like a Southern plantation transplanted to the North."

On June 11, 1965, 1,000 delegates met at the first FIGHT convention and adopted a constitution, set policy goals, and elected as president Minister Franklin Delano Roosevelt Florence, who had been acting as temporary chairman since FIGHT's founding in April 1965.

Some of the local leaders who had apprehensions about inviting Alinsky gave an unintended lift to FIGHT's cause and its acceptance among the black community by overreacting to FIGHT's initial efforts to inject itself into local civil-rights causes. For a number of years the city had contemplated the idea of bringing in the Urban League, a moderate national black organization. Perhaps it was sheer coincidence, but when Alinsky's group arrived in town, local businessmen were suddenly able to raise $40,000 and the Urban League opened an office in Rochester. Furthermore, when one settlement house attempted to join FIGHT, the manager of the Community Chest Fund denied it the previously committed funds, saying that "Chest funds could not be used to support FIGHT or IAF work in fulfillment of promises made to contributors." The directors of the Baden Street Settlement lost their nerve and narrowly decided against joining FIGHT; the dissension caused two of the directors to quit the board. Suddenly, Florence had a cause to fight for and a devil to fight against. He accused the Community Chest of discrimination and blackmail. The *New Republic* [145] quoted Minister Florence:

"The establishment feels it can plan for us and not with us," says Minister Florence: The only thing the white paternalists want to know about Negroes is whether they will riot again this year. And that all depends, he adds, "on how soon the whites learn black men are human beings. They are not their simple children."

The going was rough for FIGHT in the beginning, and its main accomplishment was simply its existence. During its second convention on June 19, 1966, one year after its birth, Minister Florence survived a sharp challenge in his second term as president of FIGHT from the Reverend St. Julian A. Simpkins, an Episcopal priest. John Kifner, reporting for the *New York Times* [78], stated that the supporters of Reverend Simpkins contended that the leadership was "too abrasive." According to Kifner, DeLeon McEwen, a barber who was a delegate from the Young Men's Progressive Club (an association of small businessmen), said that much of the opposition had come from middle-class blacks who were disturbed by his tone. "But Minister Florence's support," commented McEwen, "came from the real grass-roots people."

In the first year and a half of its existence, FIGHT's efforts were mainly directed toward federal antipoverty programs and urban renewal. FIGHT attacked as inadequate initial efforts in these areas, and was able to persuade the city to increase the number of planned low-cost housing units. It also controlled an urban-renewal citizens' committee. FIGHT was granted three seats on Rochester's antipoverty board and was itself awarded a federal antipoverty grant of $65,746 for an adult-education program. FIGHT was, to a lesser extent, involved in litigation concerning racial imbalance in the schools. [99, 144] In 1965 "FIGHT picketed a couple of landlords and got some slums fixed up as the result. The leaders also met with the police." [145] Early, FIGHT was so successful that one newspaper columnist accused Rochester of "killing FIGHT with kindness." [18] In addition, FIGHT organized a recruitment and training program, along with other agencies, with Xerox. Cooperating with FIGHT, Xerox started with 16 trainees. The program was expanded to 30 of the jobless and underemployed in 1967. [18]

FIGHT soon claimed to represent three-quarters of Rochester's black community through its component 110[1] black organizations: churches, settlement houses, pool halls, and Black Panther clubs. [18, 144] FIGHT accepted few whites as members, but a more open "Friends of FIGHT" was formed to give support. [99] Many, however, question the validity of FIGHT's claims. [144] Kodak officials[2] say that component groups support FIGHT only in proportion to the intensity of the controversy in which FIGHT is involved. Before December 20, 1966, FIGHT's active membership was low, but afterwards membership may have risen to 300 active supporters. This number dwindled after Kodak's annual stockholders' meeting the following April. [144] According to an Associated Press feature story, directors of a settlement house which FIGHT is supposed to represent "suggested the organization actually speaks for less than one percent of Rochester Negroes. Minister Florence scoffs at that, but offers no hard membership statistics." [99] Rochester's Mayor Lamb has said [165]:

FIGHT represents less than 2 percent of the Negro population of Rochester, and I think he [Florence] is losing more of his power all the time. . . . Believe me, if other firms operated the way Kodak does, this would be a better country to live in. The firm has shown an unusual concern for Rochester.

By the summer of 1966, FIGHT was ready to try something big. In its convention in June, FIGHT resolved that "Eastman Kodak be singled out for special investigation this year." [99] Because of Kodak's size, it was inevitable that FIGHT approach Kodak about jobs, but the FIGHT strategy in dealing with Kodak was to be different from its strategies with other corporations. [105] Florence said, "Taking on Kodak was something else. That just wasn't done in Rochester. But we knew if we could get Kodak in line every other business would follow." The FIGHT president claimed that the black employment of 1,400 at Kodak (of a total employment of over 40,000) was less than fair representation. [99] According to Alinsky [144],

[Rochester] is under the thumb of Eastman Kodak, which also controls the banks, local university, hospitals, etc. The effect of its rule is to shut Negroes away from the rest of the community.

Had its management agreed to work with FIGHT, it would have been a substantial step toward bringing Negroes into the mainstream of Rochester.

Eastman Kodak Company

Eastman Kodak has long been in the forefront of Rochester's industrial corporations. At the end of 1966, Kodak's Rochester plants employed about 13 per cent of the Rochester area's labor force and about one-third of its industrial workers. Kodak has been described as a paternalistic company. [99] Employee benefits are high: according to the annual report for 1966, benefits—including medical and life insurance, retirement annuities, and profit sharing—averaged about $3,500 per employee. [37] Prospective job seekers think highly of their prospects with Kodak. In Rochester alone, the ratio of job applicants to vacancies at Kodak has been 2 to 1. [182]

Kodak products, mostly photographic equipment and supplies, are well known to most Americans. About 41 per cent of Kodak sales is related to professional applied photography and 28 per cent to amateur equipment, films, accessories, and processing services. Another 22 per cent of revenue comes from the sale of fibers, plastics, and industrial chemicals. Special products, including vitamin concentrates, special military items, and government-contracted research and development, account for the remaining 9 per cent. [37]

In 1918, George Eastman, founder of the company, started the Rochester Community Service, which later became the city's Community Chest. [165] He also founded the Eastman School of Music and made large grants for medical facilities and for a community theater. [107] Kodak gave out some $1.5 million for aid to education in 1964. The company enjoys close relationships with Rochester University and other local organizations. [107, 182] It also donates employee time to work in civic causes. Kodak's influence on the community is such that merchants schedule sales to coincide with Kodak bonus checks. [99] Moreover, 20 per cent of Kodak shareowners live in Monroe County, where Rochester is located.

Business Week [47], in commenting about Kodak's position, regarded it as pervasive and its economic muscle as formidable. Though it comes in for some of the resentment dominant companies inevitably arouse, Kodak is considered both a good place to work and a good corporate citizen. Kodak's management is proud of its record and feels a sense of responsibility which as often takes the form of shepherding the flock as of enlightened guardianship of its domain. "Evidence of the company's philanthropy is visible everywhere." [99] In the past decade it has pumped nearly $22 million into the city's hospitals, schools, and Community Chest, and it sponsors a fellowship program for black teachers. Even Minister Florence, during the initial phase of FIGHT's conflict with Kodak, admitted with unusual candor that Kodak "wants to do right." [18]

However, Kodak's evident sense of social responsibility, though contributing to the betterment of community life, resembles that of the benevolent Puritan father who, while making sure of his children's welfare, does not hesitate to discipline them should they fail to measure up to his standards and values. By keeping its employees happy with generous bonuses, good working conditions, and other benefits, the company has remained free of unions and has carefully guarded the established prerogatives of management.

The benevolent-father image is very strong in Rochester and has been fostered so assiduously and for such a long time that to some extent both the community and the company have become its captives. For Kodak to take any action not in keeping with this image would be almost psychologically impossible and with consequences in other areas of its activities on which Kodak might not even want to speculate. As William C. Martin [105] put it,

It is inaccurate to think of Rochester as a company town, but he who underestimates the devotion Rochesterians feel toward Eastman Kodak does so at his own peril. One minister, relatively new to the city, who took FIGHT's side in the controversy between Kodak and FIGHT and found himself cut off from his people, said, "I had, without knowing it, attacked their grandmother. I didn't know that any American industry had so successfully fostered the 'Mother of us all' image. I had shot a mortal blow into their beloved."

In an interview with Raymond A. Schroth, S.J., a spokesman for Kodak was asked to define, in his own words, the company's social responsibility. The spokesman replied that Kodak has a special responsibility, but that since Kodak is a private business, it best helps society by being successful. Kodak did not feel under any special obligation to take extraordinary measures to solve Rochester's particular ghetto problem.[3] [156]

In that it is nonunionized, Kodak is unusual. More than half of the companies in Rochester (including General Motors, General Dynamics, and Xerox) are unionized. One Kodak executive says, "the only explanation is that . . . the laws being what they are . . . people don't feel the need to be represented." The company has said [42]:

Kodak continually reviews its employment policies to assure that they do not present any barriers to the employment of anyone because of race, creed, color, sex, or age. Pre-employment testing is limited to a few jobs which require specific skills or aptitudes.

Kodak employs a great number of scientific and technically trained people (more than 400 Ph.D.'s in 1965). [36]

The company has long had a skilled-trades apprenticeship program which, according to one Kodak brochure [42], consists of up to four years of

combined classroom and on-the-job training leading to a skilled craftsman career as an electrician, instrument mechanic, machinist, pipe fitter, sheet metal worker, or tool or instrument maker. A high school diploma or equivalent and demonstrated mechanical ability are required.

Kodak was one of the first 100 companies to join in President Kennedy's Committee on Equal Employment Opportunity Plan for Progress Program, in June 1962. [42] A management letter of April 25, 1966, describes this company-wide program, which started in June 1962.[4] According to this letter, the company had long done its best "to live within the letter and spirit of the Fair Employment Practice legislation." The company's Plan for Progress included informing all employees by meetings, booklets, and letters of its hiring and promotion policies. The brochure *How Kodak People Are Selected* states that

for any particular job, the person is chosen who appears best fitted to do that job [and] that such things as race, creed, color or national origin neither help nor hinder in getting a job at Kodak. [Moreover,] practically all employee facilities are desegregated. In a few areas where segregated facilities are required by local social custom, desegregation has not been completely accomplished. We will work toward the desegregation of these facilities.[5]

Referring to the Plan for Progress, Kodak's chairman of the board William Vaughn said, "We meant that commitment seriously and we have taken it so ever since." [42]

Kodak has been making efforts to ensure that blacks are aware of opportunities at Kodak. In recruiting nonprofessionals, the company uses a number of community agencies, such as the Human Relations Commission, the New York State Employment Service, the Urban League, Rochester's five settlement houses, high-school counselors (particularly in the inner-city schools), and adult-education administrators. In 1966 Kodak, which contributes to the Negro College Fund, expanded the range of its recruitment of professionals to include thirteen predominantly Negro colleges. During that year the company was involved, with Career Centers, in a program to help place college-trained blacks.

The management letter of April 25, 1966, which was issued four months before the first FIGHT-Kodak meeting, stated:

... you will recognize that our efforts to provide equal employment opportunities are increasingly more positive and far-reaching than in past years. Previously, our policy had been simply to try to employ the person best fitted to do the work available without regard for his or her background. We have moved actively beyond that position. We now seek to help the individual who lacks the necessary qualifications *to become qualified*. In other words, we are contributing to the training of the individual so that he or she can qualify for employment.

The letter recognized that minority-group members were usually those most in need of this training.

At the time of the letter, 156 people (half of them members of minority groups) were enrolled in a special year-long course designed to prepare them for the apprenticeship training programs. Candidates selected for this Skilled Trades Trainee Program were those felt to "have the potential ability but lack the education and training to enter into a skilled trades apprenticeship." The program, begun in 1964, combined on-the-job training with classroom instruction. Two other training programs that were announced in the letter combined classroom and on-the-job training for potential laboratory assistants and machine operators. The Laboratory Trainee Program was expected to start with 12 students in June 1966; the machine-operators program apparently was already in effect.

The teaching in these programs soon became almost tutorial, for trainees' backgrounds were extremely diverse. Kodak instructors were occasionally required to teach at the primary level, but felt inadequate to the task. The company therefore retained a professional adult-education firm, the Board for Fundamental Education (BFE), a nonprofit, nonsectarian, Indiana-based organization chartered by Congress in 1954, which was directing adult-education programs in 29 states. While the BFE handled the classroom aspects, Kodak retained operation of the on-the-job training portion of the program. [53] The BFE program started with 100 students, of whom 40 were enrolled in one of the Kodak training programs and 60 were regular Kodak employees.[7]

More than 200 people were enrolled in Kodak's five training programs in 1966 [42], and 300 more were anticipated in 1967. [99] On October 13, 1966, Chairman Vaughn told a meeting of the STEP (Solutions to Employment Problems) Workshop that he hoped the largely isolated efforts of individual firms in offering training to the disadvantaged could be brought together "in a common, organized effort, [so that] we might all go farther, faster .... Speaking for our company, we are prepared to invest the time of some of our people and, if necessary, some of the wherewithal, to try to bring this objective to reality."[8]

At the stockholders' meeting in April 1967, President Vaughn (subsequently chairman of the board) said, "I think you will find that your company takes a back seat to no company across the nation in this field [that is, civil rights and assistance to minorities]." [42]

In a statement in the *New York Times*, on January 7, 1967, Louis Eilers, executive vice president (subsequently president) of Eastman Kodak, was quoted as saying that there were from 1,200 to 1,500 blacks among the more than 40,000 employees in Rochester, "several hundreds of whom were hired in the last few months." The press report also stated that it was the first time Kodak had released such figures, which included workers for a construction company and other Kodak subsidiaries. It was about one percentage point higher than the 2 per cent that FIGHT had estimated. [74] In Rochester, the employment of the members of *all* minority groups at Kodak totaled 4.2 per cent of all employees at the end of 1967, compared with 3.5 per cent in 1966. Approximately 10 per cent of the new hirings in 1967 were members of minority groups, roughly the same percentage as in the prior year. Kodak officials say that the rate of Kodak hiring has kept pace with the increases in Rochester's minority-group population but that total minority-group employment percentages are small because 50 per cent of Kodak personnel were hired before the minority-group population became significant.[9] In addition, a Kodak official emphasized that there were not many blacks available at the professional or technical levels. In 1967 Kodak hired 20 professional-level blacks through its Negro college recruitment, Negro career centers, and referrals from the national unit of the Urban League.

The Incident

DATE: September 2, 1966
TIME: 10:00 A.M.
PLACE: Headquarters, Eastman Kodak

[Enter a stocky black man, wearing a Black Power button in his lapel and flanked by fifteen of his associates]

"I want to see the top man."

The speaker was Minister Franklin Delano Roosevelt Florence, president of FIGHT.

Thus opened what was to become a turning point in the relationship of giant corporations with the community and, particularly, with minority groups. Like the personae in a stock drama, the characters developed in this episode have subsequently become stereotyped and are today being played by many activists and management representatives in numerous cities.

The visit was not a spur-of-the-moment event. In its convention on June 18, 1966, FIGHT had resolved that "Eastman Kodak be singled out for special investigation this year." [99] This first meeting was deceptively harmonious. Minister Florence and his associates were met by Kodak's chairman of the board Albert Chapman, president William Vaughn (subsequently chairman), and executive vice president Louis Eilers (subsequently president). His voice dry and his manner direct, Florence talked intently about the painful problems of ghetto-dwelling blacks. He proposed that Kodak set up a new job-training program to hire and train people who could not meet regular recruitment standards. Vaughn responded that Kodak already had such a program, but agreed to talk further with FIGHT on the subject. According to a Kodak official, Florence was somewhat taken aback: "He had expected immediate resistance to FIGHT's proposals."

Alinsky made sure that Florence was prepared for the next meeting. At the second meeting, on September 14, 1966, the FIGHT leader put his proposal in writing.[10] Reading from a written statement that was distributed to Kodak officials present at the meeting, Florence admitted that Kodak's special pre-employment training programs were "encouraging and enlightened," but then went on to demand that Kodak hire and train, over an 18-month period, between 500 and 600 persons so that they qualify for entry-level positions across the board. FIGHT stated that *it* would *recruit* and counsel trainees and offer advice and assistance in the project, basing this proposal on its claimed status as the only mass-based organization of poor people in Rochester and its active contact and true representation of this untapped reservoir of labor in the Rochester area.

Vaughn's reply was also in writing.[11] He did not accept FIGHT's demands, nor did he reject them outright. Indeed, he reviewed Kodak's special programs for creating job opportunities for the unqualified and unskilled and the criteria used for selecting these trainees. He spoke of the company's plans to expand its programs to include special on-the-job training and classroom instruction, saying:

The Company hopes to benefit from suggestions which FIGHT may offer, as it has in the past been helped by the advice of a number of organizations on these matters. FIGHT and other interested organizations are invited to refer possible applicants for all these programs.

Vaughn noted that the FIGHT proposal and the Kodak plans had a great deal in common and that the company would be interested in meeting with FIGHT again to discuss ways in which "FIGHT might cooperate in the implementation of Kodak's plans."

Despite Kodak's refusal, the company seemed in no way to want to end the talks. Florence, however, soon discovered that Kodak had stiffened its resistance to his proposal; the company continuously repeated its "intention to retain control of all hiring. At the same time, it urged FIGHT to refer people to existing programs designed for the underskilled." [105] But Florence was not interested in Kodak's plans. FIGHT rejected Vaughn's proposal to work within the existing Kodak framework for assisting the hard-core unemployed. As Florence said, this was not what he and FIGHT were after. Vaughn refused to bind the company to hiring a specific number of people, pointing out that "jobs aren't something you turn out on a machine." [47] Among the reasons given by Kodak for not accepting FIGHT's demands were:

1. Kodak could not enter into an exclusive arrangement with any organization to recruit candidates for employment and still be fair to the more than 60,000 people who apply each year.

2. Kodak could not agree to a program which would commit it to hire and train a specific and substantial number of people in a period which would extend so far into the future. [3]

Apparently stalemated, the parties wound up their meeting after planning to meet again the following day.

According to an article in *Business Week* [47],

At this point, Kodak was admittedly sidestepping FIGHT's demands, while trying to bring its own thinking into sharper focus. Indeed, as a labor spokesman has pointed out, no major company could remain union-free in New York state as has Kodak, without considerable skill at evasive tactics.[12]

However, these talks were doomed to failure before they even started. Behind the mask of courtesy, there was a basic difference of opinion on whether FIGHT could *demand* anything by right and on whether Kodak could concede such demands without abrogating its rights and obligations.

A member of Kodak's special group formed to handle the "crisis" said that because "the nature and purpose" of FIGHT are so different from Kodak's, "I'm not sure we can ever really find a basis for the kind of cooperation you would normally expect between two organizations who are trying to accomplish the same thing." After this meeting, subsequent handling of the situation was delegated by top management to second-echelon management.

On September 15, 1966, the third meeting took place—as had the two earlier meetings—at Kodak headquarters. Vaughn's absence was particularly noted by Florence and his associates. Kodak's spokesman was Kenneth Howard of the company's industrial-relations department; other company executives were also present.

From the beginning it was obvious that although both parties were talking, there was no dialogue. While Howard was explaining Kodak's training program, Florence repeatedly interrupted, asking, "Are we talking about FIGHT's proposal?" [47] Howard's discussion made evident the company's view that the subject was ways in which FIGHT might cooperate in Kodak's expanded recruitment and training plans. Florence made it clear that he was "not interested in Kodak's plans"; he insisted that the discussion be limited to the FIGHT proposal. Howard stated that the company could not set a quota for hiring new employees; nor could Kodak enter into any exclusive arrangement for one organization to recruit candidates for its special training programs. The session broke up after the participants had again agreed to meet.

The situation seemed like a classic bargaining confrontation gone sour. Kodak did not know quite how to handle things. The overt symptoms of a problem involving industrial and public relations were there; yet the situation did not really fit the pattern. It was not even evident at this stage that Kodak viewed the problem as being very profound or having crucial long-range implications. Similarly, it is not evident whether Florence realized the full implication of FIGHT's demands. This was his first encounter with a large industrial organization, in which he had to deal with professional experts. In this situation, lack of established ritual meant that there was little likelihood of the issue being settled, since the motives and needs of the parties regarding aspects of the encounter other than economic were either misunderstood or ignored. Howard said later of the three-hour meeting: "It was a strange experience. We never really turned them down, but we were getting no place." [47]

The fourth meeting, held on September 19, 1966, was brief. Howard called on Florence in FIGHT's headquarters. His offer to discuss the problem further was rebuffed. Florence declared that he would deal with no one from Kodak except President Vaughn himself. [18] Not entirely unprepared for this intransigence, Howard then delivered a letter[13] from

Vaughn to Florence, reiterating the company's position and stating that if FIGHT wished to cooperate with Kodak, further meetings could be held; otherwise, Kodak would have to proceed with its plan without FIGHT.

Between September 22 and October 22, no meetings were held, but Kodak and FIGHT exchanged letters. The tone of the communications became increasingly cool. Florence stated in one letter:

Use of terms like "exclusively," "monopolistic," "arbitrary demands," etc., in reference to the FIGHT Proposal does an injustice to the careful thought and consideration that has gone into our suggestions. We have not even had the opportunity to discuss the details of our approach with Eastman Kodak.[14]

Vaughn replied that he was surprised at that statement. Kodak representatives, he observed, had called on FIGHT representatives for discussion on ways to implement the Kodak proposal made on September 14. The Kodak president stated further:

Meanwhile, you and other members of FIGHT might be interested in knowing that while these discussions and subsequent correspondence have been going on, the Kodak Company has continued to employ a substantial number of people in this community, including many Negroes.[15]

Within a week, negotiations had broken down. According to copies of correspondence between Florence and Vaughn from September 14 to October 22 (distributed by Kodak), the sides could not even agree on what had taken place at the meetings. Florence was insisting on FIGHT's proposal, while Kodak maintained that its usual hiring practices were already helping minority groups and that FIGHT should cooperate with these procedures. [156]

The situation, as described by Kenneth Howard of Kodak's industrial-relations department in an interview with the author, was somewhat as follows:

As a member of the corporate industrial-relations staff, I have specialized for the past number of years in these general groups like Plans for Progress, Equal Employment Opportunity, and race relations. So, when Minister Florence and his contingents came to call on the top man to try and see if we could work something out, it naturally fell into my line. . . . [Florence] put in a call for Dr. Chapman, who was then chairman of the board, and the initial meeting . . . last September was with the top brass of the company. The subsequent meetings were delegated into [my] area of specialty when it was determined specifically what [FIGHT] wanted, and [top management] said, "O.K. Meet with Mr. Howard and his group; he handles these affairs. The president of FIGHT has to meet with the specialists in industrial relations." As a matter of fact, we tried to suggest it the other way. Mr. Vaughn told the FIGHT committee that I would be working with them for the company. Anyway, I then had a small committee of people representing each of the three plants . . . . Jack McCarthy, who is director of personnel at Kodak Park, Paul Holm, who is responsible for counseling at the apparatus division, and Dick Kusela of the Kodak office were the three. So we met with them [FIGHT] only on a couple of occasions. It quickly became evident that we weren't talking about the same rules at all but it appeared to be the basis of understanding when we met with them. So, the next day we met with them again. They changed a 180-degree turn; now they wanted to fight.

So we had a couple of meetings with them, and it became perfectly clear that there was no basis for working with them. Then there were letters to Mr. Vaughn . . . and there were no further meetings . . . . In the meantime, they made the typical wild statements to the newspapers and radio. The newspapers played this up a little bit and one radio station that we call the "Voice of FIGHT," would play anything that Minister Florence said. You would call them up and they would put it on the air. Fortunately, not many people listened to it. It was a little bit of a harassment situation. It was a matter of wide interest at the time. It was the kind of thing that was an annoyance to our management. Kodak has long enjoyed an immensely favorable reputation with employees and within this community, partly because we haven't had an annual hassle with the union in which wild statements are made and so forth. We just never had that kind of exposure to this kind of thing, with people making all kinds of wild statements . . . . It bothered our president and the chairman of the board.

The situation was equally unsatisfactory to Minister Florence. In dealing with second-echelon Kodak executives, he not only saw a loss of status but also realized that he could not make any gains—these people having no real authority. He sensed, too, the danger of losing the highly potent and desirable public exposure that keeps an issue alive and that he could get only by talking to top management. Consequently, after the fourth meeting, Minister Florence refused to continue talks with anyone at Kodak except the president or the chairman.

Kodak's New Move and FIGHT's Response

On October 22, Kodak announced that it had arranged with the Board for Fundamental Education (BFE) to help expand Kodak's training programs by holding in-plant training classes. [99] The announcement said that 100 persons would be enrolled in the first classes.

FIGHT's response was swift and bitter. Florence was enraged, declaring the whole thing to be a fraud perpetrated on poor people to sidetrack them from their genuine demands. He immediately led a 45-man group to Kodak's office to seek "clarifications" of the program, and on his arrival found that all the trainees had already been selected. [18] Of the 100 trainees, 60 had been recently referred to Kodak by various community organizations and 40 were regular employees. "It's a fraud—it's a trick," Florence immediately declared. And he went on the radio to say: "We can't understand, for our lives, how a company with their creative ability can . . . take pictures of the hidden side of the moon . . . but can't create Instamatic jobs." Saul Alinsky, who accompanied Florence on the air, said: "I can tell you this. Eastman Kodak has plenty to be concerned about, because this kind of an issue . . . if it ever develops . . . and it may well develop . . . will become a nationwide issue across the board to every Negro ghetto in America." [18]

FIGHT retaliated by mounting an intensive campaign in the news media abusing Kodak and threatening dire consequences for the peace of the city and other ghettos all over America. [18] Alinsky bitterly accused Kodak of playing "an out-and-out public relations con game with FIGHT" and considered the hiring of BFE (rather than accepting FIGHT's programs) as "a backdoor deal." [149]

There followed several weeks of intense pressure on Kodak. Much of the confrontation assumed the character of a clash of "personalities," both organizational and human. To the management of Kodak, it was inconceivable that their organization, with its enviable record of good corporate citizenship and assistance to minority groups, should be accused by a militant group backed by local churches and other community organizations for not helping the cause of the black man. Kodak's incredulity was reinforced by growing evidence that the company was not holding its own in the contest. In the public forum, FIGHT repeatedly outmaneuvered and outclassed Kodak.

The human element played its role, too. Florence, described in an AP story [99] as stocky, bull-necked, with a dry voice and unvarnished mannerisms, used communications media with dramatic effect on every possible occasion. He held press conferences after every meeting with company officials, sometimes even in the lobby of Kodak's headquarters building. Vaughn, on the other hand, a quiet and somewhat aloof man who found Florence's manner "intimidating—a lot of finger-pointing and all that," [47] maintained a cool, dignified posture. His press statements outlining the company's position were legally correct but at best bland, conveying the impression that the company was trying to hide behind verbiage and clichés.

All was not well, however, under Kodak's cool surface; decision-making procedures were cracking. Management's search for alternative approaches was without much success, and its response to FIGHT was often ambiguous and ambivalent. Certain segments of the Kodak management felt that in order to resume discussions with FIGHT, a change in the negotiating team would be desirable. They believed that Howard and his associates had become unacceptable to FIGHT. There were suggestions that Howard was unsympathetic to the blacks' cause and that because of his training in industrial relations, he tended to look at the whole question as a routine problem of employment. A number of Kodak employees were also members of FIGHT and Friends of FIGHT.[16] Some of them attempted to help break the impasse between Kodak and FIGHT. In early December, for example, John Mulder, a Kodak assistant vice president, met for lunch with his friend, the Reverend Marvin Chandler, a member of FIGHT as well as one of the two associate executive directors of the Rochester Area Council of Churches. [182] They discussed ways in which discussions might be resumed. Mulder had been active in civil-rights causes, and his wife was a member of Friends of FIGHT. [99] As assistant general manager of the Kodak Park plant, the company's largest Rochester installation, he felt that men directly responsible for hiring and training might be the most appropriate company representatives in future discussions with FIGHT. [144] Mulder and Chandler agreed that new delegations should be appointed to resume talks. They submitted this idea to Vaughn, who agreed, and on December 16, 1966, he appointed Mulder to head a new Kodak team.

Kodak's Abortive Agreement and Its Repercussions

On December 19 and 20, Mulder and other Kodak representatives met secretly with FIGHT spokesmen in a room at the Downtowner Motel. Mulder had expected to meet with Chandler to pursue further their earlier luncheon discussion. Instead, although Chandler was present, Florence took charge.

At 2:00 P.M. on December 20, the two parties signed the following agreement:

A special committee appointed by Eastman Kodak president, William Vaughn, has been meeting Monday and Tuesday with officers of the FIGHT organization.

Kodak representatives stated that they have not employed traditional standards of hiring for the last two years. FIGHT hailed this as a step in the right direction as well as Kodak officers' statement that they will deal with the problem of hard-core unemployed.

Job openings, specifications and hourly rates were discussed and agreed upon by the joint group. January 15th was agreed upon as the date for a beginning of the referral of 600 employees, the bulk of which would be hard-core unemployed (unattached, uninvolved with traditional institutions).

Under the agreement, the FIGHT organization and Kodak agreed to an objective of the recruitment and referral (to include screening and selection) of 600 unemployed people over a 24-month period, barring unforeseen economic changes affecting the Rochester community. FIGHT, at its own expense, would provide counseling for the employees selected by Kodak.

Kodak agrees to the following: join with FIGHT in a firm agreement to

A. Continue semi-monthly meetings between Kodak and FIGHT to increase the effectiveness of the program.

B. Kodak will familiarize FIGHT counselors with the foremen and work skills required, and in turn FIGHT will familiarize Kodak foremen with life and environment of poor people.

C. Kodak and FIGHT will share information on the referrals.

D. Kodak and FIGHT will issue a 60-day community progress report.

JOHN MULDER
Asst. Vice President, Eastman Kodak
Asst. General Manager, Kodak Park Works
FRANKLIN D. R. FLORENCE
President of FIGHT

To say that Florence was jubilant would be an understatement. Apparently, he could not quite believe his own success. He repeatedly asked Mulder, "Are you sure you are authorized to sign this?" On Mulder's confirmation, they exchanged the signed copies of the agreement and the meeting ended amicably. Immediately after leaving, the FIGHT people made a radio announcement of the agreement to a surprised city.

The nature, content, timing, and procedure involved in the signing of the agreement were rather unusual and might indicate that Kodak's handling of the situation in terms of long-term planning, negotiating strategy, and selection and preparation of negotiating personnel was haphazard and not well thought out. Mulder's inexperience and ineptness in dealing with Florence showed in the language of the agreement. As Barbara Carter [18] pointed out,

It was a strange agreement at best. One of the six paragraphs mentioned the "referral of six hundred unemployed people," another the "referral of six hundred employees," a distinction of some importance. For a non-union company, the briefest paragraph was by far the oddest. It said simply, "Job openings, specifications and hourly rates were discussed and agreed upon by the joint group." Moreover, semi-monthly meetings on the program's "effectiveness" were also agreed on.

By 3:00 P.M. Howard's boss, Monroe Dill, had heard the news over radio station WBBF.[17] He promptly contacted Louis Eilers,[18] who was to assume the company's presidency the following week and who had participated in earlier Kodak-FIGHT discussions. Dill told Eilers that Mulder had signed an agreement with FIGHT. "The hell he has!" Eilers replied. [99] Eilers called Mulder's boss, Vice President Clarence Wynd, who confirmed the radio reports and said that Mulder was there, agreement in hand. Eilers snapped, "Get that paper up here fast!" [47] When Mulder came to his office, Eilers promptly dressed him down. [99]

On December 21, 1966, Kodak's executive committee met and voted unanimously to repudiate the agreement. The following day the board of directors met and concurred with the executive committee's decision. In a statement issued by the company, the executive committee stated that "for all its ambiguities [the document of December 20] violated anti-discrimination laws." [99] The committee stated that Mulder had not had the authority to bind the company. The company apologized profusely for the mixup, but flatly repudiated the whole arrangement. [45] It may be noted here that the company by-laws do not define the scope of authority of an assistant vice president. In an interview with the author, company executives indicated that Mulder's title was largely ceremonial, entitling him to a higher salary and certain fringe benefits that his work per se would not otherwise merit. Kodak has no record of any written instructions from Vaughn to Mulder about the extent of the latter's authority in conducting the negotiations. Nor did Vaughn publicly admit that Mulder was specifically prohibited from signing an agreement with FIGHT. Mulder, since the incident, has not talked to the press or anyone else, so that his side of the story remains unknown.

As reported in *Fortune* [3], William S. Vaughn, newly elected chairman of the board, said that Kodak had

two fundamental and critical objections to the FIGHT proposal: (1) We could not enter into an arrangement exclusively with any organization to recruit candidates for employment and still be fair to the more than 60,000 people who apply each year.... (2) We could not agree to a program which would commit Kodak to hire and train a specific and substantial number of people in a period which would extend so far into the future. Obviously, our employment needs depend on the kinds of jobs available at a particular time, and on the demand for our products.

According to an Associated Press release describing the events directly following December 20, 1966, "Another aspect of the agreement plainly horrified at least one high Kodak executive, who detected the faint odor of a 'labor contract.' " [99]

Mulder, apparently somewhat bewildered by these events, asked that he be allowed to break the news to FIGHT. [99] He took the board of directors' statement to Chandler's home. According to the Associated Press, "Minister Florence and his wife were there, celebrating her birthday." *Business Week* [47] reported that when Mulder entered the room, Florence said:

I whispered to my wife, "They've broken the agreement." You could see it in John's face. He looked like Christ must have looked when Peter denied him. . . . When I read that statement the whole thing Brother Malcolm told me about white folks hit me again. He said never trust them unless you have the power to make them deliver. . . .

When they tore up that agreement they tore up the hopes of the poor people of Rochester. The issue is, they have signed an agreement with us—are they honorable men? Do their signatures mean one thing to white man, another to black?

It was not clear what actually happened at the meeting between Vaughn and Mulder when the latter was given his instructions about contacting FIGHT. In an interview with the author, Kenneth Howard gave the following version of the meeting:

I wasn't present when Mr. Vaughn met with . . . Mr. Mulder to give him instructions, but my boss was there and I talked with Mr. Vaughn the next day and he told me what he had told [Mulder] by way of . . . instructions and they seemed to have been quite clear. But, somehow, they apparently weren't clear, or for some other reason Mulder chose to do something which was quite contradictory to what Mr. Vaughn had expected him to do. His instructions, as he [Vaughn] related them to me, were essentially that he was asking Mr. Mulder to try to accomplish the policy which we previously enunciated. Mr. Vaughn was probably led to believe that attitudes of various parties might have been hardened because of various personalities and their ego involvement. It was suggested that Kodak's talks with FIGHT might resume and a rapprochement with FIGHT easily accomplished if Kodak were to use new faces on their discussion team with FIGHT. . . . So two days later, Mr. Vaughn was out of town and we had heard on the radio that this agreement had been signed. Of course, you can imagine, this came as a great shock and it was a great shock in the community because it was only three weeks . . . after this little kit and material had been circulated which made our position very clear. On December 20, the whole thing seemed to have been reversed and no one even knew anything was going on in the meantime. Nobody, not even my friends, knew that I had been relieved of the responsibility for the discussions. For a few days people looked at me as though I was crazy or something.

The reaction of the community to this new twist in the Kodak-FIGHT conflict was one of disbelief, surprise, disappointment, and angry frustration. The involvement of a major corporation, the unusual role of the church, the unorthodox tactics used by the nationally known professional radical Saul Alinsky, and the militancy of FIGHT and its leader Minister Florence had already brought to national attention a conflict which the local community and press preferred to regard as essentially a local issue. This turn of events was certainly not going to lessen the heat which the conflict had already generated.

Kodak people foresaw the possibility of dissatisfaction arising among its supporters and negative reaction and resentment among the pro-FIGHT elements in the community. However, it is doubtful that Kodak had any idea of the nature and the intensity of repercussions that its repudiation of the agreement would cause among various elements of the national population and organized groups.

In the days immediately following denouncement of the agreement, Kodak took double-page advertisements in both morning and afternoon papers to say that it "sincerely regrets any misunderstanding." The ads repeated the company's earlier position that it could not have "an exclusive recruitment" with any group, nor could it commit itself to any specific number of jobs "owing to the uncertainties of economic conditions." Furthermore, the ads gave the company's oft-stated position on social responsibility: that Kodak was "deeply concerned to do all that we reasonably can to meet a pressing social need in this community, namely, to try and develop employment opportunities," and that "many positive steps" had already been taken by the management. [160]

FIGHT's reaction was swift and, at least in retrospect, predictable. A promise had been broken—and at the very moment of triumph. Alinsky severely criticized Kodak for breaching the agreement, caustically remarking, "Maybe their executives ought to enroll in the Head Start Program and learn to read." He charged Kodak with "playing into the hands of those who say you can't trust the white man. I don't know how much [strife] Kodak will be responsible for this summer." Florence labeled Kodak "institutionally racist" and gave a solemn warning: "I see troubled times, grave times for the total community because of the dishonesty of Eastman Kodak." [47]

Both Kodak and FIGHT held news conferences in which angry words flew. In his news conference on January 6, 1967, Kodak president Eilers[19] charged that FIGHT's "talk about employment [was] being used as a screen [for] making a power drive in this community." [74] In his statement, as reported by the *New York Times*, Eilers said that

since the Alinsky forces were brought to Rochester, FIGHT has run a continuing war against numerous institutions that help build Rochester—the school system, the Community Chest, the city government, and even organizations especially set up to help solve minority group problems.

Eilers characterized FIGHT's demands as "arbitrary and unreasonable" and asked if the group's "goal was really to get jobs for those who need them. . . .To the best of our knowledge, FIGHT has not sent anyone to us to apply for work." Concerning Mulder, Eilers said, "We all expressed the greatest of displeasure at the signing," but added that he didn't envision any change in Mulder's job. Mr. Mulder declined to comment. [74]

Writing for the *Washington Post* [67], Nicholas Van Hoffman[20] stated:

The company's statements seemed befuddled and contradictory. . . . "The only people in Rochester who are unemployed don't want to work or can't," Industrial Relations man Howard stated, but a few minutes later he was saying in a spasm of corporate self-pity, "we ought to make it clear that Kodak has never taken a position against FIGHT. If anything we were overly sympathetic. This is where we get into trouble."

In a news conference held later in his storefront office, Minister Florence said that Eilers' statement was that of "an hysterical and insecure man." Florence said that his group was trying to get blacks into the "[melting] pot at Kodak." As to Eilers' statement that no one was applying for jobs through FIGHT, Minister Florence flourished what he said were duplicates of the applications of 45 people, many of them written in shaky scrawls. He said he had sent them to Kodak in anticipation of such criticism. [74]

Thereafter, Eilers and Florence met twice, coolly. However, in the third meeting, on January 10, 1967, Minister Florence stalked out when he found that Eilers had turned over the discussions to the members of the industrial-relations department. "We thought we were going to meet with Dr. Eilers, and they sent in a group of janitors." [88]

In January 1967, Saul Alinsky began a campaign to round up national support for FIGHT. On January 3, 1967, representatives of the National Council of Churches' Commission on Religion and Race, the Board of National Missions of the United Presbyterian Church, and the Board for Homeland Ministries of the United Church of Christ visited Rochester and expressed their support of FIGHT in the Kodak dispute. [160] On January 10, 1967, the Citizens Crusade Against Poverty, a private group working with funds of the United Auto Workers Union, convened a closed meeting where it was decided to support FIGHT. At the meeting were delegates from the National Association for the Advancement of Colored People, the National Council of Churches, the Protestant Episcopal Diocese of New York, and the United Presbyterian Church. [88]

Hoping to make peace, the Rochester Area Council of Churches took a full-page ad in the two local dailies (*Rochester Times-Union* and *Rochester Democrat and Chronicle*) urging FIGHT to endorse Kodak's training programs and Kodak to endorse FIGHT's proposal. A few days later the president of the council (a Kodak employee) and two directors (one of whom was a Kodak employee) resigned from the council in protest against the ad, which they felt favored FIGHT. [99] The Associated Press [99] also reported:

Parishioners began holding back contributions to churches that had supported FIGHT. Kodak president Eilers had a device put on his home telephone to intercept abusive calls. One minister, tormented by threats and phone calls, took his own life. The calls continued to his wife.

The readers' letters to the newspapers were mostly critical of the council's ad. As reported by Barbara Carter [18], an editorial in the *Rochester Times-Union*, anti-FIGHT from the beginning, entitled "The Gulf Between Pulpit and Pew—One Layman's View" severely criticized FIGHT and its supporters.

Meanwhile, FIGHT's position was growing harder and broader, as the following report [144] shows:

"We're not interested in white hope," Florence told a FIGHT meeting. "FIGHT asks Kodak where is the black hope for the underprivileged and unemployed in Rochester."

"Tell it, Brother," yelled the crowd. "Sock it to 'em."

"They talk about America being a melting pot," said Florence, "but the question right now is not whether black can melt, but whether they can even get into the pot. That's what FIGHT has been trying to do—get some of them into the pot at Kodak."

Kodak's statement that the document of December 20 was unauthorized did not contribute to its standing in the eyes of the public, as a letter to the editors of *America* magazine illustrates: It is inconceivable that a man in Mr. Mulder's position could so misunderstand what he was or was not authorized to do. [104] Despite Kodak's insistence that they had not intended Mulder to initiate a new policy, *Business Week* quoted Vaughn as saying that Chandler and Mulder's decision to resume talks between FIGHT and Kodak "gave us some hope that there was a new deal here." [47]

One widespread opinion was that Kodak should have honored the agreement anyway. In fact, Friends of FIGHT demanded that Kodak do just that. [99] An interesting analysis of the situation was made by Barbara Carter in the *Reporter* [18]:

"Kodak made FIGHT look good," said one University of Rochester professor, who thought Florence might have had trouble coming up with six hundred people. "For a moment there," said one of FIGHT's many vice-presidents, "I wondered if Kodak was utterly cynical." He was worried not only about FIGHT's ability to produce but also about its ability to counsel the hard-core unemployed effectively, as the agreement stipulated FIGHT would do at its own expense. "If I were Alinsky," said

Benjamin Phelosof, then acting president of Friends of FIGHT, "I would have bribed Eilers to repudiate the agreement."

On January 19, 1967, two television crews followed Black Power leader Stokely Carmichael into town. FIGHT took advantage of the cameras to parade with picket signs. That night the leader of the Student Nonviolent Coordinating Committee told a FIGHT rally (approximate attendance of 200) about plans for a national boycott of Eastman Kodak products, vowing to "bring them to their knees." [99] Carmichael said, "We have been looking for a fight against a big company, and you've got everything we want . . . . When we're through, Florence will say 'Jump,' and Kodak will ask 'How high?' " The boycott was to take place on Valentine's Day. [18] Carmichael's national boycott, scheduled for nine cities, turned out to be picketing in four and involved only several dozen citizens in Detroit, Chicago, San Francisco, and Atlanta. [18]

William C. Martin, writing in the *Atlantic* [105], said:

Though stung by public rebuff, FIGHT quickly turned the December document into a *cause celebre*. Minister Florence had an issue he could get his teeth into, and he bit to the bone. He painted Kodak as the corporate symbol of the lying white Devil.

During the first week of February, Kodak announced openings for from 137 to 158 unskilled persons in training programs leading to regular jobs. These people would be hired within the five-month period following the announcement. The programs would last from several weeks to one year. Pay during training would in all cases be more than $2 an hour. The training programs ranged from technical courses to instruction designed to bring the most disadvantaged up to fifth-grade reading level. Kodak requested referrals from eleven agencies, including settlement houses, the state employment service, the Urban League, and FIGHT. [18, 99]

Four days later Florence brought 87 people to the Kodak employment office. Kodak interviewers were ready with application forms. Describing the meeting, a Kodak official said in an interview with the author:

[The FIGHT people engaged] in an hour demonstration, constantly interrupting our attempt to describe these programs to the group; they demanded that we provide jobs on the spot for those present. Our industrial-relations people offered to accept applications and interview that day any members of the group who were seeking employment. Several stepped forward to volunteer, only to be warned by Minister Florence, president of FIGHT, that they should not accept the offer.

The Associated Press [99] reported:

After an hour and a half in a closed conference room, Minister Florence said his group had been offered neither jobs nor interviews, and if Kodak claimed the opposite, which Kodak did, it was "an out and out lie."[21]

Florence also said that agencies who cooperated with Kodak in referring people for jobs were joining in a "conspiracy"[22] and that Kodak's training programs were "a sham and a disgrace." [42] In spite of Florence's accusations, referrals were made and the program moved along.

Reviewing other aspects of this sequence, an Associated Press release [99] reported the following:

Late in February, Kodak told FIGHT in a letter that it wasn't interested in any more "meetings about meetings" and that the jobless would be better served by "employment referrals that result in jobs." FIGHT called the letter a "slap in the face." In a telegram to Eilers, Minister Florence replied in part: "The cold of February will give way to the warmth of spring and eventually to the Long, Hot Summer. What happens in Rochester in the summer of '67 is at the doorstep of Eastman Kodak Co."

Eilers regards the wire as irresponsible and inflammatory. Furthermore, he doesn't believe FIGHT sincerely wants to help the unemployed. "To tell the truth," he says, "I don't know what they want. Certainly not jobs—they could have had those, and still can. Every one of the other ten referring agencies in Rochester has placed people in jobs at Kodak and none has asked for an exclusive deal. This year we'll have about 300 more in our training program. It's too bad FIGHT doesn't want to participate."

It is also true that FIGHT's aims go beyond getting jobs. They include how jobs are obtained. "We don't want any of Kodak's paternalism," says Minister Florence. "The training program we've proposed is something we can do ourselves. We know ourselves better than anybody from Kodak does, and better than any Black Man who goes home to the suburbs every night and pretends he's white. We have to help ourselves by ourselves. That's what self-determination is."

Meanwhile, FIGHT was making elaborate plans to mount a protest campaign and disrupt Kodak's annual stockholders' meeting which was to take place in April 1967 in Flemington, New Jersey. According to the *New York Times* [82] ,

In March, FIGHT bought ten shares of Kodak stock, at a cost of $1,442.65 to gain a voice at the stockholders' meeting. The organization sent out 700 letters to clergymen and civil rights groups urging them to contact fellow stockholders to protest the company's action at the annual meeting.

In response to FIGHT's call, various church organizations announced that they would withhold from the management their proxies for more than 34,000 shares.[23] In addition, 21 private investors accounting for 5,060 shares announced their withholding of proxies from the management.[24] One pension fund was reported also to have withheld its proxy vote to management in support of FIGHT. However, as John Kifner, writing for the *New York Times* [81] , pointed out, "these proxy withholdings (about 40,000 shares in all) are largely symbolic since the company's latest annual report lists 80,772,718 shares of stock."

A New Approach: Rochester Jobs Inc.

After an exchange of written communications late in February, the FIGHT-Kodak controversy was stalemated; the only plans apparent were those of FIGHT to disrupt the Kodak stockholders' meeting in April. Efforts by other groups to head off "a long, hot summer" were redoubled, and in early spring hope for a settlement began to develop. A small group of influential ministers, including Gene Barlett, president of Colegate-Rochester Divinity School, Episcopal bishop George W. Barrett, and Reverend Lloyd Peterson, executive secretary of the Genesee Valley Presbytery, decided to develop a compromise program which, while providing jobs for the hard-core unemployed, would contain the necessary ingredients to bring about an end to the Kodak-FIGHT controversy. The group, which soon expanded to include representatives of many local industries,[25] developed a program wherein local industries would hire and train 1,500 hard-core unemployed over an 18-month period. Understandably, Kodak was all for Rochester Jobs Inc., as the program was called. RJI's position, from almost the very beginning, was that the problem of the unemployed in Rochester was a citywide concern and not merely a Kodak problem.

FIGHT complained that this was another example of the white Establishment's doing something for the poor without giving them an adequate voice in the process, but the group finally joined the program. Minister Florence was elected a vice president and named to key committees. Clearly, FIGHT had gained an impressive victory and was undeniably, if indirectly, responsible for a precedent-setting partnership between private industry and the poor. Though no hiring quotas were announced, estimates placed Kodak's share at approximately 600. The solution appeared perfect. The poor—not 600, but 1,500—had the promise of jobs, FIGHT had its victory, and Kodak was apparently doing all FIGHT had ever asked of it.

Then, to the dismay of the principals in RJI, Minister Florence announced that the new program would not affect FIGHT's dispute with Kodak and that the protest at Flemington would take place as scheduled. *FIGHT still wanted some kind of direct concession from Kodak.* [105] In fact, "I don't speak for FIGHT," said Ed Chambers, Alinsky's representative in Rochester, "but FIGHT's main thrust will continue until Kodak honors its agreement." [18] Florence said that he would cooperate fully with RJI only if its broad plans included the basic points in the agreement of December 20.

As far as Florence was concerned, the issue was no longer jobs but dignity. He maintained that Kodak had arrogantly broken a moral agreement and that they had never produced John Mulder—and never would—to support their claim that he was not authorized to sign. He accused Eilers of living in the eighteenth century and said that FIGHT was only trying to solve local problems in partnership with business, rather than by resorting to the federal government. He recalled that in a previous crisis situation, during World War II, industry turned farmers into tradesmen overnight because the national good demanded it. A similar crisis situation, he said, exists today. [156]

Kodak's Annual Stockholders' Meeting

DATE: April 25, 1967
PLACE: Flemington, New Jersey,[26] Hunterdon Central High School,
    Eastman Kodak annual stockholders' meeting

After a mile-long march through Flemington, more than 700 noisy demonstrators surrounded the high school [75] carrying signs: "Kodak Out of Focus," "FIGHT," [174] "Kodak is Lost in the Dark Room," [3] "Kodak Snaps Its Shutter on the Ghetto." [98] The demonstrators included FIGHT members from Rochester, blacks from other cities, and students from Cornell, Princeton, Yale, and Dartmouth.

FIGHT was also very much in evidence at the meeting itself. Ten members had each purchased a share of Kodak stock. [99] In response to letters sent out by Florence [46] and the energies of Friends of FIGHT [99], FIGHT had also persuaded seven large church groups to withhold their more than 34,000 shares from management proxy.[27] John E. Hines, presiding Episcopal bishop, probably expressed the feelings of the seven organizations when he said, "We are very much interested in FIGHT, and we are very much interested in the responsible exercise of corporate power in the community." [22]

At 1:00 P.M. Chairman of the Board William S. Vaughn opened the meeting. Minister Florence was on his feet immediately. "Point of order," Florence shouted. "I'll be heard as long as I'm on the floor." To cries of "Throw him out," Florence shouted, "We will give you until two o'clock to honor that agreement," and then walked out of the building. Outside, Florence told his followers, "This is war," and Alinsky [75, 174] described the battlefield:

What has happened so far has just been skirmishing. . . . Eastman Kodak has always done the wrong and not the ethical thing. . . . The issue with the churches now is to put your stocks where your sermons are! . . . We are ready to move on a national scale and FIGHT is going to be the fountain head for the resurrection of the civil rights movement.

The "war" was to be waged "in Eastman Kodak's arena—the nation from Harlem to Watts." [3] Inside, Vaughn was speaking with 1,000 stockholders, not all of them friendly. [45] The chairman again explained the company's decision on the document of December 20. [165] Clergymen pressed him on Kodak racial attitudes.

Precisely at 2:00 P.M., Florence returned to the meeting, crying "point of order" until he had Vaughn's attention. [47] Florence pointed a finger at the chairman and asked, "Are you going to recognize the December 20 agreement?" Vaughn's reply was firm: "No sir, no we are not." [45] With this, Florence and some of his followers walked out of the meeting. FIGHT's attempts to disrupt the meeting were only partially successful. The meeting was not halted, nor was management challenged.

John Kifner, reporting in the *New York Times* [75], described the meeting in this way:

After the walkout, representatives of religious groups and private individuals who had withheld their proxies from management remained in the meeting to question Kodak's employment policies—to the occasional groans of the majority of stockholders present.

Several Rochester residents, including a local newspaper columnist, Mary Grooms, defended the company.

The buses and carloads of white and Negro demonstrators from Rochester and other cities and from Cornell, Princeton, Yale and Dartmouth arrived in this sleepy rural village this morning, to be met by a worried force of about 100 state troopers, many of whom were held in reserve at a nearby armory, local police and Kodak guards. There were no incidents.

It was the biggest event here since the trial of Bruno Richard Hauptmann for the Lindbergh kidnapping, in 1935, which is still a topic of conversation.

The demonstrators marched along the sidewalk on both sides of the town's three-block long business district, then walked about a mile to the Hunterdon Central High School where the meeting was held.

The police had blocked off the streets and the school and most of the stores were closed for the day.

Vaughn's defense of Kodak's record as well as its reasons for repudiation drew cheers from most of the stockholders present. [45] Nor did the withholding of proxies present any serious difficulties for management. At the meeting, 84 per cent of Kodak's 80.8 million shares was voted for management. Disappointment was perhaps the dominant emotion on

Vaughn's part when he referred to the dispute in an address to the stockholders: "If it has accomplished nothing else, however, it is only fair to say that FIGHT has helped to keep the problem of the unemployed Negro before the community." [42] All Kodak officers were reelected. A month later the company took from John Mulder his title of assistant vice president, although he retained his position as assistant general manager of Kodak's Park plant.

Outside the auditorium, it was a different story. FIGHT had made elaborate plans for demonstrations in order to get national publicity for their cause. Florence's statements and those of Alinsky, and the pickets marching outside the building, did receive national coverage on television and radio. Florence's press statements that day were more and more militant. A nationwide civil-rights candlelight pilgrimage to Kodak headquarters was planned for July 24, the anniversary of Rochester's riots, [165] and there was an intensification of efforts to persuade socially concerned groups, including the big foundations, to bring pressure on Kodak. [47] A national Black Power strategy meeting would be held to discuss tactics against Kodak. Florence promised to bring in from 5,000 to 10,000 "outsiders" and make Rochester the center of summer 1967's civil-rights movement. [98] He also suggested that they might picket the home of Kodak founder George Eastman, now a photographic museum, or perhaps pester Dr. Eilers—"Everywhere he goes, we go." Florence also suggested that FIGHT members have an "eat-in" at the Eastman School of Music and eat beans while "our white brothers pass by in their silks and satins." The Black Power leader charged that "racial war has been declared on American Negroes by Eastman Kodak." [46]

Perhaps it was the adverse national publicity resulting from the protests and demonstrations at the annual stockholders' meeting, or a combination of this as well as other factors, which resulted in an immediate drop of six points in Kodak's stock prices in an otherwise strong market.[28] However, within a week the prices were back at their regular levels. [46]

Events after the Stockholders' Meeting

On April 27, 1967, Kodak announced the appointment of Uptown Associates, a Manhattan-based black public-relations and advertising concern specializing in "ethnic marketing."

According to a story in the *New York Times* [77]:

A Kodak official in Rochester said the company contract with Uptown Associates was not related to its current conflict with FIGHT.

Reuben J. Patton, head of Uptown Associates, said "the company did not seek me out" because of FIGHT controversy. He stated that he had first offered his services to Kodak in June 1964 when they were turned down by the company advertising director who wrote to Patton saying:

"As you know we are very much interested in the Negro market.... At the moment we do not require extra services ... and if the occasion arises where we feel you can be of additional service to us, please be assured that you will hear directly from us."

Florence said he was "glad to hear that Kodak can sign contracts with Negro firms specializing in face-saving. This is proof that Kodak was never in good faith with the poor, but only wants to hire 'instamatic' Negroes."

On June 23, 1967, President Eilers sent a telegram to Minister Florence in which he said:

Kodak recognizes that FIGHT, as a broad-based community organization, speaks in behalf of the basic needs and aspirations of the Negro poor in the Rochester area.... Both FIGHT and Kodak support RJI [Rochester Jobs Inc.] which promises to be an effective way of providing job opportunities for the hard-core unemployed.... It was suggested [in discussions between Kodak and FIGHT] that FIGHT and Kodak establish a relationship under which Kodak would send employment interviewers into selected places in inner-city neighborhoods in cooperation with FIGHT. It was also suggested that it may be helpful to the people referred by FIGHT and employed by Kodak to have special guidance and advice from your organization ... [and that there be a] continuing dialogue between FIGHT and Kodak [to] cover various areas bearing on the economic needs and the aspirations of the Negro community.[29]

In FIGHT's third convention, held the same evening, the meeting endorsed Kodak's telegram and the program outlined therein. The meeting also elected DeLeon McEwen president of FIGHT to replace Florence, who could not succeed himself. The meeting also decided to change the referent of the letter "I" in FIGHT's name to stand for Independence instead of Integration.

In the fall of 1967, discussions between FIGHT and Kodak resumed on the possibility of Kodak's promoting the organization of inner-city small business. FIGHT had initially hoped Kodak would build a plant in the ghetto area[36] and let FIGHT run it. Kodak said it couldn't do this but suggested that an independent business would be best. In response to FIGHT's enthusiasm, Kodak prepared a 40-page booklet entitled *A Plan for Establishing Independently Owned and Operated Business in Inner-City Areas.* [132] The plan suggested that Kodak would take the initiative in organizing a unit called Community Development Corporation (CDC) and assist in its financing along with other organizations who would be encouraged to join it. The objective of CDC would be to support small businesses. The plan suggested three types of small businesses: a wood-products business, a plant for manufacturing vacuum-formed plastic items, and an equipment-service business. In addition, Kodak suggested forming a microfilming service. The company considered this service to be particularly feasible since it was labor-intensive, equipment could be rented, and the required training lasted only several weeks. The jobs involved would not be menial. Kodak foresaw a good-sized market in microfilming government documents.

FIGHT showed interest in the microfilming service but was somewhat disappointed by the small number of jobs involved (under 150). It asked Kodak how much financing would be required to employ 500 people. Kodak estimated that it would need between $2 million and $3 million in sales to support such a large operation and emphasized that it considered such an operation unrealistic as there was no possibility of finding such a large market.

At the same time, without any concurrence from Kodak, FIGHT telephoned the *New York Times*, which carried two news stories on the subject on November 4 and 18, giving FIGHT spokesmen as their source. The story of November 4, 1967, stated that Kodak would build a finishing plant for photographic facilities. The factory, which would employ between 100 and 150 people, would be "black-operated." "A Kodak spokesman, Charles Fitzgibbon, would not comment yesterday on the proposed plant." [148] The story of November 18, 1967, quoted DeLeon McEwen, president of FIGHT, as saying that Kodak will join FIGHT "in developing a microfilming factory that will hire and train 400 to 500 unskilled Negroes." McEwen also said that "the date the program will get underway and the capital investment Kodak will make . . . would be disclosed next week." [93]

The two stories put Kodak in an awkward position. To continue talks with FIGHT would be by "deeds reenforcing their exaggerated claims"; to break off talks would contradict Kodak's desire to help FIGHT. Kodak asked FIGHT to announce the misunderstanding, but FIGHT refused— even after Kodak said it wouldn't be able to continue talks if this were not done. FIGHT, in preserving this "barrier" to talks, kept the issue alive—but no direct talks with Kodak have occurred since.

Epilogue

On November 3, 1967, Kodak announced the appointment of Carl Byoir and Associates of New York for what it termed over-all public-relations work. The account executive, Bill Seely, said that the work would include "some of the local problems Kodak had been encountering in Rochester." The *New York Times* news story suggested that the Byoir agency was retained "probably to burnish the company's corporate image rather than increase sales in specific lines." [148]

On December 5, 1967, Kodak announced the "details of a plan to combat poverty in Rochester." The plan called for starting small businesses in the city's predominantly black slums, each employing from 9 to 15 workers. Although these businesses would be started with Kodak's help, they "would eventually be independently owned and operated by employees." [58] FIGHT was not mentioned in the announcement.

On April 1, 1968, Kodak announced that its program to train jobless persons from Rochester's inner city would continue in 1968. Monroe V. Dill, Kodak director of industrial relations, said the company expected to hire 200 persons for the program during the coming year, the same number as the preceding year. He also said that since the inception of this on-the-job program in 1964, 500 men and women, many lacking industrial skills or adequate education, had been trained in special classes. FIGHT's president, DeLeon McEwen, responding to Kodak's announcement, said that the results of the education program were "known only to Kodak" and "they have not been enlarged to the black hard-core unemployed." [84]

This program was not connected with Rochester Jobs Inc., which was a community program jointly sponsored by various local industries and church groups. Meanwhile, RJI had made considerable progress. According to the *New York Times*, [146] eleven months after its creation—RJI was incorporated on April 11, 1967—participating employers in RJI had made available 1,033 jobs. Referral agencies in the program, including FIGHT, had referred 986 persons to prospective employers, of whom 784 had been hired. Besides serving as a clearing house for job openings and referrals, RJI, with participating agencies, was also sponsoring workshops for industrial foremen on the problems that the hard-core unemployed brought with them. RJI was responsible for "carrying out the Rochester phase of the National Alliance of Businessmen project, the new industry-government attack on unemployment." [146] RJI's board of directors is composed of seven persons from groups involved with the poor, three clergymen from as many faiths, and ten businessmen. RJI's president (as of March 1968) is Donald A. Gaudion, president of Ritter-Pfaudler, and its executive director is Edward S. Croft, who is on leave from the New York State Employment Service.

The Rochester Business Opportunities Corporation

As with RJI, Kodak realized that the promotion of independent businesses to be run by minority groups could best be performed as a community effort, and it proposed a similar nonprofit corporation to set up such businesses.

In January 1968, Rochester Business Opportunities Corporation (RBOC) was formed "to promote and encourage independent business enterprises in and for the inner-city."[31] William J. Maxion, a printing-company executive, was elected RBOC's first president and soon asked the city's sixty largest companies to contribute to a fund which would be used as collateral to guarantee bank loans to finance business development by inner-city residents. "The fund would also support loans to persons with promising proposals who normally would be unable to obtain adequate financing." Government contributions to the fund were also expected. [146] RBOC has a staff of three: general manager; a black who is on leave from Ritter-Pfaudler, where he is training director; and an accountant, whose main job is helping RBOC's Business Development Committee screen loan applicants and assisting them in developing their proposals.

RBOC's 28-member board includes many of the blue-chip names in the Rochester business community: the top executives of four banks, Eastman Kodak, Rochester Gas and Electric Corporation, Xerox, Gleason Works, a division of General Motors Corporation, the Gannett Company, Ritter-Pfaudler, and other companies. But it also includes several blacks—a restaurant proprietress, the owner of a beauty-salon and barber-shop supply house, and two insurance agents—as well as a Puerto Rican grocery-store owner. [103]

Only nine months after RBOC's founding, an article in the *Harvard Business Review* [103] reported:

Because it enjoys such respect and support and also because great care and thought went into its formation, the Rochester Business Opportunities Corporation is one of the most promising organizations for furthering the economic independence of that city's minority groups, which represent about 15 per cent of the population.

RBOC's 60-odd corporate supporters have given or pledged some $250,000 so far. The money is used as seed capital for financing new businesses, usually through Rochester banks and the SBA.

. . . The newly formed businesses represent quite a variety of ventures: general contractors, a grocery store, auto body repair shops, a sign painter, building maintenance firms, a plastic molding company, a beauty shop operator, and trucking equipment companies, to name a few. In some cases the loans went to businesses seeking expansion, such as a dry-cleaning establishment. . . .

A bookbindery was initiated by local printing companies which needed one. The plastic mold shop started with a $150,000 contract from Eastman Kodak for short-run items and promises of business with other local companies. (The owner, incidentally, was able to put $5,000 of his own into the $100,000 financing package.) Kodak also helped organize a camera repair shop, Camura, Inc., and is providing it with initial technical help and training its manager. Kodak will be the shop's first customer. The Urban League, which sponsored Camura and selected its manager, hopes to expand the operation into appliance repair.

RBOC also is arranging the sale of existing businesses to minority group members. The nonprofit group is not interested in failing firms; a typical transaction which RBOC brokered was the purchase of a small department store from a couple who wished to retire. (The husband then helped the new owner become familiar with the operation.) A few of these sales have involved firms outside the black community.

On April 17, 1968, Kodak announced a gift of $150,000 to the Community Chest's Martin Luther King Memorial Fund. Prior to Kodak's announcement, many other large and small gifts had been made to the fund. Among these were $250,000 by Mrs. Joseph C. Wilson, wife of the board chairman and chief executive officer of Xerox, and $100,000 by the *Rochester Democrat & Chronicle*, the *Rochester Times-Union*, and the Frank B. Gannett Newspaper Foundation. [147]

On April 30, 1968, Kodak's annual general meeting again took place in Flemington, New Jersey. Robert A. Wright, writing for the *New York Times* [180], commented:

Kodak management appeared much more adept—and happier—at handling the pre-emptive rights issue than they did last year in a civil rights dispute. Discussing Kodak's involvement with FIGHT, chairman Vaughn said, "Late last year, we had considerable joint discussion about a possible FIGHT-operated business in Rochester. ... [T]hough I have no specific results to report at this time, I hope that something practical can still be worked out." He also said "that in 1966 and 1967 about ten percent of the new employees hired by Kodak in Rochester were members of minority groups." This was made possible, he said, "because the company had developed special education and training programs."

As of this writing, RBOC's largest project has been a $600,000 joint venture by FIGHT, Xerox, the United States Department of Labor, and RBOC to start a plant for the manufacture of metal stampings and electrical transformers. The plant is expected to employ 100 hard-core unemployed, and by 1970 to achieve a sales volume of $1.2 million. The final plans were announced on June 20, 1968, culminating discussions begun between Xerox and FIGHT during late November 1967—about the time Kodak and FIGHT broke off discussions on independent businesses. FIGHT members were to manage the new factory, while Xerox was to have the job of supervising the training of the workers. [79, 103, 164]

The corporation was to be named FIGHTON, a "people's manufacturing plant." It represented "the first attempt by Government and private industry to start a wholly Negro-owned and operated large-scale business." [181]

The Labor Department's contribution was a training grant of $445,677. This grant was reportedly increased from a smaller amount by Labor Secretary Willard Wirtz himself. RBOC's contribution is the leasing of the plant to FIGHT which the latter plans to purchase and renovate for $200,000. According to an article in the *New York Times* [79], "The plant, now a boarded-up clothing factory, is in the predominately Negro seventh ward, a few blocks from the scene of summer rioting in 1964."

Minister Florence, who again became FIGHT's president (succeeding

McEwen) on June 14, 1968, was to be the chief organizer of the new enterprise which would eventually be completely run and owned by blacks. Florence said the enterprise was "a first for the nation—more radical and militant than all the riots put together." The press conference itself, held at FIGHT headquarters, was certainly a study in contrasts: affluent Xerox businessmen stood out against FIGHT's sparsely furnished office decorated with photographs of Stokely Carmichael, H. Rap Brown, and Che Guevara. [79, 181]

Xerox promised to provide "a full-time manufacturing expert and financial analyst as well as other technical advice, and to guarantee to purchase $500,000 worth of products for each of the first two years." According to the *New York Times* [79], "G. E. Powell, manager of manufacturing for Xerox's system information division, and chairman of the study team that recommended establishing the corporation, . . . [said] the only question about the project [was] . . . 'Why didn't we do it sooner?' "

Footnotes for Chapter 2

1. According to James Ridgeway [144], the number of allied organizations was only 105.

2. Unless otherwise specified, all references to Kodak in this book pertain to either written or oral communications between Kodak officials and the author.

3. A Kodak spokesman who was present at this interview refutes Father Schroth's allegation. According to him, Schroth, in his questioning, "verbally underlined the word special to imply an obligation which might transcend all others. He did not see fit to repeat this implication in his editorial."

4. Appendix C.1.

5. These segregated facilities are in Kodak's plant locations in the deep South—the company has plants in Kingsport, Tennessee; Longview, Texas; and Columbia, South Carolina.

6. This figure was increased to 36 by the end of 1966. [53]

7. Appendix C.2.

8. Remarks by W. S. Vaughn, president of Eastman Kodak, at the luncheon session of the STEP Workshop presented by the National Association of Manufacturers at the Sheraton Hotel, Rochester, October 13, 1966.

9. One Kodak official estimated that more than 50 per cent of Kodak employees had been employed with the company for more than 15 years.

10. Appendix B.1.

11. Appendix B.2.

12. According to the Associated Press, Kodak, in its dealings with FIGHT, avoided using labor-management terms such as "negotiations," and at one meeting Vaughn quickly corrected FIGHT officials whenever they used the term "collective bargaining." [99]

13. Appendix B.3.

14. Appendix B.5.

15. Appendix B.6.

16. The latter was a predominately white association of sympathizers of FIGHT. See Chapter 4.

17. This was the station Kodak people called the "Voice of FIGHT." [47]

18. Vaughn was out of town on December 20. [47]

19. On November 17, 1966, Kodak announced changes in its top management. Albert K. Chapman retired as chairman of the board and of the executive committee; William S. Vaughn, who was then president of the company, succeeded Chapman as board chairman; and Louis K. Eilers, who was previously executive vice president, became president.

20. A Kodak spokesman maintained that Mr. Hoffman, who had earlier worked as an organizer for Saul Alinsky, was biased against Kodak. Although I have no doubt about the accuracy of statements attributed to different Kodak people by Mr. Hoffman in his article, the general tone of his article does appear to be highly sarcastic and one which ridicules Kodak and its officials.

21. The Associated Press learned that a Kodak spokesman did in fact tell Minister Florence that applicants must first be interviewed, and offered them the chance. Minister Florence replied, "We didn't come here to talk about interviews, we came for work." [99]

22. At the same time, FIGHT had a similar arrangement with Xerox. [18]

23. The church organizations included, among others, Domestic and Foreign Missionary Society of the Episcopal Church (5,614 shares), the Board for Homeland Ministries of the United Church of Christ (11,161 shares), the Board of Missions of the Methodist Church (10,500 shares), Y.W.C.A. (2,600 shares), United Presbyterian Church (3,628 shares), and Units of the Reformed Church in America (106 shares). [3, 22, 76, 82, 134]

24. The movement was started by Geoffrey Cowan, a second-year law student at Yale University. Among the investors withholding proxies were his father, Louis G. Cowan, president of Chilmark Press and former president of the Columbia Broadcasting System television network; John Spiegel, the director of the Center for the Study of Violence at Brandeis University; Mrs. Harold Ickes, the widow of the Secretary of Interior in President Franklin D. Roosevelt's cabinet; and other businessmen and members of the academic community.

25. Among these were Xerox, Bausch and Lomb, Ritter-Pfaudler, Graflex, General Dynamics, local banks, and local utilities. [46]

26. According to the *New York Times* [75], Flemington is the home of the law firm of Large, Scannel and Danziger. The tiny frame office of this firm is the official headquarters of 61 corporations, including Eastman Kodak, Standard Oil of New Jersey, American Tobacco, and United Fruit. Most of these firms originally located in New Jersey because of the liberal tax laws.

27. There were only two specific management proposals involving a vote: the election of auditors and the election of several directors. The issue at the general meeting

was, in fact, confrontation of the management, and not one of being for or against the only two proposals which came before the meeting.

28. Commenting on the drop in Kodak's stock prices, a Kodak spokesman said in an interview with the author: "As a practical matter, the market price of Kodak stock and that of most other major corporations traditionally rises in anticipation of good financial results and drops immediately after the announcement of same. . . . Naturally, we were interested in any effect which the controversy with FIGHT might have on our stock prices and we checked into this matter closely; in all candor we were not able to determine that the controversy affected the stock prices in any measurable way."

29. Appendix B.7.

30. In fact, Kodak's plants are either near ghetto areas or not difficult to reach from ghetto areas.

31. The idea for RBOC originally came from Eastman Kodak in 1967, which took the early initiative in organizing and promoting it. [103]

CHAPTER 3

How the Players Moved: Kodak

If you're not part of the solution, you're part of the problem. – A VISTA Slogan

There are two sets of causes which both give rise to a conflict situation and act as inhibiting factors in conflict resolution. The first set relates to the external factors that motivate opposing parties to seek different ends from a joint effort: higher wages for workers, against improved profit position for a company; or seniority rights, against management's right to hire the worker who is most suitable for a job. The parameters of a problem falling in this set are definable and, therefore, easier to analyze and more susceptible to an amicable solution than in the second set.

The second set relates to the problem of the perceptual bias of the opposing parties. This bias may be due to ideological commitment, past history, tradition, the particular experience of opposing groups or their representatives in similar situations, and the external environment and events which may force one or both the parties to assume a certain posture and defend it regardless of whether such a position is tenable or in the long-term interest of the party assuming it.

It is the second set of causes which is the more important. Not only do these causes color the judgment of opposing groups, but also they put the contestants in a sort of conceptual block that determines the process of information seeking and evaluation. Thus parties are likely to pursue wrong strategies, insist on wrong goals, ascribe wrong motives to the opposing group, and display general distrust by using selective information which supports their own viewpoint and avoiding information which conflicts with their viewpoint. Above all, lack of clear understanding of their goals makes them unable to identify and seek the information that is most pertinent to the issue.

Therefore, we can perhaps develop a better insight into Kodak's motives and actions if we first try to understand Kodak management's philosophy and its traditions on the one hand and its perception of the external environment on the other hand.

Kodak Tradition and Philosophy

Kodak is one of the most successful industrial enterprises in the nation[1] and is one of the oldest and largest employers in Rochester. As mentioned earlier, Kodak has contributed generously to such worthy local causes as the University of Rochester, the Community Chest, the Eastman School of Music, and so on. Thus, in terms of conventional and traditionally accepted criteria, Kodak has been a good corporate citizen in the community and has been a socially responsible company.

In terms of its philosophy of management, Kodak felt that it had a responsibility to many sectors of society. The company saw its main function to be the balancing of claims of customers, shareholders, the employees, and the community, while using sound business practices and keeping within certain legal requirements. As one company official close to the

49

FIGHT controversy said in an interview with the author:

> ... you can't do a damn thing in the community unless you're a highly successful company....
>
> The worse thing that we could do for the community in Rochester would be to go bankrupt, see—boom! this community goes right down the hole.... [T] he best thing we can do is to be successful, to exercise our resources wisely for the good of the community and this kind of thing.... You can be as successful as possible and still you can spend money on Community Chest, and contributions here and on hospitals for the poor ... but you can't do these things to the point where you really impair your effectiveness in the success pattern of the company. That will harm the community, not help it.

If we consider these attitudes, we can begin to understand the stress situation created by a confrontation between two groups with different assessments of the value of each other's earlier contributions, different negotiating styles, personalities, and motives. A study today of the FIGHT-Kodak correspondence, along with conversations with both sides in their own offices—FIGHT's shabby storefront and Kodak's carpeted tower on State Street—is ample evidence of the psychological gap between the two worlds of "black power" and "executive suite." [156] Vaughn is a proud and urbane person who regards himself at the helm of a large, successful, and socially responsible private organization. His manner is that of a person who understands the uses and abuses of power and wields the resources of his office with moderation. Florence, on the other hand, "is militant by conviction and rude by preference." Bitterly antiwhite, he sees most issues as white against black. [47]

In addition to image and management philosophy, another factor seems relevant in analyzing the nature of Kodak's strategy in dealing with FIGHT: Kodak's tradition of being a nonunion employer. Many writers who have been sympathetic to Kodak's position attributed some of the mistakes made by Kodak in its dealings with FIGHT to the former's lack of experience in labor negotiations and want of an attitude that necessarily develops through extended exposure to people with totally different backgrounds, motives, and negotiating styles. Commenting on the agreement between Mulder and Florence and its later repudiation, *Business Week* [47] quoted one of Kodak's own executives who thought that lack of labor negotiating experience accounted for some of Kodak's clumsiness: "Union negotiating teaches you when your name is on something, you have got an agreement." Commenting on Kodak's fear of anything akin to unionism, Saul Alinsky, FIGHT's original organizer, was reported in the *New York Times* [77] as saying, "When we talk about negotiations, Kodak thinks about unions, and when they think about unions, they check the airport to see when the last flight came in from Peking." To this, Kodak's chairman retorted that "our labor policies have nothing to do with this," and President Eilers accused FIGHT of making a "savage attack on Rochester's major institutions."

Now we begin to get an idea of the frame of mind of Kodak's management and the effect it had on its decision making. Kodak's management was steeped in the traditional philosophy of business. The executives had, in their opinion, nothing to be ashamed of in their record in working for civic causes and helping minority groups. The problem was that a new element had been added in the external social environment of Kodak which rendered the earlier criteria of social responsibility irrelevant to at least one segment of the population. This new element was the rise of black militancy among a segment of the local blacks who did not accept the nature, extent, or even the manner of Kodak's corporate efforts in community-oriented activities. These militants did not request help; they demanded it. And in dealing with these militants, Kodak management, according to Minister Florence, did not precisely get a little old lady holding out a slotted collection can.

One may well ask why Kodak did not foresee this change. The reasons are manifold. First, Kodak did not have any effective lines of communication with or feedback from those segments of its external environment where major changes were taking place. Second, if any information was received, it was filtered by the lower echelon of operating executives who view any problem from the vantage point of their professional specialty— an inevitable concomitant of rigidity in organizational structure. Third, when the diluted information finally reached top management, it had been so shorn of its "undesirable" elements that they could not judge its impact on their decisions. These facets are discussed in the following sections.

The Lack of Effective Feedback

A large segment of Kodak's employees was from the white professional middle class. Furthermore, the median age of the workers was quite high, and more than half the employees had been with the company for more than 15 years. The percentage of minority-group employees in Kodak's Rochester work force was only 4.2 per cent in 1967. Thus the company had no effective feedback system within its existing structure to recognize, understand, and evaluate these new problems. Problems of minorities, militancy, and reallocation of power did not fit into Kodak's existing personnel makeup and decision-making process.

Kodak's contacts with minority groups were through discussions with the NAACP, the Urban League, and other similarly moderate black organizations. However, what Kodak executives badly needed was an education about the local black community—its frustrations, anger, and changing mood. This they did not get from the conservative black organizations which were, in some sense, also not in touch with the immediate reality of the situation. Without this understanding of the local black community, Kodak managers reacted to FIGHT's confrontations in terms of their own conveniences and preoccupations. They did not or could not grasp the real meaning behind the black man's words. The parties were talking to each other, but not understanding each other. As Joseph Lyford put it [100],

The failure of businessmen generally to establish a social as well as political relationship with Negro communities explains, in part, the emphasis in management-civil rights negotiations on techniques and temporary adjustments rather than long-range programs. The corporation that becomes mired in half-programs or half-solutions will never be free of the problem, it will eventually learn what it is to be "nibbled to death by a duck," as a veteran labor reporter once described the process of perpetual negotiation.

More specifically, Kodak lacked a stereotyped role to play in forming expectations of what the other party's actions might be. However, this lack of a stereotyped role should have allowed Kodak to react in a new creative manner, unencumbered by constraining precedents. Needless to say, Kodak failed to produce any innovative actions or reactions to FIGHT's challenge.

The lack of feedback of timely and relevant information made it difficult, if not impossible, for Kodak's top management to grasp the unconventional nature of the problem, which called for a new and daring approach. Consequently, they perceived the problem as one of "community relations" and appointed those professionals in their organization who were conversant with "similar" problems. The results were not hard to predict. History tells us that in times of crises only those people flourish who rightly interpret the direction of change and lead response to them. Those who remain the same, when the same is no longer fitting, perish. In one observer's words [130], "For the most part they perished because their minds had become like the body of a dinosaur, unfit for the new climate of the world."

The sharp contrast between Kodak's problems with FIGHT and the success of Xerox, another large Rochester-based company, in dealing with the local minorities can only be attributed to the unavailability of relevant information to Kodak's top management and their resultant inability to comprehend and deal with the problem in more realistic terms. In 1965, when FIGHT was just started and was having its teething troubles, Xerox accepted FIGHT as a legitimate black organization and developed with FIGHT a meaningful training program for the hard-core unemployed. In this program FIGHT along with other similar organizations was to refer prospective applicants to Xerox and also assist in their selection and training.[2] Commenting on the reasons for their successful dealings with FIGHT, a Xerox official offered the following explanation to the author:

Several considerations come to mind as to why this relationship developed. First of all, we recognized the value of a grass-roots organization in establishing a channel of communication with the inner city. Thus we believed the success of the FIGHT organization would contribute to the community as a whole. We also recognized that FIGHT was a political organization and as such had to operate to satisfy its "constituents." They, in turn, learned to recognize that we, too, were limited in terms of areas where we could work or where it was possible to "negotiate." Thus, a mutual understanding of the functioning of our respective organizations helped us to work together constructively. Also, I believe we both recognized the value of continuing to talk when we reached an impasse. In every instance, a way was found around the difficulty. A final consideration that comes to mind is that we found the FIGHT organization responded with integrity when we discussed with them highly confidential information on reasons why we could not pursue certain courses of action they had proposed.

The attitude of Kodak officials stands in sharp contrast to that of Xerox. One Kodak official stated that he recognized FIGHT was trying to develop a power base for itself in the community, that Kodak was not opposed to FIGHT acquiring this power base, but that Kodak was not going to be the means by which such power was acquired. The mutual trust between Xerox and FIGHT and the mutual distrust between Kodak and FIGHT were evident throughout the conflict. Thus while Xerox was taking bold actions in every instance and was leading the community, Kodak's actions were notable for their timidity—being too little and coming too late. In April 1968, Kodak's contribution of $100,000 to the Martin Luther King Memorial Fund *followed* a contribution of $250,000 by Mrs. Joseph C. Wilson, wife of Xerox's board chairman. As late as June 1968, when Xerox entered into a joint venture with FIGHT and guaranteed purchases of $500,000 a year for two years from the new company, which would employ 100 hard-core unemployed and would be black-managed, Kodak was launching programs, independent of FIGHT, for the city's black slums in the manufacture of wooden pallets and plastic equipment components and in the repair of cameras, each employing from 9 to 15 workers. True to its philosophy and moral outlook, Kodak piously announced that "Independence, dignity and opportunity more than jobs are needed at this time." [58]

The inevitable outcome of this outlook and approach was that even some of Kodak's substantial efforts in alleviating the problems of minorities went unrecognized and failed to create any trust among FIGHT and its white and black supporters in the sincerity of Kodak's intentions. Joseph Wilson, chairman of the board of Xerox, said [85] :

They [Eastman Kodak] have been doing in connection with the Negroes and Puerto Ricans and other disadvantaged people as much or more proportionately than we, and they have done it quietly without much fanfare.

In terms of our theory of social systems, Eastman Kodak as an institution within the business subsystem was expecting its performance to be evaluated against a value set which was based on the aspirations and expectations of a community which had changed. By not having an adequate feedback system, Kodak did not realize that important changes had taken place in the group alignment of various segments in the community—changes which called for a redistribution of economic goods produced by the subsystem as well as a realignment of the decision-making power within the over-all system. Kodak seemed to substitute a comparatively superlative record for a perception of "system" and "system ethics." This lack of perception caused Kodak to misread the results from disturbances within the system. Under the circumstances, Kodak decided to behave exactly as it had behaved in the past; only this time the rules of the game had changed, leaving Kodak bewildered—like a person who returns to his hometown after a long time to find that everything has changed and he cannot find his way around town.

Organizational Structure

Another dimension of Kodak's problem was akin to that of any other established institution in a subsystem, which by virtue of its long history develops formal decision-making structures in order to expedite day-to-day decisions, to determine centers of authority and responsibility, and, in a way, to run the organization smoothly and efficiently. However, these formal decision-making structures also bring a certain rigidity into the organization, making it less sensitive to new and unusual situations which call for unconventional decisions. As Sethi and Votaw [159] pointed out:

Corporate management tends to be problem oriented and this is its greatest strength as well as its weakness, depending on the nature of the problem. By training and temperament, corporate management is magnificently skilled in dealing with conventional types of problems relating to its business functions.

The parameters—external environment—of these problems are well defined and are either constant or changing at a very slow rate. The only variables whose interaction needs to be interpreted, in the light of new information, are the internal variables with which the management already has the most familiarity and experience. However, the assumption of unchanging external environment is crucial to the validity of the management's evaluation of the problem, because a changing external environment will also alter the nature of the problem thereby rendering inapplicable those solutions which might have been previously tried and found effective. Facts in themselves are innate and meaningless. The consistency of interpretation of a set of data and its analysis in terms of certain hypotheses are possible *only* when exogenous variables—external environment—remain unchanged.

The problem of management decision making in the case of Kodak was further compounded by the nature and personalities of professional experts assigned by the company to deal with FIGHT. These experts came from three departments: industrial relations, public relations, and legal. They brought with them all the strengths and weaknesses associated with professionals. A professional expert is trained to look at a problem only from the viewpoint of his own specialty which becomes his point of reference. He tends to distrust intuitiveness or instinct both in himself and in others. He identifies and associates with people who talk his language and share his interests. Thus he is unable to appreciate or understand the claims of other groups whose frame of reference is different from his own. The system of reward and punishment at the operational level—where most of the experts are employed—in business corporations further reinforces this tendency. The behavior of a professional in a given situation depends on the nature of the image which he has of the organization, his bosses, and their expectations of him. As Sethi and Votaw [159] pointed out:

The quality of his decision is based on the availability of information, validity of earlier experiences and past training in analyzing that information, individual perceptual biases, the risk of failure and the cost of uncertainty both to the individual making the decision and his understanding of its costs to the corporation. It is very difficult, if not impossible, by management edict alone to make people at the operational level change their basic beliefs and operational training acquired over a long period of time.

With this background in mind, we are now ready to analyze Kodak's reactions to FIGHT's demands and the effectiveness or ineffectiveness of Kodak's strategy.

Kodak's Arguments for Rejecting FIGHT's Demands

As has been stated in Chapter 2, the initial conflict revolved around two major demands by FIGHT:

1. That Kodak hire and train, over an 18-month period, between 500 and 600 of the hard-core unemployed for entry-level positions.

2. That FIGHT, as the only organization which is close to the local poor and which has knowledge of their problems, select those people for referral to Kodak and also counsel and assist them during their training period.

Similarly, Kodak's rejection of FIGHT's demands consisted of two main arguments:

1. That Kodak could not commit itself to hiring a substantial number of people because economic conditions could not be predicted so far in advance.

2. That Kodak could not give an exclusive right to one organization to recruit people for training as it would be unfair to other organizations who are active in this area. Moreover, besides being illegal, it would abrogate management's prerogatives, which Kodak would not allow.

Let us take Kodak's arguments one at a time. First, is there any substance in Kodak's contention that it was unable to plan for economic conditions 18 months hence? Any marketing man knows that it takes between 2 and 4 years, or more, from the inception of a consumer product until it achieves mass distribution. During this period, a company spends literally millions of dollars in product development for market introduction. It is inconceivable that a consumer-oriented company would invest so much money without very careful and elaborate planning to estimate consumer demand and potential for sales growth.

Even if we were to accept Kodak's contention of the uncertainty of economic conditions, let us see how much it would have cost the company to maintain an unproductive work force of 600 people. According to government estimates, it costs between $3,000 and $7,000 to train a hard-core unemployed person, of which the government has been willing to pay the employer between $2,000 and $4,000 and even more.[3]

Now, applying this cost analysis to Kodak, let us assume that both training costs and federal contributions would be averages of the ranges mentioned above. The cost picture would look something like this:

1. Cost of training 600 men at $5,000 per man per year $300,000
2. Government contribution to the training costs at $3,000 per man per year $180,000
3. Training costs to Kodak $120,000
4. Training costs, being business expenses, are tax-deductible; therefore, savings from federal taxes at 50 per cent $ 60,000
5. Net costs to Kodak $ 60,000

In 1967, Kodak's net income (after taxes) amounted to $352,257,000 and $4.37 per share. Thus a loss of $60,000 on training costs—assuming that these trainees' contribution to production and profits was zero—would have reduced Kodak's net income by less than one-fifth of 1 per cent, and earnings per share would have declined from $4.37 by less than 0.75 cent per share. Thus, Kodak's rejection of FIGHT's first demand on economic grounds does not seem to have much substance. As a matter of fact, Kodak's subsequent actions indicate that Kodak did not think hiring 600 people would present an unbearable economic hardship. Of the 1,500 jobs proposed by RJI[4] to be filled by Rochester businesses, Kodak was supposed to have agreed to hire 600 persons. In fact, according to an editorial in *Fortune* [3], Kodak did hire 600 blacks in the Rochester area. This was over a 12-month period instead of 18 months.

Now, we turn to Kodak's second argument, on giving FIGHT exclusive referral rights and abrogating management's prerogative. It seems doubtful that FIGHT could or would have insisted on this exclusivity if its first demand had been granted. To begin with, FIGHT had already been working on a nonexclusive basis with Xerox. Second, most competent observers of the scene agree that FIGHT just did not have the resources to recruit and counsel so many people. Therefore, given a victory in its first objective, it stands to reason that FIGHT would have been happy to get out of the second one without a loss of face.

Thus it seems reasonable to conclude that Kodak's refusal of FIGHT's demands and its combining the two arguments for rejection were either a deliberate policy move or a strategic error, the reasons for which must be looked for outside the purview of the arguments publicly stated by Kodak.

Kodak's Strategy during the Initial Negotiations

From the start it was obvious that although the two parties were talking, there was no dialogue. The talks started on a sour note and immediately there was a clash of personalities between Kenneth Howard, chief of Kodak's team, and Minister Florence of FIGHT. Reverend Chandler, another member of FIGHT's negotiating team, said that in one of the early meetings Howard started a sentence with the phrase "You boys," to which Minister Florence heatedly retorted, "Go back to your bosses." Tom Robertson, director of Kodak's public-relations department, denied that Howard or anyone else made such a statement, saying, "we are sophisticated enough here to know that Negroes are obviously sensitive to that kind of talk." [55] The first few meetings were nothing but sparring rounds between the two groups and were confined to name calling and restatement of oft-repeated stands taken by the two parties. However, some points became obvious:

1. Kodak's initial posture toward FIGHT seemed to be that of an indignant parent. As a loving parent would, Kodak stated that it was always willing to start talks again with FIGHT and accept job referrals from them. [42] Kodak people implied that they would give FIGHT what it wanted but not on FIGHT's terms. Granting FIGHT's terms would have meant, from the company's viewpoint, a surrender of some management prerogatives to a crude attempt by FIGHT. This attitude, unfortunately, persisted through most of the time negotiations between the two parties were taking place. At the stockholders' meeting Vaughn characterized Kodak-FIGHT relations in this way:

We extended the hand of welcome. . . . Regrettably, our hand has been rejected repeatedly. [42] An internal company letter stated, "We have been sincere in our discussions with FIGHT. . . . we have affirmed that we cannot delegate decisions on recruitment, selection, and training for Kodak jobs to any outside group. Other organizations with whom we have worked readily understand this."[5]

2. To FIGHT, Kodak seemed to be presenting the black ghetto with proposals formulated by community representatives, but proposals which ultimately required Kodak's acquiescence for execution. In FIGHT's opinion these attitudes smacked of "white colonialism" or "Papa knows best," and were therefore unacceptable. FIGHT maintained that the ghetto should exercise this power for final decision.

3. FIGHT's proposals—outlandish, impractical, and unacceptable from Kodak's point of view—were nevertheless imaginative, and they caught the attention of both the news media and the local poor whose cause FIGHT was allegedly championing.

4. Kodak was on the defensive from the very start. Its posture in the negotiations was limited to explaining what the company had been doing in the area of employing minority-group members and the hard-core unemployed and to aver its willingness to cooperate with all interested groups.

5. Kodak did not seem to have any long-range well-thought-out plan of action or assignment of personnel to handle the situation. Personnel from the department of public relations and industrial relations were assigned on an ad-hoc basis. These people worked on the FIGHT situation along with their other normal duties.

By December 1966, no progress had been made in terms of conflict resolution. However, this statement assumes that the two parties were in fact negotiating to resolve the conflict. An analysis of the events suggests that this was not so. The rigidity of their positions did not leave room for compromise, and the personalities of the negotiators tended to arouse the worst fears in each other. The perceptual block of the professional, which was referred to earlier, becomes obvious when we analyze Howard's opinion about his dealings with Minister Florence. Looking at the situation from the viewpoint of an industrial-relations man, Howard commented to the author:

I think in a certain way Minister Florence and I understand each other. . . . I think in a way I can communicate better with Mr. Florence, but he will never admit that he understands my point of view. I think probably he does. I think to a large extent I can understand his needs and requirements and why he does what he does. We may end up on opposite sides of the table, but we have an understanding of why we are where we are.

Last January they had a big demonstration to which Mr. Florence brought 80 people to apply for jobs—a pure demonstration kind of thing. I had to sort of respond to them single-handed. Well, Minister Florence chewed me up and down and he called me names and he ranted and he raved and he wouldn't let me finish a sentence. This went on for about an hour and a half. Well, in June when we got back together to try and work out this thing, he said, "You were great. You represented that company just beautifully." I said, "Well, you didn't do too badly on your own behalf either."

Again, perhaps this attitude and strategy which created a stalemate in talks was not a mistake but a short-term objective and, if so, it was successfully accomplished.

The Industrial-Relations versus the Public-Relations Approach

Kodak's negotiating team included members from its industrial-relations department and public-relations department. These people had their own particular ways of looking at things, which were often contradictory. The industrial-relations department was interested in getting the job done with minimum cost and sacrifice to the company. Thus it was not interested in winning any kudos for itself and would have been perfectly satisfied to stand back and let the opposing party claim all or some of the credit. The public-relations department was interested in making the company look good and thus tried to make the most propaganda out of the company's concessions, making it impossible for FIGHT to claim any credit among its constituents. Thus, while on the whole recognition from the company for FIGHT's position came in small pieces, it came too slowly and whatever effect it could have was nullified by the bad timing of publicity releases. Many observers believed [55] that

Kodak was insensitive to a basic need of FIGHT's—the need to maintain face, to be recognized as an effective force in bettering the lot of distressed people it represented. Kodak failed to come up with any solutions that might have preserved FIGHT's pride and helped its people without surrendering any of the company's authority.

As a matter of fact, a study of Kodak's actions and timing of its public announcements and press releases seems to indicate that Kodak went out of its way to deny FIGHT any credit for gains in the employment of local minorities or for success in dealing with Kodak. The following examples will make the point:

1. On October 22, 1966, Kodak announced its retaining of the Board for Fundamental Education (BFE) to help Kodak's training program for the hard-core unemployed. The announcement came two days after the last exchange of letters between Kodak and FIGHT since the termination of their meetings on September 19, 1966. It is beyond my comprehension why Kodak could not take FIGHT into its confidence and enlist its cooperation in retaining BFE and expanding the training program, thereby sharing the limelight with FIGHT. As it turned out, an effort by Kodak in the right direction was mired by bitterness and distrust on the part of FIGHT and its supporters.

2. Kodak repudiation of the agreement of December 20, 1966, one day after it was made, without any effort to salvage it and help FIGHT maintain its self-esteem was another action which was bound to deteriorate the situation further.

3. Two weeks after repudiating the agreement, Kodak announced openings in their training programs for between 137 and 158 unskilled persons. Although Kodak invited FIGHT along with ten other agencies to refer applicants to the company, the entire program was kept under cover before it was announced. Moreover, the company's press release gave the impression that this was an independent effort by Kodak in its campaign to help the hard-core unemployed of the community.

4. On April 27, 1967, two days after the demonstrations at Kodak's annual stockholders' meeting, the company announced the appointment of a black public-relations and advertising agency, Uptown Associates. The company blandly announced that the firm had offered its services to Kodak first in June 1964, but at that time those services were not needed. It seems more than a coincidence that Kodak felt a need for those services two days after it was faced with the biggest demonstrations ever staged against a major corporation.

The Agreement of December 20: Internal and External Repercussions

In early December 1966, sympathizers of both Kodak and FIGHT felt that a change in negotiators was necessary if the talks between Kodak and FIGHT were to resume and make any progress. Accordingly, John Mulder, an assistant vice president and the assistant general manager of the Kodak Park plant, who was ostensibly more sympathetic to FIGHT, suggested such a change to Vaughn with the assurance that a similar change would be made at FIGHT's end.

According to a story in the *Wall Street Journal* [55],

On December 16, a FIGHT delegation headed by Mr. Chandler met with a group of top Kodak executives. Mr. Chandler recalls that Kodak chairman Vaughn told them that he was "turning the entire matter over to Mr. Mulder" and said he hoped both parties could agree on a program that would benefit the people in need of help.

However, at the stockholders' meeting, Vaughn gave a different version of this meeting:

The points that were proscribed that were out of bounds for discussion were some of the very points that were included in the agreement and this was carefully explained not only to Mr. Mulder and other Kodak gentlemen present at the meeting on December 16 before the conversations began, but also to several members of FIGHT who were present at that time, including Mr. Chandler, who had been delegated by Minister Florence to lead a group to reopen discussions. Cannon Simpkins, Mr. Jones, and Mrs. Davison were all present, and heard this, and we went over this ground very carefully so there could hardly be any doubt in anybody's mind that we could not agree to a specific number in advance or any exclusive tie-up with people.

Furthermore, there was no thought on anybody's part in Kodak that any agreement in the form of a contract or written agreement was to come from this at all. Nothing whatever was said about this and nothing whatever at the time was contemplated. The only thing that was hoped for there was that we would learn, or that Mr. Mulder and others would be able to work out means of implementing, first the referral from one side, and second the selection and induction into training programs on the other side.

A great deal of emphasis has been put by the FIGHT people on the fact that these unemployed and unemployable, as they call them, not only lack the cultural background, education, acquaintance with industrial life but they lack motivation. They use this term a great deal, and, of course, I believe it. They need to be motivated. They need to get up in the morning. Somebody's got to follow them and all that. We recognize that perhaps they [FIGHT] could be of great help on this. It was purely in the implementation phase, and nothing else, that we contemplated any working arrangement of that kind. But no agreement was ever contemplated.

Furthermore, Mr. Mulder did not have authority to sign an agreement of that kind.[6] I specifically told him if he got into matters involving industrial relations questions or legal questions—I said: "This thing bristles with legal implications, John, so get in touch with the Legal Department or the Industrial Relations Department!" That's the last word I gave him. Well, it didn't happen, that's all. It didn't happen. It was a misfire, of course, and we regret it very much.[7]

Vaughn also said that Mulder signed the document "through an over-zealous desire to resolve the controversy and to succeed where prior discussions had failed." However, the board chairman said, Mulder "did so without realizing the implications involved," and Vaughn admitted that "there was a failure in our communication. Neither I nor anyone else in the company's general management knew of the document before Mr. Mulder signed it." [42]

Mulder has not given his side of the story to the news media or to any other person inside or outside the company. However, in the face of it, Kodak's position of a misunderstanding between top management and Mulder's group seems a bit too innocent and, if true, reflects an incredible lack of sophistication on the part of Mr. Mulder—an assumption which seems very tenuous in view of the facts that we know about the man. To begin with, he had been with the company for almost thirty years, had held an executive rank for quite some time, and was the second top man in one of Kodak's largest film-manufacturing facilities. Moreover, he was president of the city's Council of Social Agencies, his wife was a member of the Friends of FIGHT, and both he and his wife had been active in settlement-house work in Rochester's black ghetto. It seems inconceivable that a man of his ability and breadth of outlook would misunderstand either his boss's instructions or the implications of his actions. Although it is conjectural at this point, it is probable that the misunderstanding lay in the interpretation of the words exchanged between Mulder's team and Vaughn rather than in the words themselves. Mulder probably thought that the problem between Kodak and FIGHT was one of personalities and mutual distrust and that his appointment by Vaughn—in view of Mulder's open sympathy with black causes and his wife's association with the Friends of FIGHT—showed that the company was genuinely interested in doing something. What was needed, in his view, was a fresh approach which would reestablish rapport between the two parties and make possible a mutually acceptable compromise.

Mulder was an operations man, and he saw the problem as that of absorbing 600 additional people into the company's plants without severe effect on its costs. His sympathy for the poor and the hard-core unemployed made the objective all the more desirable. The agreement, despite all its ambiguities, showed this dual concern. To protect the company's position, the period of employment was extended from 18 months to 24 months and was further hedged with the qualification of "unforeseen economic changes affecting the Rochester community." There was more emphasis in the agreement on joint efforts by Kodak and FIGHT rather than exclusivity of FIGHT's recruiting privilege, which was never made clear in the agreement.

Chairman Vaughn, on the other hand, was still looking at the problem in the traditional framework and had not changed his views. He was still a captive of his conceptual blocks and viewed the situation of FIGHT as that of a recalcitrant and irresponsible group which was trying to humble a respectable corporation. All he was offering FIGHT was the same medicine but with a different coating so that it could be swallowed more easily. He and the members of his top-management team still could not properly size up the problem because these men were surrounded by nothing but praise and respect for Kodak's contributions to the society.

The rigidity in the corporation's approach and the somewhat tenuous nature of their arguments became more apparent in the events immediately following Kodak's repudiation of the agreement. FIGHT desperately tried to patch things up and salvage the agreement on almost *any terms acceptable to Kodak, but was rebuffed by company officials.* Earl Gottschalk, writing in the *Wall Street Journal* [55], gave the following account of Kodak's attitude:

On December 23, a delegation headed by Mr. Chandler met with the executive committee. According to Mr. Chandler's account of the meeting—which Kodak agrees is accurate—FIGHT asked Louis D. Eilers, president of Kodak, to sign the agreement. He declined, saying the company simply could not give a second party any voice in determining its labor relations and employment practices. Then, says Mr. Chandler, "We asked them to put into the agreement anything they wanted to, or to change it in any way they desired. Again, Mr. Eilers said no."

"At that point," says Mr. Chandler, "Mr. Florence even suggested that the entire document could be dispensed with if he and either Mr. Eilers or Mr. Vaughn could go on television and make a joint statement saying simply that FIGHT and Kodak would work together to get more jobs for ghetto Negroes. This idea met with no enthusiasm either."

Thus the issue of whether or not Kodak should accept FIGHT demands merged, in some people's minds, with the personality of Ken Howard. In an interview with the author, Howard stated that he didn't know how widespread this feeling was. "I am aware of some of it, but most of the people who are mad at me do not talk to me about it. It has been the same here since I got this assignment. People who do not agree with you do not talk with you about it because essentially you are following the management policy and position in this area."

After the repudiation of the agreement, Kenneth Howard was back in the saddle as Kodak's chief negotiator. However, it would be erroneous to assume that Howard had something to do with the repudiation of the agreement or that he was a better negotiator than Mulder. It would be more correct to say that Howard's views of the situation and of what Kodak ought to do were more congruent with those of top management than were Mulder's. Howard may have been wrong for the situation but he was right for the management. As a second-echelon official, he was simply presenting the management's views as faithfully as he could. The fact that he happened to agree with that position only made him more suitable for the job.

Kodak did not envisage the effect of its repudiation on the nation. For a company of its size and resources it is hard to comprehend how Kodak could have been so far off the mark in taking the pulse of the social system. While the company was handling the problem in the confines of Rochester as a local issue, the controversy had received national attention largely because of the efforts of FIGHT and its supporters, the National Council of Churches, the Catholic church, and because it involved a large corporation. To an outsider it looked like a fight between David and Goliath. Gottschalk [55] reported that according to Edward L. Bernays, a well-known public-relations counsel and author,

[It] fell like a bombshell into the pro-civil rights milieu of contemporary America. A company dependent on good will went against all the current social mores and folkways. It was a colossal public relations blunder that will go down in history.

The Public-Relations Strategy after Repudiation of the Agreement

In general, Kodak's public-relations strategy during the height of the crisis had been to "cool it." However, misunderstanding was so widespread by the middle of November 1967 that Kodak prepared a kit of relevant documents relating to the controversy. The kit included all correspondence between FIGHT and Kodak, summaries of the meeting discussions, newspaper clippings, excerpts from speeches by Alinsky, Vaughn, and Florence, and extracts from Kodak management letters concerning its "Plan for Progress." Also included were descriptions of Kodak training programs, including the BFE program. This kit was sent to all Kodak foremen and supervisors, to local business leaders and clergy, and to some people and groups outside Rochester.

After the repudiation of the agreement, Kodak stiffened its attitude toward FIGHT and started publicly attacking FIGHT and its motives as well as defending Kodak's own position. The company took a full-page ad in the local newspapers explaining why it could not honor the agreement and describing its past and future plans for helping the disadvantaged. [99] Kodak was now on the offensive and its entire public-relations machinery was geared to discredit FIGHT in an effort to distract the public mind from Kodak's act of disowning the agreement. However, this strategy also had the effect of keeping the issue alive before the public and thus complementing FIGHT's efforts. As reported in the *New Republic* [144], on January 6, 1967, Eilers held a news conference during which he stated:

From what I have been able to learn of other Alinsky efforts this one seems to be developing according to his pattern. . . . An issue is picked. Community conflict is created by much talk, noise and pressure and the creation of confusing ideas.

In our case, the issue the Alinsky forces chose seemed to be related to the employment of Negroes. It is more and more clear, however, that all the talk about unemployment is only an issue or device being used to screen what FIGHT is really doing—and that is making a drive for power in the community.

Kodak officials closest to the FIGHT controversy cited Alinsky's book *Reveille for Radicals* (published in 1946) as the blueprint for his operations. Alinsky tactics, they claimed, were styled on union-organizing tactics of the 1930's. [99]

Business Week in its issue of April 29, 1967 [47] stated that President Louis Eilers, looking back over the troubles with FIGHT, commented: "I think we used too much patience." With regard to the press, one Kodak official outlined the company's strategy thus, in an interview with the author:

We tried to make as few statements as possible in the paper. We said nothing at all against FIGHT or against Florence. We just didn't respond most of the time. If the newspapers would call with some particularly erroneous statement, we would try to set the record straight.

Company industrial managers also kept the community groups they belonged to informed of company policy and progress.

Why did Kodak change its public-relations strategy after the agreement of December 20? To answer this question, we must first analyze Kodak's motives. Prior to its repudiation of the agreement, Kodak regarded FIGHT as a small militant organization which, although a nuisance, was not a serious threat to Kodak. The use of mass media meant bringing the issue to a large body of people who, according to Kodak, were members of its own subsystem and believed in the same values. These people therefore needed no convincing on Kodak's position. On the other hand, any airing of the controversy would have elevated FIGHT to the same level as Kodak in the eyes of the members of the subsystem. Publicity would have made FIGHT an institution within the same subsystem and therefore subject to greater consideration than Kodak was willing to accord it. Such publicity would also have aroused the curiosity and suspicion of some members in the subsystem who might not otherwise have concerned themselves with the controversy.

However, after the agreement of December 20, Kodak changed its objectives. It wanted to prevent FIGHT from achieving an objective which Kodak considered detrimental to the interests of the organization. The company resorted to a multiple strategy. First, it mobilized all its resources of generating publicity to create an atmosphere of critical and dangerous urgency in the mind of the public. Second, it attempted to create a long-range and generalized image for the corporation while at the same time diverting public attention from the immediate issues. Third, to establish the legitimacy of its objectives and their conformity with socially accepted norms, Kodak used "good" symbols to characterize its actions and "evil" symbols to identify its opponents. Thus, in its publicity releases, Kodak called itself a "progressive" organization and emphasized its community-assistance programs, including those involving blacks. Simultaneously, Kodak branded FIGHT as a "radical" organization whose leadership was more interested in grabbing power for personal aggrandizement rather than in helping the poor. It further accused FIGHT of attempting to destroy all similarly "good" and "constructive" organizations in the community.

Although the theory behind Kodak's public relations was right, the strategies employed by the company to put this theory into practice were wrong—with the result that Kodak's campaign to win friends and humiliate enemies was a failure. The problem again lies with Kodak's value set. Kodak used symbols of "good" and "evil" which belonged to a bygone era. Thus while Kodak considered the word *radical* to be derogatory, it was regarded as a synonym of *progressive* in the minds of an increasing number of people. Its "good" symbols of the company's record were also not identified as such by a large segment of the population. Furthermore, its efforts to discredit FIGHT failed because

1. FIGHT was successful in keeping the immediate issues before the public, and Kodak could not answer them convincingly.

2. FIGHT had developed effective working relations with other large organizations in Rochester, such as Xerox, and therefore could not be considered as bad as Kodak wanted it to look.

3. A large part of the membership of the Establishment—church organizations, influential white liberals, trade unions, intellectuals, and the black community—believed in and agreed with FIGHT's position and was not persuaded by Kodak's publicity campaign.

Changes in Organizational Structure and Strategy

Another aspect of the problem was that of making both top management and operating staff comprehend the nature of changes taking place outside the corporation in terms of their effect not only on corporate policies but on operating procedures and methods as well. As one Kodak industrial-relations official responsible for dealing with minority problems put it in an interview with the author:

There is an urgent need for doing something other than the traditional approaches if we are to comprehend the problem. I do not think people outside of my particular field realize what revolutionary changes have already taken place. For example, take the case of hard-core unemployed. Think what you are doing to an employment interviewer. Here is a person who has been taught, trained, and paid to select the applicant who is best qualified for particular jobs out of hundreds of people that he interviews every month. "Try to get them as best qualified as you can for that job." You have a company that has spent literally, and I suppose it goes into billions of dollars, making itself an attractive place to work. The only justification is so that you can maintain the best possible work force for getting out your products. All of a sudden I say to this employment interviewer, "Forget everything that you have learned. You are going to go with me over to FIGHT headquarters and we are going to interview some hard-core unemployed and you are going to hire some." All of a sudden here is a guy who for twenty years has been taught to do the best job he can, to find the person best suited for a job, and now he is told to hire somebody who just walks in off the street and who is hard-core unemployed. Well, by what standards does he do this? How does he interview the guy? What questions does he ask? He is not looking for somebody who is best qualified for the job. We have asked him to turn himself upside down and do things just the opposite.

And it is worse than that in a sense because we have these special training programs. . . . The training programs are set up specifically to accommodate people who could not otherwise qualify for a Kodak job. Now if the interviewer makes a mistake and picks a guy who might have made it on his own, you know, might have walked in the door and been able to be hired, he is occupying one of these positions and he should not even be in there.

Summary

An analysis of Kodak's posture toward FIGHT and its strategies in dealing with FIGHT and other elements of the community reveals that Kodak eventually realized the ineffectiveness of its public-relations strategy. The firm tried to amend its strategy by hiring outside agencies, such as Carl Byoir and Associates, for further help in dealing with ethnic groups. Kodak also approached other professional experts in urban and ghetto problems to aid specifically in dealing with FIGHT. In May 1967, Kodak invited Daniel P. Moynihan, former Assistant Secretary of Labor and then Chairman of the President's Council on Urban Affairs, for consultations. Moynihan talked with both Kodak officials and FIGHT people to seek ways of possible compromise. A week of secret meetings between the two parties resulted in an agreement. The controversy was ostensibly resolved on June 23, 1967, when Kodak's president Eilers sent a telegram to Minister Florence which was endorsed by FIGHT the same evening.

It is, however, doubtful that Kodak changed its basic attitude or value system. Even after the telegram of June 23, Kodak and FIGHT accused each other of misrepresentation in the press concerning Kodak's part in starting a microfilming plant in the black ghetto of Rochester. Direct communications between the two groups were either at a minimum or nonexistent. Kodak was for the most part going on its own—without FIGHT—in announcing plans for its projects to help the urban poor and the hard-core unemployed. This was at a time when other large Rochester companies, such as Ritter-Pfaudler and Xerox, were maintaining good relations with FIGHT. Commenting on Kodak's problems with FIGHT, Donald A. Gaudion, president of Ritter-Pfaudler, contended that Kodak had made its basic mistake when it allowed discussions of the basic issue— jobs for blacks—to be diverted into a "battle over management prerogatives." [55]

In the end, Kodak granted to FIGHT essentially what had been asked for and conceded to FIGHT—although not explicitly—what it had strenuously objected all along that it would not do. Moreover, its policy of piecemeal action, which had been a defensive response to outside pressures, eventually cost Kodak perhaps as much as if it had agreed to FIGHT's proposals in the first place. Yet Kodak did not gain the respect of many important and vocal segments of the nation's population which it had desperately sought and which a company of Kodak's size would always need.

Kodak treated the issue of minorities and its problems with FIGHT in terms of making "concessions" to these "people" rather than of undertaking a necessary social obligation. Kodak's record of helping the underprivileged reflected a status anxiety. The company was proud that its record was one of the best and was distressed and unhappy that new demands were being made by a militant group when, from the company's viewpoint, it had already done so much for the local minorities. Kodak could have anticipated the confrontation and in a sense treated it as a challenge. The company could have approached the problem as one that must be solved rather than as charity which must await the convenience and good will of management. As Joseph Lyford [100] pointed out,

Where the Negro succeeds in opening up employment and promotion opportunities, he will apply greater and greater pressure for more until he has achieved full equality. The businessman who makes "concessions" under pressure then asks, "When will they stop? How far will the civil rights people go?" The question need never have been asked had these same businessmen acted on their own initiative, with some imagination and understanding. Concessions that have to be extracted by pressure are seldom appreciated and they never satisfy. The white business executive should consider the issue of Negro employment from the Negro's angle. The more progress the executive makes, the more progress he should seek. In other words, he could become a little more competitive about success in his dealing with the Negro.

Footnotes for Chapter 3

1. According to *Fortune's* directory of the 500 largest manufacturing corporations in the United States, Eastman Kodak, in 1967, ranked 29 in terms of sales volume (up from 34 in 1966), 23 with assets, 9 in income, and 20 in number of employees. In 1967, it earned 14.7 per cent on its sales and 21.4 per cent on invested capital. Between 1966 and 1967, Kodak's earnings per share grew by 14.7 per cent.

2. It might be noted here that in its dealings with Kodak later in 1966 FIGHT demanded an *exclusive* right of referral for hard-core unemployed trainees.

3. In the case of AVCO, which was planning to train about 350 people for skilled jobs in a new printing plant to be opened by the company in Boston's Roxbury ghetto, the federal government offered to pay about $5,000 per person. In a similar arrangement with another company, the government agreed to pay about $3,500 per man. [136]

4. See Chapter 2, page 38.

5. Appendix C.2.

6. The By-laws of Eastman Kodak Company state that the duties of an assistant vice president are those "required of him by the Board [of Directors]."

7. Transcript of Chairman Vaughn's comments at the stockholders' meeting.

CHAPTER 4

How the Players Moved: FIGHT

I think the aura of para paramilitarism among the black militant groups speaks much more of fear than it does of confidence. Negro agitation is requiring America to reexamine its comforting myths and may yet catalyze the drastic reforms that will save us from social catastrophe. — Martin Luther King, Jr.

"We are celebrating the first anniversary of black power in Rochester . . . the first anniversary of our declaration of manhood and independence." Slamming his fist down, Minister Florence said: "Our proudest claim is that our proud name, FIGHT, is feared and hated in every quarter where white men still believe they're entitled to live off the sweat of black men's brows." [78]

"We aim to incite" might well have been the rallying cry of FIGHT under the leadership of Minister Florence, who felt that Rochester provided an important forum for blacks. "Rochester will never be the same because FIGHT exists. The white folks at least know we poor black folk exist." [99]

Are these the cries of a paranoiac bent on destroying himself, the cause he purportedly espouses, and the community whose support he must have if he is to achieve any success? Or are these the slogans designed by a shrewd, calculating man determined to bring black people under his influence and to make the white Establishment not only accept him as a leader but also view their response to his demands as granting favors to the black people of Rochester?

FIGHT within the Context of the Social System

Florence has been heavily criticized by the local news media and even by some of his white supporters (who were FIGHT's financial backbone) for his extreme, militant posture and for his violent anti-Establishment, antiwhite, and even anti-Semitic statements.[1] Probably, FIGHT could have achieved greater success with Kodak if it had taken pains to praise Kodak for the efforts being made to hire people from minority groups rather than brand the company as institutionally racist. Kodak executives might have responded to new demands more readily if their past efforts had received proper recognition.

Moreover, instead of taking on a giant corporation like Kodak, which was also a nonunion company, FIGHT could have started with small local businessmen—retail merchants, gas stations, slum landlords—who probably depended to a greater degree on the patronage of the local black community, whose record of discrimination was more obvious, or who had less staying power and therefore were more vulnerable to such pressures. FIGHT could have then built a power base, broadened its support in the community, and would have been in a better position to confront a big corporation like Kodak. Such an approach was successfully tried in Philadelphia, where a group of black clergy launched a project called the Selective Patronage Program (SPP). In this program various companies like bakeries, soft-drink bottlers, fuel-oil distributors, and oil companies were successively persuaded to hire a certain number of additional workers in skilled or "status" positions. The means of persuasion was a boycott of the companies' products in campaigns organized through sermons from the pulpit. The number of positions allocated to each company was determined by the SPP, but was generally quite small in proportion to a company's total work force. Thus, although individual companies hired only a few more workers, the over-all gains in black employment were substantial. [95]

It would be overly simplistic to compare Minister Florence's approach to that of the SPP in Philadelphia and declare the former as less effective. Such a comparison would be valid if we could assume that in both cases the external environment and the balance of power among various subsystems and institutions were similar. However, as we shall see in the subsequent section, such an assumption is untenable, so that a comparison between the two situations is irrelevant.

In order to understand FIGHT's motives for following a militant strategy and to apprehend the effectiveness of that strategy, it is necessary that we view FIGHT within the context of the over-all social system. This will involve a study of (1) the conditions which led to the creation of FIGHT, (2) the needs and expectations of local minority groups which FIGHT aspired to fulfill in competition with other institutions working in the same area, (3) the problems which FIGHT faced in its struggle for survival against these established institutions which held the balance of power, and (4) the philosophy and outlook of FIGHT's leadership. In terms of our theory of social systems, we are talking of three sets of factors which have an important bearing on FIGHT's actions:

1. The value set of the over-all system and the rate at which the total system is changing its goals to satisfy the needs of all members in the system, to bring about a greater congruence between the value sets of the various subsystems and that of the total system, and to maintain enough flexibility in the system so that disgruntled individuals can form new institutions and subsystems.

2. The need of an emerging institution to define its value set in such a manner that it can develop a new identity for itself and seek allegiance from individuals who currently belong either to competing units within the same subsystem or to different subsystems.

3. A new and developing institution or subsystem must also innovate in its operational strategies if it is to succeed in changing bargaining relationships with established subsystems which have heavy odds in their favor if the game is to be played according to the existing rules. Operational innovation becomes more important if the over-all system is rigid or if the changes sought by the disenchanted minorities call for a major realignment in the spheres of influence of various subsystems and institutions within those subsystems.

We shall now focus our attention on Rochester and FIGHT and analyze the situation within the conceptual framework outlined above.

The race riots of July 1964 vividly brought home to the Rochester community the plight of the black man. Of the 893 individuals arrested for involvement in the riots, 90 per cent were either unskilled or unemployed. In all, 720 blacks were arrested, 660 of whom were born outside of New York State. [178] About a year before the riots, William Vogler, of the *Rochester Democrat & Chronicle*, wrote five articles (April 22-27, 1963) reviewing the economic and social conditions of the Rochester Negroes. As reported in *Crisis* [173] Vogler had said:

A major factor behind white and non-white income difference is the unemployment rate. The male unemployment percentages in 1961 nationally were non-white, 12.9 and white, 5.7. The comparable Rochester rates in 1960 were non-white 14.5 and white, 4.8.

These non-white figures contrasted sharply with the affluence of the white majority and the almost full employment among whites. The problem was further complicated by the fact that a large number of Rochester's black people had migrated from the South. They had no affinity with the city's past and the contributions made by its large and successful corporate citizens. On the other hand, these people considered it their right to share equally in the prosperous conditions prevailing in the city and were not to be denied equal opportunities because they did not share its past.

However, one year after the July riots, things seemed to have changed but little for the poor. In April 1965, before resigning as Rochester's city manager, Porter W. Homer submitted a report on the riots of 1964. After reviewing the progress achieved since then, he concluded: "it is apparent that the city is tragically close to talking itself into another riot." [173] Some progress had indeed been made, in reorganizing the police department and in establishing a "crash" program of summer employment. However, most other programs were still in the planning stage, and their implementation was obstructed by disagreements between the white community and the black. Consequently, little if any benefits had filtered to the poor, the angry, and the frustrated. The situation was well summed up in the *Reporter* [178] by a white woman employee of one of the stores which was looted during the riots:

We see no changes in the condition that makes these people restless and without hope. An awful lot of people are trying to help but as far as I can see they just aren't reaching the people who rioted.

Insufficient Support from the Local Black Community

The black community of Rochester was fractionated and without political leadership of any kind. As one observer [145] put it,

There is not much of a civil rights movement; and since only 3,000 people go to church regularly, Negro churches are not much help. . . . The Negro community is united only in its detestation of the white police; this spills over into a general dislike of whites which finds an outlet in an ill-defined sentiment for black nationalism.

The only black organizations in the city were CORE and NAACP,[2] but both had little influence either on the black youth or on a large majority of the black poor. Despite various attempts, neither had any success in broadening its base or strengthening its local chapter. Both organizations are presently functioning in the city, but few community leaders consider them a major force. Although the NAACP provided legal defense for those arrested in the July riots, it also severely criticized the rioters for creating civil disorders. In an address to the rioters, Reverend Richard A. Hilde-brand, president of the New York branch of the NAACP, said [2],

No responsible community leadership condones the rioting, the reckless provocation of police officers, the destruction of property and looting. We condemn such actions and we sternly warn those guilty of such acts that they are betraying their own people and the cause of racial justice everywhere.

Notwithstanding this assistance, the local black community just did not believe that the NAACP's moderate and conservative approach to their problems and its insistence on using legal means would accomplish any-thing. They had long since given up hope of seeing the white man give up anything willingly. Robert A. Rhodes, of Rochester's NAACP chapter, blamed the local white Establishment for the NAACP's lack of influence among the city's poor, saying, "Negro leaders are and always will be avail-able, but they must be recognized." [178] However, in more somber moments, the area's highest elected black official, Mrs. Constance Mitchell, supervisor on the Monroe County board, admitted a lack of rapport be-tween the local civil-rights leaders and the black youth [178]:

Civil-rights always was a bourgeois movement here. There never was room for the kids. . . . I went down to Selma, and when I came back the kids said, "Hey, Mrs. Mitchell, why did you go down there? What good did it do you?" Why, they don't even know what the civil-rights movement in this country means.

The city's poor were also affected by the growing militancy of black people in other parts of the nation and their dramatic, if not always substantive, success in achieving their goals. The Northern cities and their business and civic establishments had not comprehended the changes that had taken place in the composition and goals of the civil-rights movement. The movement was, for a long time, dominated by middle-class blacks whose primary goal was equality of status with whites, according to white standards, but in an integrated society. To prove that he was civilized and therefore worthy of that status, the middle-class black scrupulously ob-served the rules of the prevailing social system to achieve his objectives. However, as Charles Silberman has pointed out, the entry of the poor forced a change in the protest movement's goals. It also meant that the great majority of blacks were more concerned with where they worked than with where they ate. A shift of emphasis from civil rights to jobs brought with it the danger of violence when whites began to fear a threat on their pocketbooks. [161]

A trend toward militancy and mistrust of the white Establishment, its value set and its *modus operandi*, among black people seems to have been inevitable when considered in the light of different environmental condi-tions in the North as compared to the South. In the South, even peaceful civil-rights movements had a hard time surviving because of an almost uniform animosity of the dominant majority and an active suppression tacitly condoned and even supported by the local and state governments. No movement started by a minority group with little or no material re-sources could withstand such an oppressive assault. In the North, however, conditions were different. Blacks had the support of a substantial number of influential whites, and local laws were administered more fairly. These were, however, only necessary but not sufficient conditions for the growth of militancy among blacks in the North. Other important factors contributed to this trend.

According to Robin Williams [177],

militancy, except for sporadic and short-lived uprisings, is not characteristic of the most deprived and oppressed groups, but rather of those who have gained considerable rights so that they are able realistically to hope for more. . . . [A] militant reaction from a minority group is more likely when (a) the group's position is rapidly improving, or (b) when it is rapidly deteriorating, especially when this follows a period of improvement.

A group conscience, coupled with an overt struggle for recognition, is further intensified where a minority group is concentrated in large numbers in a small area, where the extent of relative social deprivation is more apparent, where there is intense competition for jobs with the dominant group in its lower strata—which comprises the largest segment of the dominant group and has to fear real economic threat for the minority group —and where a rising level of education causes an awareness of the collective power of the group and raises their level of expectation.

Moderation and proponents of moderation therefore have no appeal, at least in the interim period, to the black people. As James Baldwin once said,

The brutality with which Negroes are treated in this country simply cannot be overstated, however unwilling white men may be to hear it. In the beginning—and neither can this be overstated—a Negro just cannot *believe* that white people are treating him as they do; he does not know what he has done to merit it. And when he realizes that the treatment accorded him has nothing to do with anything he has done, that the attempt of white people to destroy him—for that is what it is—is utterly gratuitous, it is not hard for him to think of white people as devils.[3]

Many scholars have predicted that the militancy of the black movement will continue to grow because of lack of commitment by the majority group to make a determined attack on the problems of the ghetto and the refusal of the black people to wait any longer for things to change gradually.[4] As Silberman [161] has noted,

Lower-class Negroes do not want to be represented to the whites as non-violent. Their anger has been suppressed far too long, and they are deriving too much pleasure from the discovery that it is the white man who is afraid of them rather than they who are afraid of the white man.

The black minority does not have trust in the promises of the white society; the evidence of the broken promises and the injustices done to the American Negro are amply documented in the pages of American history. Moreover, the blacks refuse to accept the leadership of those blacks who appear to have faith in the values and premises of the white society. To them, there is scant difference between legal and illegal means—for the means seem to them to be designed to deny them of their legitimate claims—and the achievement of ends is the only relevant question. They view tokenism as a gimmick and exploit token gestures for what they are. But such tokens of help—like training programs without specific jobs, larger welfare payments, summer youth employment—do not buy any long-term peace because the blacks refuse to feel grateful for these tokens of charity and will always come back for more.

These, then, were the environmental factors which faced Northern cities and the blacks living in them. Rochester was no exception. A year after the race riots, the problems which caused them persisted, and the frustration of blacks continued to grow. The local church organizations realized that one reason for the lack of progress in solving the problems of the city's poor was the absence of an organization which could effectively present the complaints of the poor to the city's administration, industry, and civic organizations. The Board for Urban Ministry first tried Martin Luther King's Southern Christian Leadership Conference. However, the SCLC team soon realized that it would not be able to make much headway with the local blacks and, consequently, suggested that the Urban Ministry invite Saul Alinsky.

The fragmented nature of the local black community would have presented a formidable challenge in organization, but Alinsky's techniques did not call for organizing the masses. A small, dedicated cadre of workers was all Alinsky needed to make the organization move. It is easier to maintain control, achieve discipline, and provide for cohesiveness in group objectives and leadership in a small organization. A not unusual phenomenon in emerging groups with no prior familiarity in the acquisition and use of power is an internal struggle for power that severely limits the effectiveness of the group itself and its ability to work with other groups. To some extent this struggle is to be expected because new leaders, not accustomed to working together, see their influence as diminished if they must share the limelight with others. Their concept of power is limited and defined in personal terms; their time dimension is confined to the present. The lack of a long-term time perspective (the result of poverty or fear of the future) also leads to an emphasis on immediate and personal needs by the members of the group and detracts attention from underlying causes, whose elimination is a slow, undramatic process. The loyalty of the members of such a group, therefore, is always shifting to the leader who can most closely relate to their immediate needs and who can promise quick and dramatic results.

FIGHT, therefore, had to start with a very small base of actual power. But to extend its sphere of influence and maintain it on any sustained basis, it had to seek support from the local poor and from the liberal and intellectual elements of the white Establishment both locally and nationally. Thus FIGHT had to satisfy two groups of constituents: the city's poor and FIGHT's white supporters. This dual constituency posed certain problems for FIGHT. To win the poor and wean them away from other organizations as well as from their own apathy, FIGHT had to adopt a constantly militant posture, promise larger gains to the poor, and also buck the Establishment. However, its white supporters frowned on militancy for its own sake, preferring moderation and a somewhat slower rate of gains as opposed to FIGHT's unyielding attitude with its accompanying danger of a disruption in the social order. An analysis of FIGHT's strategy is a study of FIGHT's attempts to satisfy two groups whose viewpoints were often opposed to each other.

Unfortunately, neither Kodak nor local leaders subjected the situation to the kind of dispassionate analysis that could have both helped the local minorities and avoided the bitter divisiveness between whites and blacks that resulted. Because of its small power base and its need to enlist wider support among the black community, FIGHT was obliged to pick up *every* black grievance and champion its cause, exaggerate the issues to achieve dramatic effect, confront the most powerful among the whites to foster among black as well as white sympathizers the image of the underdog, and make maximum use of the news media to keep the issues alive. In these activities, FIGHT and its president, Minister Florence, were following Saul Alinsky's advice to the letter [55]:

Don't just ask—demand! Back up your demands with constant friction, constant pressure to win concession after concession. In short play the role of a hard-nosed leader of a powerful union—the very role Kodak could be expected to view with most distaste, the very approach it could be expected to resist almost instinctively.

Support from White Liberals

Though FIGHT may have lacked sufficient black support initially, it had more than enough from white liberals. As reported in the *New Republic* [145],

One of FIGHT's big problems is to keep white liberals from swallowing the organization whole. FIGHT permits any Negro to join, but demands that whites be sponsored by a member organization. This is disconcerting to some of the white ministers who played a major part in bringing FIGHT into being in the first place. But Florence and Alinsky argue that FIGHT must reach the bitter, frustrated Negroes before it becomes encumbered with white liberals.

And so, Friends of FIGHT was organized as a parallel organization to engage the white liberals. According to the *New Republic* [144],

Friends of FIGHT now has a membership of 450 and looks like the beginnings of a grass-roots political organization that in the end may have more influence in Rochester than FIGHT could ever hope for. Friends of FIGHT wants to substitute a city income tax for the sales tax, throw out the city manager and get in a strong mayor. They want to run the Gannett press out of town and abolish the human relations commission, which is regarded as useless. Employees of Kodak and Xerox are among those active in Friends of FIGHT.

However, there is some friction between the two groups. As one reporter noted [18]:

Friends welcome their own exclusion from the councils of FIGHT on the theory that for too long in helping the Negroes the white man has told them what to do; now the Negroes are to have their innings. The Friends have, therefore, followed Florence's dictation, and while this has worked well for a time—Florence's prestige is certainly enhanced by telling whites what to do—certain problems are beginning to arise. How long, for instance, can Friends of FIGHT be effective if it is merely an echo? There are signs that the two groups have differed over education, with FIGHT pressing more for quality schools in the Negro districts and Friends tending to emphasize integration. Some Friends would like to organize research on school segregation or housing, research FIGHT badly needs, but Florence will not give them the go-ahead. Some are concerned about the unemployed whites in Rochester, too. "I think FIGHT prefers that we sit around and save our energies for things they think up," said the former acting president of Friends, Benjamin Phelosof. "Friends," said Florence, "only do what they are directed to do." The first president of Friends had resigned, citing the press of other business. Now Phelosof has resigned, too.

Kodak officials also had little faith in the ability of Friends of FIGHT or similar groups to bring about a rapprochement between FIGHT and

Kodak or to build a communication bridge between the white and the black leadership. If anything, there was more cynicism in their attitude toward the white liberals than toward FIGHT. Perhaps the remarks of one of Kodak's officials during an interview sum up this attitude:

Florence got up there in Immaculate Conception Hall here last spring, March, and he had a large group of people, amongst them a bunch of priests and nuns and clergymen. They were there because they wanted to be a part of this thing. And what does Florence tell them, he says, "You hate me . . . [B]ecause I'm black and you're white so you've got to hate me, and you hate me." So what did these people do? They said, "I'm here because I love him. What can I do to show him that I love him more" and they get drawn in further.

Some of these white liberals aren't really interested in knowing the true facts or anything else. They've made up their minds. There are one or two that I know in this Friends of FIGHT group that have a perspective on this, that understand the nature of the process and you can talk with them, but with most of them, there's not much point in talking with them.

Friends of FIGHT, of course, do not comprise all of FIGHT's white support which in effect is a mixed bag of left-wingers, do-gooders, some church oriented, some politically oriented, a coalition now of Voters for Peace, Friends of FIGHT, Women Strike for Peace. They support whatever the big issue is, and in early 1968 the big issue was Vietnam, but if FIGHT gets another big issue they'll be right back there again.

The New Organization: Goals, Leaders, and Attitudes

The primary goal of FIGHT was to become the most effective spokesman for the city's poor. In achieving that goal, Minister Florence was running afoul of the moderates not only among the whites but among the blacks as well. This was to be expected because the objectives of poor blacks did not agree with those of middle-class blacks who seek identification with the white majority rather than with their low-status minority group. Kurt Lewin [97] has described this phenomenon as "peripheral theory" thus:

In a minority group, individual members who are economically successful, or who have distinguished themselves in their professions, usually gain a high degree of acceptance by the majority group. This places them culturally at the periphery of the underprivileged group and makes them more likely to be marginal persons. They frequently have a negative balance and are particularly eager to have their "good connections" not endangered by too close a contact with those sections of the underprivileged group which are not acceptable to the majority.

FIGHT wanted to develop a power base by drawing support from the community and by uniting the black people. Probably more than anything else the group wanted society as a whole to understand the squalor of ghetto life, to be conscious of the problems of the black in the ghetto. Another objective of FIGHT was that it needed to differentiate itself from other peer elements attempting to gain power as the representative of the minorities, and its method of differentiating itself was through the use of new tactics which were unpredictable given the conventional or prevailing management wisdom.

Most important of all, FIGHT aimed at controlling and representing the *whole* black man, not just some aspects of his life. Perhaps under the present circumstances, this may be a desirable short-term goal, but if

FIGHT and other similar militant organizations succeed in entrenching themselves as the sole voice of the black people, the prospects can be frightening, as their effect will reach far beyond the issues of economic and social equality. A black militant organization is different from earlier ethnic organizations—the Jews, the Irish, or the Italians—in the United States. Although these organizations also represented the whole man, their emphasis was to shepherd him and protect him only until he achieved equality of opportunity with the majority within the existing subsystems like business, politics, education, and professions. Once members of their organizations had achieved this equality of status, they were free to join rival institutions within various subsystems (for example, different political parties), to subscribe to different business and social philosophies, and to follow separate modes of life. They could do all this and yet maintain an identity with their ethnic background and organizations, and enjoy commonly shared cultural traits and beliefs.

The black militant leader of today is not trying to represent the whole man as an interim device only. He intends to make his organization a full-fledged subsystem superseding all other subsystems—as far as the black man is concerned—which aim to represent only some aspect of an individual's life. Unlike the other ethnically oriented organizations, the black militants do not subscribe to the ideals of the existing social system, which they consider as irrelevant for the black man in America. Black militants are attempting to mold the whole black man into their own image, regardless of whether the majority of the black people want it or not, and to project on them the militants' own needs. These militant leaders are prone to use coercive techniques both against outsiders and against members of their own organizations, thereby extending their tyranny over the widest possible arena of human institutions, values, beliefs, and options. If successful, they are likely to create a subsystem from which an individual member cannot escape without incurring serious penalties. They are, therefore, launching an assault against flexibility in a social structure which is so essential to the survival of the over-all system. In their attempt to remove the rigidities in the over-all system, they are trying to impose new inflexibilities which are equally pervasive and damaging not only to the system but also to the black men whose interests these miltant black leaders seek to espouse. If the changes in the system must be made through violent means, the black men, being a minority in numbers as well as in social, political, and economic influence, are bound to lose.

FIGHT's leader, Minister Florence, practices this philosophy of militancy perhaps even more militantly than many of his followers and supporters would want. William Martin [105] described him thus:

Minister Florence (ministers of the Churches of Christ do not use the title "Reverend"), had served as the first vice president of the Rochester NAACP, but he was better known in the streets as a close friend of Malcolm X's.[5] Malcolm's picture hangs on the wall at FIGHT headquarters. Florence wears a hat Malcolm gave him just before his death and plays records of Malcolm's speeches for white visitors in his home. And like Malcolm, Minister Florence bears a deep, flashing hostility toward most whites.[6] From the earliest meetings, Florence made it clear that FIGHT was to be a black group. Most of the white liberals who were part of the original organization were soon squeezed out. Black power became more than a slogan.

Florence's "abiding distrust of most whites" even extended initially to

Saul Alinsky. [99] This admiration for Malcolm X certainly influenced FIGHT strategy in its dealings with Kodak, particularly Malcolm's statements about never trusting white men unless you have the power to make them deliver. This "power" to make them deliver seemed almost more important than the deliverance itself.

A further glimpse into the personality and beliefs of Minister Florence can be had from the following statement which he made at the first convention of BUILD—Build, Unity, Independence, Liberty, Dignity—a militant black group in Buffalo which was also organized by Saul Alinsky. This convention took place in May 1967 to form a coalition between BUILD and FIGHT. Among many other remarks, Minister Florence was reported [7] to have said:

A lot of blackies will say go slow ... take it easy. We've found in Rochester three kinds of [Uncle] Toms ... one, who's after money ... one, who cares more for being "in," and the "house negro."

This is a generation that is more selfish than the past. I am not working for my sons. I am working for me, because I know if I get [freedom], they'll get it.

Right here in your own community they [the whites] will love you to death, they'll be sweet and receptive, but just as soon as you get ready for the marriage, they'll fall out. They'll tell you we don't have a race problem in Buffalo ... they will try to buy you off, separate you, can you.

... What you're after is power. ... Power gives a person the right to affect change on the daily issues which affect our daily life.

Florence believed that to be anti-Florence was to be anti-black. His white-baiting tactics probably did his cause little good. One middle-class black who helped draw up the FIGHT constitution complained of the leadership: "They want to use us while they abuse us."

Apparently Florence felt that he had nothing to lose and much to gain by castigating the middle-class black. Thus when Kodak offered to expand its training program and to take referrals from several agencies and Florence responded by saying that any cooperating agency would be joining a "conspiracy," his attack was aimed mainly at the local Urban League and its new head, Laplois Ashford.

The local branch of the Urban League had been primarily middle-class-oriented. Ashford hoped to broaden its base, but in so doing he unavoidably came into competition with Florence and was caught in the middle of FIGHT's struggle with Kodak. Ashford said that Florence "told us outright" during the earlier discussions with Kodak, "You don't send any of the six-hundred down." When Ashford protested, Florence's followers began calling him "an Uncle Tom" and "a traitor to the cause." [18]

The most painful split occurred between the poor and the few middle-class blacks, as reported by Barbara Carter [18]:

The alignment of forces is not a simple polarization of Negroes against whites. There also are whites against whites, Negroes against Negroes, and Negroes against Jews. It has caused dissension among the ranks of the Protestant Rochester Area Council of Churches.

The same observer [18] commented on Florence's tendency to make inflammatory statements:

Jobs and job training are not the only or even the major issues. FIGHT's basic struggle is for recognition and, through recognition, power. Many of Florence's statements such as "The plague of black democracy will . . . sweep Main and Exchange Streets" are addressed to the black community, not the white. Yet, it is often the whites who react most volatilely.

In the heat of a public argument last fall with Superintendent of Schools Herman Goldberg, for example, Florence said, "That's the trouble with you Jews when you get your color up." The Jewish community was thunderstruck. "I got more phone calls that night than over anything FIGHT has done," one Jewish matron who supports FIGHT told me. She shrugged. " 'What's there to be surprised about?' I asked them. 'Is this news?' " Alinsky tried to patch things up by explaining to the Temple B'rith Kodesh that Negroes were impartially hostile to all whites. It was simply that the most visible whites in the Negro community, "the ones you can get your hands on," are often Jews.

Commenting on Florence's attitude, *Business Week* [47] wrote:

In accepting a personality as jarring as Florence's for leadership, Alinsky was following principles. One of his primary aims is to insist on dignity for the poor, and rudeness can indeed amount to an assertion of equality. If you win demands even while being obnoxious, runs this line of thought, it's proof you aren't taking charity.

FIGHT's Strategy and Use of the News Media

The initial support of FIGHT was confined to a minority of the black people. Thus, to seek gains in membership, FIGHT had to secure influence among local blacks as well as among white liberals. In terms of pursuing selected options, choice of opponents, and use of news media, the objective of FIGHT was not to influence a wider public but rather to use widespread public support in order to extract favorable reactions from those in a position to make meaningful decisions which were beneficial to FIGHT. Thus FIGHT's leadership was not looking for converts to the cause but was trying to reach those people who, for a variety of reasons, might support FIGHT's drive for a voice in the community and might be in a position to help FIGHT achieve it. FIGHT probably believed that it could get all the poor it needed behind its banner if only it could persuade the existing centers of power in the community to share some power with FIGHT. Thus in the beginning, it was logical that FIGHT used the city's poor as a tool to gain power for itself which it hoped to use in the future to the greater advantage of the poor.

The use of propaganda differs in both technique and objective between small and large groups. As Key points out, small groups are attracted to extensive propaganda campaigns since "they can readily subscribe to the doctrine that they must carry their cause by the generous support of propaganda to shape the opinions of the general public." [73] Thus, while mass organizations look on public relations as a device to mobilize *membership* behind the position of the organization, small organizations aim toward general public opinion. [184] The use of propaganda by small organizations suffers one handicap, however, when their propaganda competes with mass or established organizations. It is easier to mobilize public opinion when an organization is espousing current mores and widely held public beliefs—which is generally the case with established organizations. Small organizations, which tend to attack basic attitudes and deeply rooted prejudices, lack this advantage. [184]

The simplification of issues seems to be a prerequisite for the effective use of mass media. Large organizations thus have an advantage over small ones since they can resort to vague statements about current values and beliefs, leaving the public to make its own interpretation. Small organizations, on the other hand, find it difficult to simplify complex issues because in so doing they are forced to assume extreme positions and therefore become vulnerable to attack by established organizations. Faced with this dilemma, small organizations tend to resort to two techniques:

1. They attack the positions taken by their opponents (that is, large organizations), showing their inherent inconsistencies.

2. They attack their opponents' integrity, exposing them as hypocrites and nonbelievers in their own position.

FIGHT's strategies against Kodak and other local organizations and its use of propaganda were a combination of these two techniques. FIGHT's first year was not spectacular; the group registered some significant gains, suffered some defections, and managed generally to maintain its stance of uncompromising militancy. Prior to its confrontation with Kodak, FIGHT's principal claim to fame resulted, not from its activities, but from the Establishment's response to FIGHT's tactics. The response ran from one extreme to the other, being more emotional than rational. The supporters of FIGHT tended to smother the organization with kindness, thereby giving the leadership the feeling that militancy, for its own sake, paid and also creating the impression among the city's poor that FIGHT could deliver. A large segment of the city's Establishment, fearing the radicalism of Alinsky and his followers, overreacted, with a response well out of proportion to the situation. By doing so, the Establishment played straight into the hands of FIGHT leadership which increased its following among the city's poor and escalated into local and national prominence in direct proportion to the magnitude of the Establishment's reaction.

The local civic leaders killed any chance of the Urban League's gaining influence with the city's poor, when they delayed establishing a local branch until after Alinsky had started organizing FIGHT. Furthermore, the local press, by being blatantly anti-FIGHT, strengthened FIGHT's image as the underdog and true representative of the poor. The biggest publicity plum to FIGHT was provided by Richard P. Miller, executive director of the Community Chest, who was accused by FIGHT of pressuring Baden Street Settlement, a black organization, from joining FIGHT under the threat of withholding previously allocated Community Chest funds. Although Miller denied any coercion, his denial and further explanations were such that there was no doubt in the minds of the poor that the criterion for help used by the Community Chest was not genuine need of the recipient but his guarantee of "good behavior" as defined by the Establishment. Jules Witcover, writing for the *Reporter* [178], quoted Miller as saying:

When we had our last fund drive we said very positively that no Chest money would be going into FIGHT. When it was learned Baden Street was considering affiliation with it my telephone began to ring. . . . We never said Chest money would be withdrawn from Baden Street, and we are not saying that now. . . . We've simply asked Baden Street, What does joining FIGHT mean? What are the responsibilities? What if FIGHT decides to picket Bausch and Lomb (a big Chest contributor)? Where does this leave Baden Street? We asked the question because we want them to know what they are getting into.

FIGHT against Kodak: Choice of Target and Course of Events

One of the big questions the events of 1966 and 1967 raise is: Why did a group as small as FIGHT choose to take on a corporation as large as Kodak? FIGHT's pressure might have been sufficient for success against a small firm; but if anyone could resist such pressure, it would be Kodak. Kodak officials stated that jobs were available and that Kodak hired *more* than 600 minority-group people in the period FIGHT demanded. By attacking one of the largest and most respectable companies in Rochester, FIGHT was guaranteed either a "villain" to help raise sympathy and hence support for establishing a power base or job openings for 600 people which would also give FIGHT a source of patronage and therefore a power base.

Malcolm X's advice about never trusting white men unless you have the power to make them deliver helps explain the why of FIGHT's strategy toward Kodak. The power to make Kodak deliver was to be the force of general public opinion or at least a segment of public opinion. To attract public attention, FIGHT-Kodak relations had to be newsworthy, preferably controversial. One reason FIGHT had singled out Kodak was that a settlement with such a major company would have created a "guideline for the nation and the world." [18]

It is debatable whether FIGHT's choice of target—granting its objective—was strategically right or timely. However, at that time it must have seemed to FIGHT that it had nothing to lose by such a confrontation. Kodak's record of good community relations, involvement in civic causes, its national prominence, and the publicity caused by such a confrontation would almost ensure some kind of positive action on Kodak's part. Even if FIGHT were not successful in establishing itself as the only spokesman for the blacks, its underdog image could not be destroyed and it could always try again. Another probable reason for FIGHT's choice of Kodak as an antagonist was that FIGHT's role did not actually place it in a position of assuming much responsibility for those it claimed to represent. Thus FIGHT could pursue tactics without regard for the costs which might be sustained by its constituency, for those costs of a tangible nature were likely to be minimal. FIGHT was not in a position of being evaluated against any previous success that might now be lost.

From the very beginning, Florence insisted upon talking to the "top man" at Kodak. Confrontations with corporation presidents and board chairmen are that much more newsworthy. Discussions with lower-echelon executives can get bogged down for months at a time with little outside repercussions; for example, the later meetings led by Kenneth Howard, a second-echelon executive, may have been doomed to failure before they began.

At the first meeting between FIGHT and Kodak executives, when Florence presented a proposal that Kodak set up a program to hire 600 people who could not meet regular company-employment standards, Vaughn replied that the company already had such a program. However, to FIGHT, the concept of black self-determination was just as important as jobs. FIGHT's contention was that a training program for disadvantaged blacks should be run by those who know the black man's problems, and FIGHT felt itself better qualified than any Kodak executive[7] to run such a program. FIGHT had little success in dealing with Kodak prior to the agreement of December 20. On every occasion Kodak rebuffed FIGHT's efforts to make any gains at Kodak's expense. At the same time the company moved independently to announce programs—somewhat similar to those demanded by FIGHT—to blunt the public effect of FIGHT's accusations against Kodak. Apparently Kodak was worried about the *indirect* implications of FIGHT's demands on the social system as it existed in Rochester at the time. In addition to a surrender of management prerogatives, Kodak probably believed that yielding would give FIGHT tremendous patronage power in the ghetto areas—a power which FIGHT could use to undermine more moderate influences—and would render Kodak more vulnerable to future demands and, possibly, to increased militancy on the part of FIGHT. What Kodak did not appreciate was that every "clever" move by the company made FIGHT that much more of a hero with the black people and made its demands appear that much more reasonable to its white liberal supporters.

FIGHT's first big break came with the signing of the agreement between the organization and John Mulder, representing the company. Minister Florence was stunned with disbelief and repeatedly asked for Mulder's assurance that he was in fact authorized by Kodak to sign such an agreement. As reported by William Martin [105],

The document was a loosely worded affair and some doubt it actually bound Kodak to anything. *But it was an agreement, and FIGHT clearly regarded it as a major victory.* [Emphasis added.]

To make it difficult for Kodak to back off from its promise, Florence immediately announced the signing of the agreement on the radio. Despite this precaution, Kodak repudiated the agreement two days later, and that repudiation was a serious blow to FIGHT. Minister Florence was in a dilemma. He did not have any real power, direct or indirect, to force Kodak to abide by the provisions of the agreement. He could visualize himself being ridiculed by his followers for not delivering what he had promised. To save face, he tried to get Kodak to agree to *any* kind of agreement. He even went so far as to offer to scrap the agreement if one of Kodak's top officials, either Vaughn or Eilers, would make a joint statement with Florence on television promising *only* cooperation between the two organizations to get more jobs for the ghetto blacks. Kodak declined both offers. It seems now that Kodak could have averted all that followed if the company had seized that opportunity and compromised with FIGHT in the spirit of give and take. However, as has been stated in Chapter 3, Kodak officials were still captives of their own conceptual blocks and were adamantly opposed to making any concessions to FIGHT which might appear to their constituents as a surrender to a militant organization.

Minister Florence then embarked on a strategy of extreme militancy, coupled with public abuse of Kodak and the entire white community. In retrospect, it seems strange that a man of Minister Florence's competence —who had used the news media so adroitly that he was able to build a power base from nothing and to confront Kodak—should let himself be cornered into a position which not only endangered his support from the black community and from white moderates but also led nowhere in terms of his short- or long-term objectives.

By this time, Kodak had changed its strategy also. Instead of passive acquiescence or studied silence in response to FIGHT's virulent public abuse, Kodak decided to fight head-on in public forum, thereby pushing Florence into further extremism. The results were damaging to the peace of the community and, more important, to the cause of helping the city's poor.

FIGHT wanted to develop its conflict into a national issue—a cause with which all blacks and whites could identify. The National Council of Churches had already come in on it. Walter Reuther's Citizens' Crusade Against Poverty planned to establish a citizens' committee to investigate the situation, much as it had with the Child Development Group of Mississippi (CDGM). There was also talk of running ads against Kodak in the New York papers, boycotting Kodak products, attacking major stockholders in the company, and demanding that the federal government cancel contracts with Kodak because of discriminatory labor policies. [144]

On January 19, 1967, at the encouragement of Minister Florence, Black Power leader Stokely Carmichael came to town. But the scheduled national boycott announced by Carmichael barely materialized in the form of some picketing. As *Business Week* [47] reported,

Most observers regard Carmichael's visit as a tactical error, but it assured Negro militants that FIGHT was not knuckling under to Whitey, and it convinced cooler heads that some alternative had to be found before the anger in the ghetto became uncontrollable.

Here again we can see Minister Florence's problem of trying to satisfy two different constituencies. Failing to make any real gains against Kodak, FIGHT resorted to ever increasing doses of militancy to keep the black poor from doubting his unflagging determination to bring Kodak to heel. However, these desperate measures were also costing FIGHT the support of moderate liberals locally as well as nationally. His trick was to pursue those strategies which neatly balanced the needs of the two groups. It seems that in inviting Stokely Carmichael, Minister Florence erred on the side of excessive extremism which cost him dearly in local and national support both with the blacks as well as with the whites.

FIGHT's Strategy at the Stockholders' Meeting

Florence's strategy on the occasion of the stockholders' meeting consisted of creating as much disruption as possible both inside and outside the meeting to force Kodak to answer embarrassing questions and so garner national publicity. To this end, FIGHT bought 10 shares of Kodak stock to give its members entry into the meeting. It also sent letters to 700 clergymen and civil-rights organizations asking them to persuade other shareholders to withhold their proxies. [46] Although FIGHT received tremendous national publicity, it is doubtful that the group gained any additional public support for its cause. Florence's antics may have had something to do with the adverse effects. "In the aftermath of Flemington, most observers agreed that Florence had done FIGHT's cause serious damage." [105]

At FIGHT's third annual convention in Rochester on June 23, DeLeon McEwen, age 29, was elected president. (Florence was ineligible to succeed himself.) The convention also voted to change the word "Integration" in its name to "Independence." [86] Both Florence and FIGHT evidently recognized their limitations, because the dire predictions of riots and civil unrest made at Flemington did not come off. Without any specific public announcement of a change in policy, FIGHT thereafter began to cooperate with other local groups.

Saner heads prevailed at both Kodak and FIGHT in the period immediately following the stockholders' meeting and eventually resulted in the telegram of June 23, 1967, from Kodak's president Eilers to FIGHT. The telegram recognized FIGHT's claim as a major spokesman of the black poor and also promised to seek FIGHT's help and counsel in recruiting and training the hard-core unemployed. Thus ended, at least officially, the conflict between FIGHT and Kodak.

The Outcome

How do the gains and losses of FIGHT's strategy add up? Was FIGHT successful in achieving its objectives? It is difficult to give an unqualified "yes" or "no" answer. In one sense FIGHT achieved its objectives by keeping the issue alive and accelerating the process of changing the attitudes of local business corporations in favor of additional job opportunities for minority groups. It also increased its power base by developing, operating, and managing a commercial enterprise called Fighton, with the help of Xerox.

Furthermore, as William Martin [105] stated,

[FIGHT] gave the Negro poor a sense of pride and a power base from which to influence urban renewal projects and the new plans for better school desegregation. It has drained off frustration that might have erupted into violence. Some have also credited FIGHT and its 400-member white middle-class auxiliary, Friends of FIGHT, with a general rise of popular democracy in the city.

According to another observer [145],

[FIGHT and Alinsky] have done the work the city never undertook, that of reaching down into the Negro wards and pulling them together, not as a political fiefdom for a ghetto politician, but into a democratically constructed organization.

But FIGHT's success may have come in spite of, rather than because of, its strategy. According to most observers of the FIGHT-Kodak controversy, FIGHT really failed in its attempt to make a national issue of its demands. Rather than unleashing public opinion against Kodak, it unleashed opinion against the clergy for supporting FIGHT in the first place. One could make a point that if FIGHT had chosen its opponent well or handled its strategies realistically, as it had started out to do, instead of being blinded by earlier success, FIGHT could have probably achieved greater success in terms of obtaining jobs for the poor and also enhancing its sphere of influence.

FIGHT's basic mistake was that it picked the wrong enemy. Granted that Kodak could have done more, the company nevertheless had a record of concern for minority workers that defied many of FIGHT's charges, such as Florence's statement that Kodak was "institutionally racist." Like Kodak, FIGHT overplayed its hand by exaggerating the issue in an effort to dramatize, and in the process—again like Kodak—FIGHT lost some of its credibility and claim to sincerity. As *Fortune* [3] stated, "It is hard to imagine a worse way for Negro organizations to try to beat down employment barriers than to attack a company that has set an example for other companies to follow." The probable outcome if FIGHT had selected a different target would have been more tangible results for FIGHT to point to, broader support from ghetto residents, and more sympathy from the press, the local community, and the larger society—in essence, the power and respectability that FIGHT so badly wanted.

Given that FIGHT decided on Kodak as its target, additional errors should be pointed out in the way Minister Florence and his group conducted that campaign. Although FIGHT fought a bruising battle against Kodak, it would probably have scored more points if it had worn thicker gloves over its clenched fists. A more pragmatic approach at critical moments might have gained more than did the spirit of intransigence which characterized FIGHT throughout the controversy. Eventually, Minister Florence did realize, as Martin Luther King had discovered earlier, that a black leader in these days must walk a thin line between moderation and militancy if he is to command support.

Footnotes for Chapter 4

1. According to Earl Raab, executive director of the Jewish Community Relations Council of San Francisco, "Black militants, frustrated by unrealized social and economic expectations, are developing an anti-Semitic ideology as part of their political strategy." Raab believes that although many middle-class Negroes are horrified at this trend, they nevertheless are reluctant to oppose it at the community level because it might seem to be an attack on the militant movement itself. [176]

2. Immediately after the Board for Urban Ministry asked Saul Alinsky to organize the city's poor, the city's businessmen and civic leaders, through the Rochester Community Chest, allocated more than $40,000 to invite the national Urban League to open an office in Rochester. The civic officials contended that the move had been in the discussion stage for several years, so that Alinsky's arrival and the invitation to the Urban League were merely coincidental.

3. Quoted in Charles Silberman's *Crisis in Black and White*, p. 153.

4. See, for example, Clark [25, 26], Pettigrew [131], and Silberman [161].

5. Minister Florence once tried to persuade Malcolm X to help organize Rochester's blacks. [99]

6. Florence, like many of Rochester's blacks, is not a native and in fact was visiting his former home in Florida when rioting broke out in Rochester in July 1964. "My first impulse was to rush back and try to help calm things down. Then I decided, No, let the brothers speak!" [99]

7. Or, in Florence's words, "any black man who goes home to the suburbs every night and pretends he's white." [99]

CHAPTER 5

The Church: Mediator or Intruder?

The church is not an impersonal edifice, although all too often it seems that way. The church is what we have made it. Its dilemma is that while its mission should be the righting of wrongs and the active pursuit of the great Judeo-Christian values, we have instead made it for the most part a force for the status quo. — John D. Rockefeller, III

The activities of the church[1] played a very important role in the Kodak-FIGHT controversy. It was an agency of the church that was instrumental in bringing Saul Alinsky to Rochester and thus creating FIGHT. Moreover, it was the local clergy who provided FIGHT with its initial momentum and sustained it in the early stages. Even after FIGHT was a going concern, the church was one of its strongest supporters at both the local and the national levels. The Protestant as well as the Catholic church organizations consistently supported FIGHT, although they were predominantly white in membership. These groups were under constant pressure, especially at the local level, to disengage themselves from this controversy. Obviously, it was not the most usual activity for the church to engage in. Granted that members of the clergy had been involved in civil-rights actions in the South and had participated in sit-in demonstrations and peace marches. Still, their action in Rochester was unprecedented in many ways. It involved a deliberate attempt at organizing local minorities through techniques which were unorthodox and unacceptable even to some of the most liberal groups in the United States. These techniques carried with them the potential for violence. In a city like Rochester, which had been the scene of race riots, this action seemed particularly foolhardy. It was sure to incur the displeasure of a majority of the town's citizens who were, after all, church members and had the right to ensure that the churches satisfied their spiritual needs rather than become rabble-rousers.

The Institutional Church and Social Systems

Why, then, did the church become involved in this controversy? What were the motives behind the actions of individual clergymen as well as church organizations? What is the role of the church in our society or, better still, what *should* be the role of the church in society? To whom are the church and the clergy responsible? Even if we were to recognize the legitimacy of the church's action in economic issues involving social injustices, the question arises as to the extent the church can pursue this objective without impairing its other objectives. In other words, is there an order of priorities which the church should pursue? To what extent are these priorities determined by the membership, and to what extent are they imposed by the official church hierarchy?

It is very important that these questions be carefully studied because the church is a powerful social institution and its involvement in controversies which have been hitherto considered primarily economic, and therefore outside the church's sphere of influence, may have a profound influence on the distribution of power and may permanently alter our social system. Moreover, a dramatic shift in the nature of the church's activities might also affect its own organizational structure, the composition of its membership, and the degree of allegiance owed by that membership. The result would be to change the character of the church into something which the sponsors of the church's present involvement in social action might not have intended.

Just as in the case of Kodak and FIGHT, the activities of the church can be understood within the framework of the theory of social systems explored in Chapter 1. The church as a subsystem has a value set of its own which reflects the expectations of its membership. The *success* of the church therefore depends on the degree to which it can satisfy the aspirations of its membership. Otherwise, this being a voluntary association, its members may leave it to form new institutions whose value set will more closely identify with their needs. The necessity of a congruence between the value set of the subsystem and that of the over-all system on the one hand and closer identity of the value set of the subsystem with its own membership on the other hand represents the area of potential conflict. The desire by the hierarchy of a subsystem to bring closer these seemingly conflicting objectives provides the motives for various strategies which a subsystem follows, because on the success of these strategies depends not only the survival of the subsystem but also the continuation in power of the established hierarchy.

As with all other subsystems, a change in the value set of the church must also be determined by its past (as reflected in custom and tradition), by its orientation toward the future, and by the dissatisfaction of its members with the existing goals of the subsystem or with their own role and influence within the subsystem. The strategies which the church must use can be understood only within the framework of this goal orientation. Moreover, these strategies involve the redistribution of power *between* various subsystems, the rearrangement of spheres of influence *within* a subsystem as between its various units, and the interpersonal relationships between the individual members *within* as well as *outside* the subsystem. Therefore, the strategies employed by a subsystem and their effects can be understood only when we analyze them not in isolation but in relation to all other subsystems.

The problem of understanding the behavior of the church is complex, involving a variety of factors. One, there is a conflict between the goals of Christianity which the church purports to represent. Two, the traditions of various units of the church in many cases differ widely. These units disagree among themselves as to the goals of Christianity and the function of the church. Moreover, these units have different ideas of the church's obligations to its members as against nonmembers or society at large.

What is the role of the church in the life of the individual? Should the church tend the soul alone and leave matters of body for the individual to tend for himself? The problem is not new; the church has always been thus vexed. The church considers itself the guardian of the human soul and the tender of the spiritual needs of man. Since the church regards these spiritual needs as of primary concern to man, it considers its value set to be more in congruence with the over-all objectives of society than is the value set of any other social system.[2] Despite the belief of the church in the primacy of its goals in the over-all system, there has been a gradual but persistent erosion of the power of the church. This diminution of power is probably due to a rigidity in church attitudes, to the lack of believers in its hard line, and to the changing needs of society which gave rise to other, secular institutions. Faced with the dilemma of alienation from within and lack of identity with over-all social goals, the church has adopted one of the following ways to adjust itself to the changing realities of the social system:

1. The church has stood aside in ascetic aloofness and regarded the materialistic values held by members of society as being in their very nature unrighteous and ungodly.

2. The church has taken these values for granted and ignored them as matters of indifference.

3. The church has thrown itself into agitation for some particular reform to give vent to frustration and to bring righteousness back to earth. These agitations have often taken on the aura of revivalism, invariably hysterical in nature, and have had little if any lasting effect on the over-all system.

4. The church has at once accepted and criticized the gross nature of human greed and appetite and has tended to work within the framework of human frailty to improve both the moral and the material conditions of mankind.

The last of the four has of late been the most typical means of accommodation by the church in the United States, for several reasons. The increasing efficiency of the economic system has produced wealth of unprecedented magnitude; yet a substantial minority of people has been left outside the mainstream of affluence. The younger generations, born into affluence and unaccustomed to economic insecurity, have become disenchanted with material possessions as the sole aim of life. Yet these young people are equally unimpressed by the exhortations of traditional church doctrines, with their promises of the good life in the hereafter. What the youth of today seek is an idealism which urges doing something *now* and alleviating human suffering through action, not prayer.

The church, therefore, finds itself in a quandary. If it is to keep the allegiance of the younger generation and bring them back into the fold, it must "swing" with them through positive action in correcting social injustices. The church has always recognized the need to alleviate human misery and suffering whether caused by nature or by deliberate social action of fellow human beings. However, the church's *modus operandi* has been to deal through prayer, charity, and service rather than through economic pressures or other measures of direct action.

This shift in the church's direction in the field of social action raises another set of questions which must be faced because they have profound implications for the future of the church as well as of society. Various segments of the church and the clergy, regardless of their denominational affiliation, differ on what the philosophy of the church should be in terms of involvement in the problems of social inequality and injustice. Proponents of church involvement believe that poor people will be further alienated from the church—they are to some degree now—if the church does not identify itself with their problems and stand with them on the side of justice and fair play. It is not easy to ask poor people to pray for mental peace, spiritual enlightenment, and communion with God when they find their fellow Christians enjoying the good things in life while they are expected to suffer in silence. However, the church's involvement in poor people's conflicts raises a host of other problems which must be carefully considered.

Involvement in the community's internal conflicts is likely to expose the church and the clergy to kinds of strains with which they are ill-prepared to cope. The solution of social problems is necessarily a result of compromises between various social groups, with the haves giving up—albeit grudgingly—some of their privileges to the have-nots. Active participation by the clergy in community problems generates resentment among the groups against whom such action is being directed. Under these circumstances, it is extremely difficult, if not impossible, for the church to provide spiritual guidance to those who resent the church's involvement in what might be considered nonchurch affairs.

There is, furthermore, no guarantee that such involvement is an unmixed blessing even for the poor in general and for minority groups in particular. The minority groups not only have causes but leaders professing to support these causes. In its endeavor to support certain causes, the church may unwittingly support certain leaders who do not agree with the church's philosophy or strategies on these issues. Furthermore, these leaders may not even be acceptable to a large majority of the people they are supposedly representing.

Another problem is that of the future. Suppose a time comes when the church and other like-minded institutions have succeeded in fully integrating American society and everyone has equal opportunity for personal advancement. What would be the role of the church under those circumstances? Affluence does not lessen the need for spiritual guidance or comfort for the soul. Would the church be able to resume its role as shepherd of all souls and not only those belonging to the minorities? Would those groups against whom the church had worked as an activist accept the church as their spiritual guide, or would they simply come to regard it as one of many pressure groups in the social system?

American churches have become conspicuous in causes of race prejudice and economic inequality for the poor only during the past twenty years or so. Thus the National Council of Churches went on record in 1954 to work against those forms of economic injustice that are expressed through racial discrimination. [112] It is also on record in support of equal employment opportunity for all [111], the use of nonviolent demonstrations to secure social justice [115, 116], the elimination of segregation in education [117], and the prevention of discrimination in housing. [114]

The use of economic pressure in racial issues was specifically proposed and approved in a background paper prepared for the National Council of Churches [110]:

We believe it is of primary importance that Christian people everywhere recognize that what may be called bread-and-butter injustice can be equally as devastating to human life and well-being as civil injustice, if not more so, largely because bread-and-butter pursuits are so necessary to the maintenance of life. Because these forms of injustice are so closely related to habit, local mores, and man-to-man relationships, they can only partially be opposed or regulated by law or civil authority.

The General Board, therefore, resolved on June 8, 1963 [118]:

When other efforts to secure these rights do not avail, to support and participate in economic pressures where used in a responsible and disciplined manner to eliminate economic injustice and to end discrimination against any of God's people based on race, creed, or national origin.

The National Council of Churches has since then gone even further and recognized that the churches' own purchases must be based on other than strictly economic criteria. The basic philosophy of the council was very well articulated in the policy statement adopted by the General Board on September 12, 1968 [113]:

The institutional church enters into the economic life of society in a variety of ways.... The economic activities and financial transactions of the church total many billions of dollars annually. As a result, the church is inevitably involved in the exercise of substantial economic power.... We reaffirm that all economic institutions and practices are human structures conceived and designed by men; that they affect the conditions and quality of life of persons, many of whom cannot exercise any control over their functioning .... The market system which characterizes the American economy is one such institution. When the church approaches the marketplace in its role of purchaser of goods and services, it inevitably becomes a participant in an intricate network of economic forces involving ethical issues, policies and decisions.

... Most purchasing decisions by the church involve a selection among competing vendors. Such factors as quality, performance, convenience and price—conventional determinants of most purchasing decisions—although relevant to the economic activity of the church, are not sufficient criteria for its selection among vendors. The nature of the church requires that as an economic institution it also consider the social impact of its purchasing decisions in terms of justice and equality.

... In cases where injustice is found to exist, the church should make vigorous efforts through moral persuasion to secure correction of the abuses.... Where such measures prove to be inappropriate in securing justice, or where past experience demonstrates that these means alone are ineffective, the church is not only justified, but in faithfulness to its nature, is required to give its patronage to sources of goods and services which it finds to have policies and practices that better serve social justice.

... When such action is taken, the church is free and indeed may be impelled, as a form of witness, not only to inform the vendors involved but also to announce publicly the nature of its action and the reasons for it.

The problem of the church's concern for economic issues and its involvement in conflicts where it is not a direct party has another dimension which is equally explosive: the choice of strategies. The National Council of Churches has supported the use of nonviolent methods in securing economic justice for minorities. [118] However, what should the church do if nonviolent and peaceful means do not succeed? When is a violation of man-made laws justified if there is a superior law of conscience? Economic pressures can be used not only by the church but also by other groups which the church is opposing. If these measures by the church can be justified because of the righteousness of the cause, how can they be condemned when used by other groups if the latter are equally honest in their belief of the justness of their cause and are not motivated by bigotry, selfishness, or prejudice. The mere existence of power, be it legal or implied, is not enough justification for its use. However, if ends are to be used as criteria for legitimizing means, the church as a party to the conflict has no more right to proclaim that its values are the "justifiable" ends than have the other parties to the conflict.

The National Council of Churches, recognizing some of these issues, justified its approach thus [110]:

Use of economic pressures also involves the possibility of violence. Though violence may sometimes result from an action, this possibility does not necessarily call for opposition to such action, particularly on the part of those who seek to use non-violent economic means to eliminate or decrease discrimination.

The council also recognized that there may be occasions when a firm might lose its present clientele if it were to cater to the special needs of a particular group. It is thus argued that such a firm is only an innocent bystander, not the offending party, and therefore should not be subjected to economic pressures by the church. These measures might involve yet another party—those people who give tacit support to discriminatory practices used by some businesses by not actively opposing those firms and their activities and by continuing to patronize them. Notwithstanding, the council maintained [110]:

These factors make more difficult, but no less necessary, the understanding of and resistance to the use of economic pressures as a means to enforce racial discriminations or oppression. They serve to highlight the importance of looking with broad historical perspective at the full sweep of economic injustice which the victims of economic injustice now seek to remove, or at least alleviate through the use of economic pressures being made against them.

These problems aside, the trend of events is clear. The church is becoming increasingly involved in social affairs. It can do so either by exhorting the haves from the pulpit or by actively helping the have-nots to demand their fair share from the haves. The trend is toward the latter and it is causing tremendous strains not only between the church and its followers but among the churchmen themselves. The case of Kodak vividly mirrors this situation and should give us pause to reflect about the long-term implications of this involvement.

Church Involvement in the Kodak-FIGHT Controversy

The first chapter stated that a subsystem's objectives are self-defined and more closely oriented toward the needs of its members than are the objectives of the over-all system. It was also stated that when a subsystem has been in existence for a long time, it develops a momentum of its own which may alienate it, at least partially, from various units in the subsystem as well as from individual members of various units. The goals pursued by the leadership of the subsystem may not be those desired by the majority of its membership. Conflicts may arise because an entrenched minority, which may be overrepresented in the leadership, has been effective either in resisting change or in pursuing change at a faster rate than the membership is willing to accept.

All these elements of both an internal and an external nature were present in the Kodak-FIGHT controversy. The Board for Urban Ministry certainly took a daring step when it decided to invite Saul Alinsky and his Industrial Areas Foundation to Rochester with a view toward encouraging organization among the local minorities and giving them a new voice in representing their views to the city and its establishment. Why did the Board for Urban Ministry invite Alinsky? Undoubtedly, the board knew his reputation as a radical organizer and a "rabble-rouser" and knew that this action might not be acceptable to the city's other powerful and equally well-meaning groups? To understand the board's action, we must appreciate the environment in which it was made and the source of the board's authority.

The Board for Urban Ministry was a semiautonomous offshoot of the Rochester Area Council of Churches (RACC). Although the RACC endorsed the board's action, it was the board and not the council that was actually responsible for bringing Alinsky to Rochester. The distinction between the two, often overlooked, is strategically important. As William Martin, writing in the *Atlantic* [105], put it:

The Council is composed of more than 200 member congregations and is ultimately answerable to them. The Board for Urban Ministry is composed of representatives from eight denominations and is thus not directly answerable to individual churches. According to the policy of the two organizations, the Board could have invited Alinsky without the Council's approval, and the Council was not obligated to poll its member churches as to their desires in the matter.

It is, therefore, no wonder that the board was more in tune than the council with the trends of national church organizations and more willing to use less conventional approaches to solving the problems of Rochester's minorities. The board was assured of the support of the National Council of Churches in view of the latter's public statements and official resolutions favoring the use of economic pressures and other direct action to promote the cause of the minorities. Moreover, financial independence and only indirect representation of the local churches insulated the board from local pressures and in a sense made it insensitive to the feelings and desires of the local clergy and citizens.

In inviting Alinsky, the board knew that it was creating "an atmosphere of controversy" [47], but the ferocity and, to some extent, the direction of opposition were unexpected. The RACC and its member congregations came under immediate attack from media and laymen alike. The local newspapers accused the council of bringing in the "outsiders" and troublemakers and of supporting militants who were intent on creating unrest among the people of Rochester. As reported in the *New Republic* [145], the city's most powerful radio station, WHAM, an ABC affiliate, in an editorial warned that

if the clergy persisted in bringing Alinsky into town then the ministers must start paying $275 for the hour-long Sunday morning church service the station had been broadcasting free. WHAM said Alinsky was a "troublemaker" . . . . [T]he Council held its ground against WHAM—and the Sunday morning radio program was cancelled.

Commenting on the intensity of local hostility to the council's action, the same observer [145] stated:

In the face of this intensive barrage, many laymen found themselves in a quandary over the role their pastors and denominational leaders were playing. For weeks, representatives of the Board for Urban Ministry and the Council of Churches spent their evenings interpreting the realities of life in the ghettos and the dynamics of the Alinsky approach to groups of troubled laymen.

It was easy and perhaps spiritually comfortable for most of the educated, suburban, affluent laymen to support their clergy's involvement in social action, as long as it did not go beyond the discussion stage and as long as any action was confined to peaceful methods of protest. However, these parishioners could not reconcile themselves to the idea of their clergy being involved in an open struggle for power between different groups in the community. The lack of precedent, the absence of a clear-cut philosophy, and the feeling of uncertainty about possible achievements further added to the laymen's confusion and frustration, as reflected in the nature and intensity of their response. There was a widespread cancellation of pledges—sometimes running into thousands of dollars. William Martin [105] reported:

Resentment of church involvement ran so high in some congregations that church leaders would not pass out brochures presenting FIGHT's request for third-year funding until after the annual pledge drive.

There was a serious question as to how long clergymen could function under such strain and still maintain their sanity. One minister, tormented by threats and telephone calls, took his own life; the calls continued to his wife. [99] Others were victims of anonymous letters circulated among the congregations and of telephoned threats against their families. A minister who had been attacked for supporting FIGHT found that the lug bolts had been taken off the wheels of his car. [144] In a large number of cases parishioners simply stopped talking or being friendly to their clergymen. William Martin, writing in the *Atlantic* [105], commented:

The loss of members and money affects a minister because they are tangible signs of his professional "success," however much he may wish they were not. But the confusion, bitterness, and hostility that he sees in his people cause him the greatest pain. In [one] case, members made a point of telling the minister's children that the church could never make progress until their father left. In some churches dissident laymen organized attempts to get rid of the offending minister. In others, leaders withheld salary increments or warned the pastor not to spend too much of his time in activities related to FIGHT.

The resentment of the local citizenry against the Rochester Area Council of Churches was even more vocal and violent. According to William Martin [105],

Letters and telephone calls—some reasonable, others obscene and threatening—poured into the council office. Numerous churches and individuals decided to "teach the council a lesson" by lowering or canceling contributions for the coming fiscal year. One church, recognizing that FIGHT was only one part of the council's activity, raised its contribution $500, but accompanied its pledge with a letter strongly critical of the council's stance. Others were not so charitable. At the final tally, the council's annual fund drive for the coming year missed its goal by $20,000. Ironically, the attempt to punish the council has had no effect whatever on FIGHT, which has in fact been guaranteed third-year funding by the various denominational bodies and church agencies, nor on the Board for Urban Ministry, which is also funded denominationally and has never been more secure financially.

Church Activities after the Agreement of December 20

When the executive committee of Kodak's board of directors announced that the company was not bound by the agreement signed by one of its assistant vice presidents, John Mulder, on the pretext that Mulder had not been authorized by the company, the RACC found itself in a worse dilemma than ever before. The community was already hostile to its earlier actions, and any support of FIGHT would further intensify the conflict. FIGHT's actions immediately following the repudiation of the agreement did not help. On January 19, 1967, against the advice of many of his supporters, Minister Florence invited Stokely Carmichael to Rochester. In his speech Carmichael made very inflammatory statements against Kodak, Rochester, and every other organization which did not agree with FIGHT.

The council was really concerned about the danger of the situation getting out of hand; yet it could do nothing but support FIGHT's cause since it felt that Kodak had indeed broken a promise which the other party had accepted in good faith. The council's hand was further forced when, the day after its repudiation of the Kodak-FIGHT agreement, Kodak took full-page ads in the local newspapers to publicize the reasons for its rejection of the agreement. The council wanted to avoid a further deterioration of the situation, but it could not desert FIGHT's cause without losing all the work that it had done so far and perhaps permanently discouraging the minorities from putting any faith in the white man's promises. The council took double-page ads in the papers urging Kodak to honor the agreement while at the same time asking FIGHT to support Kodak's training programs. However, in a community whose passions had been aroused to a high emotional pitch by both the supporters of FIGHT and Kodak, the council's appeal to patience and reason was lost in the hysteria, while its support for FIGHT was overblown. The reactions were predictable though unfortunate.

Denominational Division of Opinion on FIGHT

The controversy caused division among individual denominations in the Council of Churches. Stokely Carmichael's visit prompted six of Rochester's eighty Presbyterian churches (FIGHT's largest church supporters) to consider withdrawing their support of FIGHT while their parent body's Health and Welfare Association condemned Kodak. [18] The Episcopalians were reportedly the second-largest church supporters of FIGHT. In response to criticism of FIGHT by the Gannett newspapers, the bishop of the Episcopal diocese of Rochester appointed a committee to "assess FIGHT and to determine" by April 1967, "whether the diocese which has already contributed $19,000 should continue its support." [156] The third-largest church group, the Baptist, decided to continue its contributions, but a third of the delegates voted against the proposal. [18]

Reverend Elmer G. Schaertel, pastor of the Lutheran Church of the Redeemer, openly dissented with the council's stand in a letter to the *Rochester Democrat & Chronicle* [154]. Schaertel equated the disrespect for authority that was sweeping in the country with that of FIGHT's for Kodak—

... the disrespect sweeping our country of youth, of college students, of ministers, and leaders like Adam Powell and James Hoffa for the law and courts and of FIGHT for Kodak which is the most community minded company that I know. ... [T]he demands of FIGHT call for a special privilege because of color. ... This seems crazy to me and would do great harm to both company and all the workers who would resent the man coming in by paternalistic power rather than qualifications for the job. If one asks why Florence and FIGHT are so insistent in this, one can only answer that it is for power and would be used in that way rather than for benefit of workers, or company or Rochester.

As to the Council of Churches and the denominations supporting FIGHT, I do not believe the majority of either their ministers or their people are in sympathy with the stand their leaders have taken or the support they have given.

Several other ministers used their pulpits to advocate reason and even some rethinking on the part of the church. However, none advocated as harsh a stand as that advocated by Reverend Schaertel. One minister said that many church people were "facing the future with some misgivings" and that "we must find our way back to the true image of the church and lessen the gap between clergy and laity." Another minister commented that "part of the reason why we have this controversy and the strong difference of opinion within the church is that we are in new times and the church is facing new and greater issues for which we have no sharp guidelines from the past." Another minister asked that Kodak and FIGHT "call it a draw," saying that the struggle between Kodak and FIGHT is "like that between the elephant and the whale, which are different animals living in different environments and moving in different worlds." [129] Some ministers perhaps could not support FIGHT because of individual circumstances, such as age, health, or special situations in their churches. [105]

There followed a spate of letters by irate citizens to the newspapers opposing the church's stand on the controversy. Many strongly supported Reverend Schaertel's views. Few, if any, sympathized with the position taken by the Rochester Area Council of Churches. Here is a representative sample of the comments made by some of the readers [126]:

I commend Pastor Elmer Schaertel for expressing his opinion so clearly in his letter to the D. & C.

In the long run more could be accomplished if everyone were allowed to devote full time and attention to his own problems. Eastman Kodak to the business of manufacturing and selling its products, FIGHT to send its people to the proper place—the school—for education, the Rochester Area Council to preaching the Gospel.

The local crusading knights of the cloth, johnny-come-latelys in the civil rights bandwagon, cloaked in their spiritual aura of infallibility, are quite ready to order others to place their houses in order according to their views, integratively speaking, but have woeful shortcomings in their own houses of worship.

Every day we read that more and more people believe that religion is becoming less meaningful. Therefore, why don't preachers either return to the pulpit and extol an almighty and just God, or leave the church to campaign for Minister Franklin Florence, Saul Alinsky and other radical dissidents under their own names.

Let those disenchanted clergy look about them. Hardly an area in or about Rochester has not benefited from the Eastman Kodak Company. There isn't a major company in the United States with a more liberal and higher standard of employment ethics.

The expression of resentment and dissent also took other forms. The president of the Council of Churches (a Kodak employee) and two directors of its board (one of whom also was a Kodak employee) resigned from the council in protest.

Fundamentalist and evangelical churches kept out of the Kodak-FIGHT controversy, perhaps because of theological conviction. These groups believed the primary function of the church was to prepare individuals for life after death and saw no relationship between socioeconomic and religious issues. The deed of one church specifically prohibited the discussion of social or political issues anywhere on church property. According to William Martin [105]:

... some are simply not aware of what is going on in their city. One insisted that Negroes "are basically a happy, satisfied people who like to work as servants and live in a haphazard way." He doubted many in his church would object if Negroes tried to become members, "but, of course, if too many came, then we'd start a colored work." Another admitted he was not too well informed about FIGHT, but he hoped Hoagy Carmichael would not get to be its president. Most, however, are as concerned as their more liberal colleagues but cannot reconcile conflict tactics with their understanding of the gospel. "We feel," one evangelical minister said, "that you will never get rid of slums until you get rid of the slum in men. You have to start with the individual man, and you don't start by teaching him to hate."

The Position of the Catholic Church

For the most part, the Catholics (not represented in the Protestant Council of Churches, of course) steered clear of the Kodak-FIGHT dispute. However, on January 3, 1967, when the turmoil in Rochester was at its peak because of Kodak's repudiation of the agreement of December 20, Bishop Fulton J. Sheen asked Reverend P. David Finks—a FIGHT sympathizer—to advise him on the problems of the poor by appointing him an Episcopal vicar of urban ministry. Finks was a member of FIGHT's advisory council and was on the executive board of Friends of FIGHT at the time of his appointment. Bishop Sheen admitted that the appointment was "a very unusual step," but said, "I do not follow traditional methods, except in the faith." He also raised the possibility of strong cooperation with other faiths "even to the sharing of houses of worship ... in poor neighborhoods." According to the *New York Times* [160],

Spokesmen for the Roman Catholic diocese declined to say whether the priest's appointment was connected with the current controversy between the Negro group and the Eastman Kodak Company. They commented that the letter naming Father Finks to the post speaks for itself.

Speaking before the city's Chamber of Commerce on January 23, 1967, Bishop Sheen said [156]:

As the Church had to learn that the world was the stage on which the gospel was preached, so the world has to learn that the inner city is the area where the secular city will find God. Could not all the industries of the secular city begin to give a proportion of their blessing to the inner city—not just "tokens" but something more substantial? The whole world looks at Rochester, he said, but it does not see the city's beauty: it sees the blemish on its face.

Father Finks expressed his views on FIGHT and his philosophy on religion and church in an address to the Pittsford—Perinton Council on Human Relations [14]:

Those seeking social justice for the have nots of this world should support a viable community organization of minority groups dedicated to bring about the necessary social change. The most viable group here is FIGHT. . . . Christianity is not a mere belief or ritual, but is basically living like Christ did. We will be judged on whether we respond to the urgent call for social justice. . . . [T]ensions are necessary and can be used creatively in making the democratic process work. . . . [M]embers of the clergy have been chaplains of the establishment too long.

The Part Played by National Church Organizations

Minister Florence was quite successful in his appeal to various religious and other organizations to withhold their proxies from the management and also to boycott Kodak's products and demonstrate against Kodak's plants in all parts of the country. At the Kodak stockholders' meeting in April 1967, seven of the eight dissenting groups, which represented 40,000 of the 80.7 million outstanding shares, were religious organizations. Although the stock represented by these groups was but a small fraction of the total, it would be misleading to measure the impact only in terms of the number of shares. Unlike FIGHT, these church organizations were well-established institutions representing a large number of churches. They had access to the public forum which, though not equal to that of business institutions, was quite important. Kodak—or for that matter any other business corporation—could not afford to treat the voice of this group as merely representing one-half of 1 per cent of their stock.[3]

Bishop Dewitt, who represented the Episcopal church at the annual stockholders' meeting, read a statement prepared by the church's executive council for the press. This statement perhaps sums up the feelings of many other churchmen who were also present at that meeting [22]:

Possession of power conveys the obligation to use that power reasonably. Corporations—and indeed investing churches—must measure the responsible use of their resources by social as well as financial yardsticks. . . . We stand with Negro communities in their real grievances and their urgent need for organizational power to participate in an open society. And we stand with the management of corporate enterprises which seek to manage their affairs for the well-being of the total community.

FIGHT's request for national demonstrations against Kodak's plants was not enthusiastically received by some of the church organizations. In an editorial entitled "Re: Church Strikes and Boycotts," the *Presbyterian Journal* [138] rejected the Presbyterian church's activities in the area of community organization:

For those who see the church as an organization existing for the purpose of helping achieve certain needed social, economic and political objectives (in much the same way Kiwanis Clubs work for the betterment of boys generally) these developments are a logical outgrowth of their concern. But for those who still hold to the Scriptural mission of the church, to win men to salvation in the Lord Jesus Christ, these developments must be viewed as radical departures from the assignment given the church by her Lord.

The same editorial reported that the Nashville Presbytery, when asked to support Project Equality, which involved sponsoring official boycotts of businesses that did not practice fair employment, turned it down by a vote of 2 to 1.

FIGHT's popularity waned somewhat among the clergy when Florence escalated his demands to Kodak and threatened to start a nationwide demonstration in Rochester that summer. The Rochester Area Council of Churches, in its first official criticism of FIGHT, passed a resolution criticizing the organization's intemperance and urging a cancellation of the candlelight demonstration. [105] Church pressure, as well as lack of interest in Florence's planned demonstrations, may well have speeded the "reconciliation" between FIGHT and Kodak on June 23, 1967.

Kodak officials were also not happy with the stand taken by the RACC in the Kodak-FIGHT controversy. During an interview with the author, some Kodak spokesmen expressed the opinion that the RACC's involvement in originally hiring Alinsky kept it from objectively assessing the company's side of the dispute. This bias spread to other churches locally and to the communications the RACC had with the National Council of Churches. As evidence of this bias, the Kodak men stated that in only a handful of instances across the country did clergymen attempt to check into the Kodak side of the story. Even when Kodak officials tried to present the facts as they saw them, their efforts were rebuffed by the clergy.[4] Kodak spokesmen gave the impression that the RACC was not only primarily responsible for creating FIGHT and for the resulting tension in the community, but also largely instrumental in engaging the National Council of Churches in the conflict and in generating adverse national publicity and reaction against Kodak.

After a careful study of all the data, it is the author's opinion that the situation was in fact the reverse of what Kodak spokesmen believed. It seems that the Board for Urban Ministry and the Rochester Area Council of Churches were encouraged in their efforts to organize local minorities as well as in their stand against Kodak by the publicly announced position of the National Council of Churches on similar issues. If anything, the Rochester Area Council of Churches, probably because of intense local opposition, was quite subdued and strove to maintain harmony between the warring groups and to keep the channels of communication open. Action by the National Council of Churches nationwide resulted either independently or in response to the urgings of FIGHT.

The Ramifications of Church Involvement

Where has the involvement between Kodak and FIGHT left the church? The Rochester Area Council of Churches certainly has not won any kudos for its efforts from any group in the community. In fact, as Reverend Paul R. Hoover pointed out, "the loudest condemnation of the RACC's actions has come from inner-city citizens of all races." [68] The dissatisfaction of the community's affluent is reflected in the financial problems of the RACC. Referring to the slump in the council's financial support, the

Rochester Democrat & Chronicle said that it indicated disillusionment with sponsorship of FIGHT and disappointment in an approach to helping blacks based on acrimony and upheaval rather than on goodwill and orderly processes. The newspaper further said that it would be more in keeping with reality "if the Council just admitted a misjudgment and went on from there." [31]

The dilemma of the church can best be summarized by asking the question: Whom does the church speak for, and what does the church stand for? Parishioners go to church for a reinforcement of belief and, to some extent, for an escape from today's reality and for hope in a better tomorrow. In a nonderogatory sense, going to church for many people may be like watching television soap operas for many housewives. The congregation listens to the problems of the world and tries to identify itself with the human suffering. And just as the housewife turns off her television set after the end of an episode and returns to her daily chores, the congregation also prays for the poor and suffering, contributes to needy causes, and then goes out to tend to its daily activities. By and large, this is the extent of their involvement. The personal and family problems of an average churchgoer, no matter how minor they might appear in the context of problems of other fellow human beings, have more immediacy and relevance to him. A large number of parishioners have hitherto been able to avoid the gruesome reality of the ghetto either by living in high-income areas of the city or by moving to the suburbs. The riots in the streets, followed by demands for active participation by their ministers in the cause of the minorities, come to them as a cultural shock. They hate to admit that the problem has always been next door and may have been compounded by their failure to act earlier. Since the problem cannot be solved by adding to their Sunday contributions, they take the next course possible; that is, they deny their ministers the right or even the opportunity to bring up the problem before their congregations.

It is hard to predict the effects of the Kodak-FIGHT controversy and similar actions on inner-city churches. Their proximity to the poor and their clergy's realization of impending explosion by the frustrated minorities force the clergy of these churches to resort to unusual and often radical techniques. However, the balance of power and financial muscle in the local church organizations is gradually shifting in favor of the more affluent and generally conservative suburban churches. The ministers in these churches find it difficult to go along with their colleagues from the inner-city churches for fear they will alienate the membership of their own churches. Even when they can sympathize with the needs of the inner-city churches, they consider the magnitude of demand for action coming from the inner-city churches as exaggerated and abhor the techniques advocated by the impatient and the radical among their brethren clergy. Therefore, at the very time when the inner-city churches need all the help, moral as well as economic, they can get, their very survival seems highly uncertain. As Reverend Paul R. Hoover, writing in *Christianity Today* [68], put it:

The frightening events in Rochester have left behind two tragic consequences: (1) a growing lack of confidence in churches and church leaders, not excluding inner-city ministers whose motivation and actions over the years were hardly open to question; and (2) a growing fear of what the future may hold in view of the reckless threats of members of the FIGHT organization at the Kodak annual meeting in Flemington, New Jersey. . . . Part of the soul-searching on the part of ministers, particularly those working within the city, centers on how long they can physically and mentally stand the pressures that stem from the difference in attitudes and professional experiences between the suburban congregation and the mission-oriented inner-city congregation.

The conflicts in outlook and approach between various churches become more apparent and understandable when we consider all organized church as a subsystem, with individual churches as its constituent units. The spiritual goals of the organized church, while relevant to its membership, are equally relevant to those nonmembers who appeal to the church for its help and suggest that by helping them the church would be fulfilling its self-proclaimed mission. However, when these spiritual goals are given operational definitions, complex problems emerge. These relate to the order of priorities for various goals preferred by different units—churches —in the subsystem. The closer a unit is to its membership, the greater is the pressure on it to tailor its actions to the needs of its members. Thus individual churches are highly vulnerable to the influence of their parishioners on any course of action they can take in a given situation.

The freedom to initiate action by the leadership is inversely related to the directness of contact between the parishioners and the clergy. This is why we find that the National Council of Churches and the Board for Urban Ministry could initiate actions which, although in congruence with the broader national interests, faced local opposition. This will also explain the often extreme radical approach pursued by the inner-city churches and the seemingly ultraconservative suggestions offered by the suburban churches—one would imagine much to the distress of their respective clergy—because in both cases the church leadership is constrained by their membership and must give vent to the feelings of their parishioners. It is more like the followers deciding the strategies for their leaders to follow rather than the latter initiating action on their own.

The validity of the above argument was essentially confirmed in the Rochester situation by a church observer, Reverend William C. Martin [105], when he made the following remarks about the role of various church agencies that are relatively free to initiate and execute action on their own:

The Board for Urban Ministry issued the invitation to Alinsky and led in providing his fee. Over half the fee came from church agencies such as the Presbyterian Board of National Mission. Much of FIGHT's most articulate support at Flemington came from similar denominational offices. These agencies and their staffs are ultimately responsible to a constituency, but even if that constituency opposes a policy decision strongly enough to try to countermand it, it is likely to move too late or hit the wrong target.

In the first chapter of this book it was stated that each individual satisfies his needs and aspirations by belonging to multiple units—associations—in different subsystems. Moreover, his associates in different units are not the same people. In other words, his basis for joining is not only that the association satisfies his goals but also that the other members in the association agree with the means to be used by the association in pursuing those goals. When this agreement does not exist, the association splits into numerous smaller units, with all units agreeing on the over-all goals but reflecting varying emphasis on different means. Any shift in the goals or the means *within* a subsystem and also *between* subsystems involves on the one hand a redistribution of power among the participating subsystems and their units and on the other hand a reassignment of individuals' various freedoms of action to different units. The latter becomes more important when such a redistribution of power results in a net loss of power for the individual members because this power has been given to nonmembers without the former's consent, either express or implied.

This situation was very much in evidence in Rochester. The activists among the clergy were advocating action by their membership against another subsystem, that is, the economic institution, and in favor of a group which did not have any substantial stake in either of the subsystems. To begin with, these ministers were attempting a redistribution of power to which the membership had not consented. If this action had involved only a power struggle between different subsystems, it would probably have been more palatable to the individual members, since they would gain the power through another subsystem that they would lose in the first. But their total power, that is, their control over resources and the availability of options together with the freedom to choose among options, would remain substantially unchanged. However, when this redistribution results in a drainage of power to outsiders, it is not acceptable to the current members in the various subsystems. Kodak, as an economic institution, was a part of the existing structure whose benefits were being shared by the membership. On the other hand, the minorities did not consider themselves part of their structure. Therefore, any increase in the power of the minorities would mean a loss of power for those groups and their members who now enjoy disproportionate gains within the over-all system and are naturally reluctant to give them up. The situation becomes all the more explosive when the minorities refuse to seek their share by the rules of the system and when the members of the favored subsystems find that even some of their own spokesmen are supporting the cause of these minorities.

The question then arises as to whether these spokesmen could legitimately claim to be representing the members of these subsystems. It is implicit in the voluntary nature of the subsystems that the leadership reflect the ideologies and views of the membership or they will be replaced by others more acceptable to the members. However, as was stated in the first chapter, a long-established institution develops a life of its own where the leadership adopts techniques to insulate itself from the pressures of the membership and thereby becomes able to initiate independent actions. Although these actions might be better for the long-run interests of the institution, the insulation from the membership has its adverse effects as well. Protected from the active scrutiny of the members, the leadership could become inbred and self-perpetuating and might act in arrogant disregard of the wishes of the current members in pursuit of self-gain, membership expansion, or some self-proclaimed ideals, virtuous or otherwise.

As an example to support this argument, we have the observations made by Reverend Martin on the Rochester situation [105]:

[A key factor affecting developments in Rochester was the existence of a] small group of activists who formed a close-knit team during the period when the invitation of Alinsky was being considered. This team, which included most of the staff of the Board for Urban Ministry and the Council of Churches, plus a handful of parish ministers, established its leadership at the outset by selling the Alinsky program to governing bodies of their respective denominations. Once this core group got things under way, they were joined by others who shared their aims, if not their innovating spirit.

These men had different motives from their parishioners, and shared with their fellows certain professional objectives. As Reverend Martin [105] put it,

The enlarged team is certainly not a homogenous group, but discernible patterns do emerge. Most are young and relatively new to Rochester. Most studied at liberal interdenominational seminaries, often under men considered too radical for the parish ministry. They talk of the church's mission primarily in this-worldly terms— "bringing about authentic relationships," "making people whole," "making human beings truly human." One explained half-apologetically, "I'm not old enough to think in otherworldly terms. I've just lately become aware of my own finitude."

  . . . To a man, they accept the doctrine that power is necessary to bring social change and that change comes from the bottom up. Some concede the existence of a sizable reservoir of goodwill in Rochester, but they doubt its gates would ever have been opened voluntarily. "Don't underestimate the intransigence of the privileged," one man cautioned. "Nobody with four aces ever asks for a new deal."

As to their personal interests and objectives, Martin [105] declared:

Ten years ago, these same men might have been more reluctant to run the risks of controversy, out of fear of endangering their careers. A note of encouragement from the denominational social actions board is scant compensation for a parish in the boondocks. As leading denominations have identified with the civil rights movement, however, sanctions and rewards have been rearranged. Now, the man who attacks social problems aggressively may stand a better chance of career advancement than his more cautious colleague. One activist explained, "This is where the action is going to be for the next few years. Sure, some churches won't want me, but most that I would be interested in will be looking for men with experience in this area." As evidence that this is not just wishful thinking, several key members of the "team" who were under heavy pressure from their churches left Rochester during the past summer for more attractive positions in other cities. And for those who prove too radical for the parish, there is always the possibility of a good staff job at the denominational headquarters.

  For better or for worse, Rochester will never be the same again. These men and their ideas have left a lasting imprint on the life of the city and its inhabitants. However, the anomalies and disruptions created by these clergymen in the established patterns and modes of behavior between various subsystems will not be confined to Rochester. Unless these men recognize that the impatience of an ideologist must be tempered by the tolerance for the daily realities of life and the limits to which mortals can be exhorted to self-denial and action, their attempts to change the social system are not likely to be successful or lasting. Unwilling to compromise, these members of the clergy will be unacceptable to the suburban conservative churches, where the need for change will become more pressing as time goes on. They will thus hire and work with people with like ideas. With little or no feedback from "the outside world," they are likely to become inbred and intolerant of those who dare disagree with them.

Footnotes for Chapter 5

1. *Church* is defined here as all organized Christian religious bodies in the United States.

2. As was discussed in Chapter 1, business regards the economic welfare of individuals to be the primary goal of society. Since business believes that maximum freedom for the pursuit of individual self-interest, as represented in private and voluntary economic institutions, leads to maximum social welfare, it considers the objectives of the business subsystem to be similar to those of the objectives of the total social system.

3. For example, the Episcopal church has 3,340,759 members in 7,547 churches, and the United Church of Christ has 2,067,233 members in 6,957 churches. [82]

4. One of the executives interviewed said that a "member of the Presbyterian clergy in Missouri was urged to send us a telegram of protest by a clergyman in New Orleans. The clergyman in Missouri called Kodak to hear our side of the story. I had a long talk with him and sent him some information. He never sent the telegram to Kodak."

   Kenneth Howard, of Kodak's industrial-relations department, said in an interview with the author, "The amusing sideline to this is that I am also a graduate of a divinity school. In the middle of this network of communications, we discovered that a former very close friend of mine in the divinity school was sending out his literature to clergymen all over the country. So I called him and said that I had heard he was interested in the Rochester situation and asked him whether he had ever visited Rochester and he said yes, oh yes. So I told him that since I was also involved in this issue from the other side, it might be worthwhile if we got together sometime and talked about it. I pointed out to him that I believed there were certain inaccuracies and half-truths that were being circulated about Kodak and that I was sure he wouldn't want to be a party to them. But he never called me, he never came to see me, he wouldn't send me a copy of what he sent out around the country. This was typical of the whole problem. He wasn't in the least bit interested in knowing the facts."

CHAPTER 6

The News Media: Onlookers or Participants?

The media report and write from the standpoint of a white man's world. The ills of the ghetto, the difficulties of life there, the Negro's burning sense of grievance are seldom conveyed. Slights and indignities are part of the Negro's daily life, and many of them come from what he now calls "the white press"—a press that repeatedly, if unconsciously, reflects the biases, the paternalism, the indifference of white America. This may be understandable, but it is not excusable in an institution that has the mission to inform and educate the whole of our society. — Report of the National Advisory Commission on Civil Disorders (1968)

Analysis of the social conflict explored in this book would not be complete without the evaluation of another important institution: the news media. It was noted in Chapters 3 and 4 that both Kodak and FIGHT were aware of the role mass media could play not only in informing the public but also in influencing public opinion. The news media were, therefore, an important variable for Kodak and FIGHT, and the strategies of the two parties were carefully designed to *manipulate* and *use* the media to their best advantage.

One may speculate whether the Kodak-FIGHT controversy would have received national attention if it were not for the coverage given by radio and television networks, wire services, national newspapers, and magazines to Stokely Carmichael's visit to Rochester, the press conferences of Minister Florence, and the demonstrations at Kodak's annual stockholders' meeting. It was apparent that the news media played an important role in bringing the issue before the public. Furthermore, it is also becoming apparent that the role of the news media in molding public opinion is becoming increasingly crucial in similar situations and that all parties to a conflict must take the media into consideration before deciding on a course of action.

The News Media and American Society

The extreme elements within the Establishment as well as those who oppose the existing social order have long criticized the mass media in their reporting of social conflicts. The current turmoil in American society—arising out of issues like civil rights, black extremism, campus unrest, youth revolt against all established institutions, and the general dissatisfaction of the masses with the deterioration of the nation's physical and social environment—presents the news media with many conflict situations in which their reporting is going to draw criticism from many segments of the society. However, in this case the criticism of the mass media is not confined to the extremist elements in the warring groups alone, but is more widespread, extending to the intelligentsia of moderate leanings as well as to the man on the street. This difference is primarily due to two interrelated factors: (1) the ability of television to convey news instantly, reaching millions of homes in a fraction of the time required by newspapers, and (2) the visual nature of television, which makes for heavy emphasis on the dramatic or emotional aspects of news stories. Moreover, because of the limitations of time, both radio and television tend to give "spot" news, which is generally fragmented, thereby exaggerating the action side of the story and understating the analysis side of the story. Unfortunately, newspapers, in order to compete with television and radio, have also been leaning more heavily on the immediate and more dramatic or sensational aspects of the news, with the result that rather than providing a counterbalance to the telvision coverage of news they have tended to compound the problem. According to the National Advisory Commission on Civil Disorders [142]:

Our second and fundamental criticism is that the news media have failed to analyze and report adequately on racial problems in the United States and, as a related matter, to meet the Negro's legitimate expectations in journalism. By and large, news organizations have failed to communicate to both their black and white audiences a sense of the problems America faces and the sources of potential solutions.

That the news media have failed to deliver a satisfactory product to its constituents is evidenced by the broad criticism leveled by virtually all segments of society. The white Establishment accuses the media of resorting to sensationalism, promoting seemingly insignificant local conflicts into events of national magnitude, creating instant leaders by giving unusually large publicity to militant leaders and radical causes, and not emphasizing the positive aspects of news. It is not uncommon to hear remarks against the press like "If you didn't report Stokely Carmichael he wouldn't exist" [57] or to read letters to the editor asking for "happy news," for example:

If the problems of America are to be solved without us killing ourselves in one big bloodbath, your paper would do well to avoid the news that divides people . . . instead of publishing it to sell papers and in the name of informing the public on controversial issues. The news media are corrupting the country. This is a certainty. [96]

The moderate wing of the establishment also accuses the news media of being "not rooted in the great mass of Middle America and also in their systematic bias toward young people, minority groups and the kind of Presidential candidates who appeal to them." [71]

Minority groups of all shades and political beliefs have also been unhappy with the news media. They view the media with hostility and suspicion, regarding them as a tool of the Establishment which intrudes into their privacy and whose reporting is partisan and biased. Although minority groups and the extremist elements among them deftly manipulate the news media to their advantage, as will be seen later in this chapter, their contempt is not any the less. The black militants regard the mass news media as "institutionally racist" and therefore untrustworthy. The report of the National Advisory Commission on Civil Disorders also noted the existence of a lack of any but the most superficial interest on the part of the news media in the problems of the black people. The report also stated that the news media tended to look at the black problem from the viewpoint of white people and noted, as reported in *Newsweek* [71], "about the only time the white 'down town' press went into the ghettos was behind police skirmish lines during riots." The feelings of the black people about the news media were perhaps best expressed by Reverend Charles E. Cobb, a black minister, during the annual Race Relations Institute held at Fisk University, Nashville, when he said, "The institutionalized press is today's real criminal of the hour." [57]

Why is everybody against the news media? Are the news media doing anything "wrong," or has the external environment—within which the news media operate—changed so radically that yesterday's "right" is no longer relevant? Why, as James Reston asks, is disbelief in the press a national joke? Should the news media rethink their role in society in view of the clamor of their critics, or should they stand firm on their past and present performance, leaving the judgment to history? Even if the news media were amenable to suggestions of a change in role, a whole set of new questions needs answering: What kind of changes should be made? In whose favor should those changes be made? How should those changes be brought about?

It is the contention of this book that the present confusion about the role of the news media and the dissatisfaction with their performance expressed by virtually every segment of society have arisen largely because of a failure to evaluate and analyze the performance of the news media as a subsystem which must operate within the over-all social system. This failure to understand the news media as a subsystem applies equally to publishers and editors of various news media on the one hand and their critics on the other hand. One can begin to appreciate the possibilities of both uses and misuses of news media, if one sees the media as a subsystem, with its own value set and its own units. In other words, different media have value sets that are likely to vary among themselves as well as between individual units and the subsystem. Furthermore, viewed in this light, the dissatisfaction with various news media by society can be analyzed in terms of the movement of membership from one subsystem to another, of the changing composition of the membership, or of the changing needs of the membership within the subsystem. All these changes create stress situations necessitating a rearrangement of relationships among different units in the subsystem as well as among their members, a redefinition of goals and objectives of the subsystem, and a redistribution of power among various units. The dissatisfaction of the masses reflects a desire by the warring groups to seek a more favorable place for themselves in the reconstituted subsystem.

The News Media as a Subsystem

Although the over-all goal of the subsystem may be simply stated as informing the public, the operational specifics of this goal vary widely within the media because various news media

1. Cater to different audiences, for example, local, regional, and national; and to special-interest groups, for example, business, religion, and ethnic minorities.

2. Operate under different competitive conditions.

3. Have different financial and personnel resources.

4. Have different images in the eyes of the public as to their credibility and, therefore, are under different kinds of pressure to provide not only news but analysis and editorial comment. News media are, therefore, not

merely vehicles of communication but have a personality of their own, and this personality is imprinted upon the news they carry, giving this news a distinctive character and emphasis not inherent in the news itself.

5. Function under different federal, state, and local statutes which regulate different aspects of their operations.

In order to facilitate our analysis, it would be convenient to divide the news media into two groups: mass news media and special-interest news media. The former group comprises those media whose purpose is to reach all audiences within certain geographical boundaries. Moreover, their coverage is of a general nature and includes a large variety of subjects. The latter group comprises those media which either aim to reach certain specified audiences (for instance, city dwellers) or cater to specialized subjects (for instance, a particular professional group).

The general-purpose media are the more important of the two groups because they have greater reach, density (they approach the same audience with more than one instrument), and frequency (they carry similar messages more than once). They also have greater financial and personnel resources which they can mobilize to provide news coverage. In theory, these media—which include nationally known newspapers, nationally distributed news magazines, other general-purpose periodicals which comment on issues of general interest, and network radio and television—represent all segments of the population and, therefore, should provide fair and adequate coverage for all their "constituents." However, in practice, this ideal is seldom approached or even attempted by the news media because of two main factors. First, unlike constituents of other subsystems, there is less commonality of interest among various members of the subsystem or even among members of individual units. Second, for different units in the subsystem, some groups (for example, businessmen) have greater influence in shaping editorial and news-coverage policies of individual media than their mere numbers would indicate.

In an attempt to satisfy all their constituents, the news media have been resorting to what they call "objectivity," which is variously interpreted as either giving all sides of an argument or refraining from expressing one's own opinion. However, as Bill Moyers, former President Johnson's press secretary, said, "Of all the myths of journalism, objectivity is the greatest." [71]

"Objectivity" is a relative term; it cannot be achieved in the absolute. The very decisions about what news to cover, what prominence to give it, and what kind of followup to accord it require a process of deliberate editorial selectivity which is based on the subjective assessment of an editor as to what is relevant and important for the audience of the medium. This argument is even more relevant in the case of special-interest news media, where there is greater identity of outlook between a medium and its audience. Thus a news magazine catering to businessmen will not only provide more coverage (compared to other news media) of news which is of interest to its audience, but, more important, is likely to look at (read: interpret) the news from the businessman's point of view. Although this news magazine might sincerely believe that it is being very objective in its reporting, such a contention might be questioned by opposing groups. As with the rape incident in the Japanese film *Rashomon*, it is not uncommon to see a given situation reported differently in different news media. Facts themselves are seldom in dispute, but they assume a coloration from the environment in which they are presented. The role of a medium in presenting and even creating this environment is the crucial factor which influences audience reaction to the news.

Even if strict objectivity or neutrality were possible, it is not certain that objectivity would either help the audience or enable a medium to discharge its function properly. The news media's attempt to separate news from opinion is inefficient at best, and dangerous at worst. A reporter, in his attempt to be objective, presents issues in a balanced scale, giving various sides of the issue, point-counterpoint, "and the opinion omitted is the one that would mean most to the reader—the reporter's own." [29] Thus various official spokesmen are quoted who outline their positions in a manner which best serves their own purpose, while the reporter is effectively barred—under the pretext of professionalism, balanced reporting, or the medium's own rules of conduct—from telling his readers what he thinks of the credibility or motives of various spokesmen.[1]

Finding objectivity difficult to achieve and to justify, media spokesmen have resorted to two approaches. One, instead of being objective, they have claimed to be "fair." As David Brinkley, of the National Broadcasting Corporation, said, "Objectivity is impossible to a normal human being. Fairness, however, is attainable, and that is what we are striving for—not objectivity [but] fairness." [166] A professor of journalism at the University of Illinois, Gene S. Graham [57], went even further:

Those who fancy that mass media should have no conviction at a time when conviction is a life's essential are naive at best and insulting our intelligence at worst. We can be fair minded without ignoring the obvious fact that this is not yet a land of its stated ideals. Lincoln Steffens, in his day, did not shrink from a judgment between good and evil. But he was objective and fair and honest.

The other approach taken by the news media is that of "personal journalism," as typified by Nicholas Van Hoffman of the *Washington Post*, in which a reporter makes his own feelings evident in his copy and leaves it to the audience to decide for themselves how much of the reporter's views they want to accept. Such reporting is, however, very rare and is still not regarded as professionally desirable.

But the news media are neither fair nor objective when analyzed in terms of our theory of social systems. The mass media have hitherto paid more attention to achieving their current goals and maintaining past traditions. They have failed to anticipate the changing conditions in their external environment which might call for a change in their own goals. Moreover, their proportionately greater emphasis on the needs of the dominant groups in society has alienated the minority groups. The latter, disenchanted, are now developing new approaches to seek better coverage from the existing media as well as developing their own media. Thus, despite the media's claims to libertarianism, the young, the black, and the militant regard the mass media as fellow travelers with the rich and the powerful and, therefore, as part of the Establishment. The evidence points to a certain truth, and the charges have a certain bite.

As far as the minority groups are concerned, the news media "until very recently have run with the hounds rather than held with the hares." [71] They have failed in their responsibility to report the grave shortcomings of our society. They have looked at the black community *not as part of the social system but as an appendage which always lies on the periphery.* Thus the only news events they consider worth reporting concerning the black community are the ones which present some danger to *their* community, the white community. That the ghettos have too few streetlights, that their streets are potholed, that the slums have poor sanitary conditions, indifferent or callous law enforcement, and consumer fraud—are all "normal" conditions and therefore not worth reporting. However, let there be riots or looting and the reporters will race to the scene because riots represent danger to their social system and are therefore news. The very fact that slums exist side by side with more affluent neighborhoods in a city and remain unreported is a condemnation of the claims of objectivity by the news media. The report of the National Advisory Commission on Civil Disorders [142] has indicted the news media for their "failure to report adequately on race relations and ghetto problems":

By failing to portray the Negro as a matter of routine and in the context of the total society, the news media have, we believe, contributed to the black-white schism in this country.

As Leslie R. Colitt of Reuters News Service [29] has pointed out,

Perhaps the greatest and least excusable failing of American newspapers has been their indifference toward the quality of their environment. Newspapers (with a few exceptions) have refused to deal with the very factors in the cities which have been producing the "urban crisis," a phrase they never tire of repeating.

How else can one explain that on a typical day a newspaper of the stature of the *New York Times* provides from three to four times more society news than news about what was said in the blacks' churches or neighborhood bars? Why is there better coverage of killings, burglaries, and auto accidents than of poor schooling, high rents in the ghetto, and lack of jobs for the black people. The situation in the few other metropolitan newspapers reviewed by the author—*San Francisco Chronicle, Los Angeles Times, Chicago American, Daily News and Tribune, Oakland Tribune, Milwaukee Journal*—was, if anything, worse than that in the *New York Times.* The conditions prevailing on network and local television stations are no different. In one survey, in San Francisco, the author monitored local evening news of the three network stations. Each station was viewed on seven separate days. Of the 21 viewings, only four contained any mention of the poor conditions of the blacks; none tried to analyze the causes of those conditions. The only news concerning the black people was about picketing or striking by militant students on local campuses or about confrontations between the police and the Black Panther Party. On all the stations, sports news dominated all news concerning black people by a ratio of more than 3 to 1.

Nor is the news-media partisanship against different groups confined to minorities; it extends to all those segments of our society which espouse causes detrimental to the Establishment or to the dominant members within the subsystem. In a recent panel discussion on the Public Broadcasting Laboratory's program in New York, Federal Communications Commissioner Nicholas Johnson strongly indicted the networks for allegedly refusing to annoy their heavy advertisers. As related in *Newsweek* [166], Johnson said,

We are never told that cigarette smoking was associated with anything other than football and good times. Automobile manufacturers are big advertisers. When do we ever hear about the unsafe automobile?

It is no wonder that the man on the street distrusts the news media, for it was not until the publication of Ralph Nader's *Unsafe at Any Speed* in 1966 that the news media recognized this issue as of vital concern to the public. Moreover, television's entertainment shows are full of episodes in which daring detectives chase outlaws, run down members of the Mafia, use ingenious devices to thwart single-handedly communist plots at home and abroad. Yet we do not find a single show that deals with frauds and deceptions carried on in the corporate headquarters of many a big business.

The problem of incomplete and biased reporting, from the viewpoint of minority groups, is even more acute and pervasive in the case of special-interest news media, whether local newspapers, local radio and television stations, or special-purpose magazines. These media are not only unfair in presenting the viewpoint of affected minorities but, in being unfair, also hurt the long-term interests of the dominant group with which they identify.

In the case of local mass media, a demonstration or riot by local minorities implies a reflection on their communities. Thus, instead of facing the issue for what it is, the local news media present it as part of a national pattern and, therefore, outside the control and beyond the power of the local community. Alternatively, they present such news when it conveys a danger to the local Establishment. The focus, then, becomes "law and order" rather than the alleviation of the causes which are behind the problem. If possible, the local media often try to either ignore the news or understate it under the lofty ideal of preserving the peace of the community.

An example of this partial approach occurred in 1960 among the newspapers of Philadelphia. Early that year, a group of black ministers successfully organized a series of voluntary boycotts against the products of certain local businesses in order to persuade the businessmen to hire more black people in jobs which were above the entry-level positions and were not dead-end positions. The white community of Philadelphia was in almost total ignorance about the conflict because the city's three largest newspapers completely ignored the news on the boycott. The editors' rationale was that they did not want to aggravate racial tensions. As Kuhn and Berg [94] wrote:

Noting that newspaper publicity for boycotts would almost certainly increase their chances of success, one editor said, "We did not want to be put in the position of helping with publicity something we don't know whether we can agree with, either morally or legally."

Interpretation of the news by the special-interest media is also biased and detrimental to the long-run interests of their audience. Thus, when a business magazine analyzes issues like air and water pollution, conservation of natural resources, civil disorders, or city slums, it presents the problem to its audience as a "crisis situation" and suggests ways and means by which business can avoid facing regulation, becoming involved, or coping with the conflict. Seldom, if ever, are the businessmen told that what they have been doing may have caused the problem in the first place. Thus, by giving their audience only what it wants to hear, the special-interest media keep their audiences ignorant when the problem is in its embryonic stage and can be solved. The businessman wakes up one morning to find facing him a situation of crisis proportions—a situation he didn't even know existed.

Manipulation of Media by Opponents in a Conflict

The established institutions of society have always used the news media to disseminate information about their activities and to reinforce among the public the value system they represent. It has always been easy for them to do so. First, what these institutions do or say is "news." Second, their values are the values to which most of the public subscribe. Third, these institutions have their own special-interest media to provide further coverage for the news which the mass media will not carry. Over a period of time, the rules of the game by which various news items were to be covered by different media were established by convention and by the spokesmen for established institutions. Thus, for example, business executives, political leaders, church leaders, academicians, and other professional experts could take the media for granted and could predict with some degree of certainty that their views would receive due publicity.

The dissatisfied groups, which in our case are the black minorities, do not have such advantages. They lack media of their own which could be utilized to disseminate information and to communicate with their own group. Furthermore, they have limited access to the news media belonging to the Establishment and little hope that their views will receive the kind of attention which their opponents customarily receive from the mass news media. Moreover, in order to succeed, a minority group must seek the cooperation of the majority group, and this cannot happen unless the dominant majority has a chance to hear the views of the minority.

With the tremendous expansion in news coverage now provided by the mass media, both the established institutions and the minority groups have come to appreciate the importance of the news media in airing their views and molding public opinion in their favor. Their understanding of the possibilities and limitations of various media has reached a high degree of sophistication. When different parties to a conflict act only in response to each other, hoping that the various media will carry the news, they are treating the presence or absence of the news media as a limiting condition, or a fact of life, with which one must live. Instead, opposing groups now decide which of the news media they want to carry their news. As such, the news media become not the limiting conditions, but rather alternative strategies to be employed in order to give their "news" a particular dimension and character. Thus news items are created by different parties in such a manner that they are likely to be carried by a particular medium.

An established institution, like a business corporation, uses the news media through press releases, publicity handouts, and press conferences where the spokesmen of the institution give their opinions on issues of importance to them as well as to the public. However, this group suffers a disadvantage in terms of reaction from that part of the community which supports the views of its opponent group. In the first place, this audience is hostile and does not believe the pronouncements of the spokesmen of the Establishment. Second, to this audience the mass media are also tools of the Establishment and therefore suspect. Third, the minority group does not have well-established media which could be used by the Establishment to communicate with the hostile audience via a medium which has greater credibility for this audience. Consequently, the Establishment ends up communicating with the people who already believe in its position. It has little or no communication with the followers of the opposing group, and the news of the opposing group which is carried by the Establishment's media is biased and therefore does not convey the feelings, motives, and reasoning of the opposing group. The communication gap between the two groups therefore continually widens, and with that their mutual distrust increases.

A minority group or an emerging institution does not have the resources to command the attention of the news media. Yet its need for reaching the majority group and enlisting its support is crucial for survival. Consequently, small groups create what is called "contrived events" to attract general-purpose and special-interest news media. These contrived events may be press conferences staged by militant leaders where the reporters are assured of shocking and headline-making statements against the Establishment; demonstrations with pickets and placards, staged at a time most convenient for the television cameras to make the six o'clock news; or similar other techniques such as sit-ins, sing-ins, and peace marches.

The news media, especially television, have been accused by various groups of giving undue publicity to these contrived events, thereby "dignifying" their leaders. However, those people who are against giving publicity to these contrived events—and there are newspaper editors as well as reporters in this group—fail to understand either the nature of these events or their implications for the future.

First, these contrived events are unusual, and the unusual *is* news. Second, the size of an event is not related to its importance. Just as large numbers cannot be ignored, large causes cannot be ignored. Third, by ignoring these contrived events, the established group stands to lose much more than by allowing it to be reported. One does not have to give Stokely Carmichael a forum when he enters the town with fanfare—the fanfare obviously designed for the benefit of television cameras—and holds a press conference. However, what Stokely Carmichael has to say is known by his followers, and regardless of whether or not the press covers him, his followers know of his arrival and through word-of-mouth publicity know of his views. The only people who are not familiar with his views are members of the Establishment, and they are the ones who must become familiar with what he has to say simply because they live in a society where a significant minority is going to be influenced by what Carmichael and others like him have to say.

What about the contention of some people that the mass media's coverage of the activities of militants further inflames racial tensions and creates unrest in the society? The report of the National Advisory Commission on Civil Disorders provides impressive evidence to the contrary. The commission found that television coverage of riots in various communities was both "cautious and restrained." The findings tended to dispute the commonly held belief that the riot intensifies television coverage, thus in turn intensifying the riot. The content analysis indicates that whether or not the riot was getting worse, television coverage of the riot decreased sharply after the first day. [142]

Apart from the obvious charge of censorship if the news media were to avoid all so-called contrived events, one may contend that the reporting of all events, including contrived events, is indeed the responsibility of the institutionalized media. In Graham's [57] words:

Otherwise how can the grass roots be heard? How can the minorities? Sam Jones, dirt farmer, member of the NFO [National Farm Organization], does not own a newspaper. Amos Simpkins, unemployed Negro, doesn't have a TV station to his name.

It should be noted that although some observers consider the use of the news media in this manner as unorthodox, it is certainly not unethical. Business corporations and established groups and institutions have both the resources and a strong traditional base for gaining national attention. In many cases, they simply take it for granted that their position entitles them to such limelight. A new or emerging group is, on the other hand, handicapped by the lack of sophistication in articulating its objectives, by the absence of a broad power base, and by a scarcity of resources to challenge the vested interests of the established groups. Still, their goals are no less important or urgent. What they lack in material resources, they often make up in dedication, ingenuity, and improvisation, all of which are surprisingly successful in developing operational strategies.

Keeping in mind this background and analysis of the nature and character of the news media in the present social system, we now turn our attention to the Kodak-FIGHT controversy and to the roles played by the various news media in that conflict.

The conflict between Kodak and FIGHT was covered nationwide by the major news services and by national magazines and journals of all types and political persuasions. Although events were reported throughout the controversy, national coverage was heaviest immediately after Kodak's repudiation of the agreement of December 20, 1966, with FIGHT, and at the time of Kodak's annual stockholders' meeting on April 25, 1967, in Flemington, New Jersey.

The news media are of interest in this case because to some extent they helped to create the news they reported. FIGHT's attempts to make its disagreements with Kodak a nationwide controversy were aided by the media. Several times throughout late 1966 and the first half of 1967, Minister Florence was able to win support among various segments of the American public because he kept the issue at a controversial level. This strategy, to a large degree, accounts for the often bizarre manner in which FIGHT's spokesmen and supporters acted before television cameras to attract public attention. By focusing solely on its sensational aspects, the news media chose to elevate the controversy to a national level and at the same time distorted and exaggerated its impact.

The Local News Media[2]

The only English-language daily newspapers in Rochester are the *Democrat & Chronicle* and the *Times-Union*, both of which are part of the Gannett newspaper chain with headquarters in Rochester.[3] The president of Gannett is Paul Miller, who also acts as the publisher of the chain's two Rochester newspapers.

Prior to the Kodak-FIGHT controversy the Gannett chain had a reputation for progressive thinking and constructive work in the area of civil rights. In 1960, the *Times-Union* developed and published a series of five articles under the title "Winds of Change," outlining the deplorable social and economic conditions of the black people in Rochester and accurately predicting the dangers of racial unrest and tension. The *Times-Union* published an updated version of the series in 1962 under the title "Winds of Revolt," which showed "how badly the Negroes were housed in a city famous for its homes, its trees and lilacs, its culture, its generosity, and its depression proof economy." [72]

In 1963, Paul Miller assigned Gannett's executive editor, Vincent Jones, to undertake an investigation of the different ways Northern cities were coping with racial unrest and urban crisis. More than 40 editors and reporters contributed to the investigation and over 100 articles were prepared and distributed within a year, starting in July 1963 under the general caption of "The Road to Integration." This series won journalism's highest award, the Pulitzer Prize, the first ever awarded to a group or chain. [72] The same series won a Brotherhood Award from the National Conference of Christians and Jews.

However, when the Board for Urban Ministry invited Saul Alinsky to Rochester, Gannett raised a strong protest. The reaction probably reflected the views of the publisher, Paul Miller, who since 1966 has led a one-man crusade against FIGHT, church organizations supporting FIGHT, Saul Alinsky, and all other persons sympathetic to FIGHT.

The *Times-Union* and its radio and television affiliate WHEC dispatched a three-man team to Chicago to study the operations of Alinsky's Industrial Areas Foundation in the Woodlawn section of Chicago. The outcome was a three-part series in the paper as well as two one-hour television documentaries during prime time. According to Vincent Jones [72], "both sides praised these presentations as objective and informative."

However, neither this series of articles nor the opinions expressed by local clergy changed any minds at Gannett. As Jones [72] put it,

We have tried to keep our feet on the ground and to pursue a moderate, practical policy.... The invitation [to Saul Alinsky] was issued by the Council of Churches without first consulting the community. Because of the way it was handled, and a belief that Alinsky's controversial methods would do more harm than good, the *Times-Union* questioned the whole project. It was a moderate editorial stand, but left no doubt of the newspaper's belief that the move was risky at best.

An analysis of various feature articles, editorials, and the manner of news presentation in the *Times-Union* and the *Democrat & Chronicle* gives one the impression of extreme hostility toward FIGHT and raises serious doubt as to the impartiality of the coverage during the Kodak-FIGHT controversy. Why was such an animosity expressed by the Gannett papers against FIGHT and its supporters? I presume that to some extent it was a case of hometown boosterism and a defensive action against outsiders who were likely to destroy the good image of "their town." In that sense, the two papers were reacting much like the news media and the Establishment of Southern towns who blamed so-called outside agitators and trouble-makers for disturbing the peace and inciting riots. There might also have been a problem of personal ego, since Miller was not consulted by the Council of Churches about inviting Alinsky.

Miller's wrath was directed as much, if not more, against the Rochester Area Council of Churches, as it was against FIGHT and Saul Alinsky. According to an article in the *New Republic* [144],

At a church breakfast in late 1966, Miller was once more belaboring the ministers for "sneaking" the organization past responsible citizens, and bringing into their midst this "ill-mannered tiger" [Alinsky] to preach "his hate."

"Rochester, New York, is not Rochester, Alabama," said Miller, who sounds like an undertaker. "We have primarily a refugee problem, not a racial problem." How inappropriate it was, he went on, for church people to cultivate in Negroes the idea that in Rochester as in the South, they must take something away from somebody to make progress. Miller recommended to the ministers an article in the December *Reader's Digest* entitled "Are We a Nation of Hoods?" It provided a valuable perspective on the teachings of Jesus.

"If the organization you finance be continued," he said, "why not see that it gets a name somewhat less offensive to the total community. How about W-O-R-K instead of F-I-G-H-T, how about L-O-V-E, how about T-R-Y, how about D-E-E-D-S?"

Again in January, Miller made an editorial attack in the *Times-Union* on those clergy who had supported FIGHT. The editorial, entitled "The Gulf between Pulpit and Pew—One Layman's View," drew a large number of letters to the editor of both papers, most of which were critical of FIGHT and its supporters. However, it is not so much the letters, but the captions given to them by the newspapers which reflected the bias of their editorial staff and management. Thus, under the caption "A Pastor Speaks Up for Kodak," the *Democrat & Chronicle* on January 15, 1967, published a letter by Reverend Elmer G. Schaertel, which strongly supported Kodak. The readers' responses to this letter were published by the newspaper under such titles as "Too Many Churches Condone Alinsky," "Let Kodak, FIGHT Fill Own Roles," "Minister Applauded Council Stand," "Pastor's Comment Was Stimulating," and "Do Church Members Support Council?" [126, 154]

The two papers gave extensive coverage to the views of Kodak and generally accorded front-page space to the company's press releases. Again the titles were invariably pro-Kodak or anti-FIGHT; for example, "Alinsky Defends Black Power" [1], "FIGHT Vows New Push for Kodak Jobs" [48], "Kodak Questions FIGHT Job Demands" [90], and "Kodak Reviews Record on Job Talks with FIGHT" [92]. The newspapers' coverage on FIGHT's activities and its position was small compared to that on Kodak or to that accorded FIGHT by the national news media. This bias was carried further into 1967 when an editorial in the *Democrat & Chronicle* of June 16, 1967, entitled "Council's Defense," derided the attempt of the Rochester Area Council of Churches to defend their support of FIGHT. [31]

Gannett newspapers were not the only media who did not like Alinsky and FIGHT. As noted in Chapter 5, in retaliation for the council's support of FIGHT, radio WHAM, an ABC affiliate, canceled a free hour which it had been giving to the RACC. In an editorial attack on the council, reported in the *New Republic* [145], WHAM said:

thinking members of Rochester area churches have admitted many times over that the solution to the plight of any minority cannot be solved overnight—that demands are one thing, but that people do not become economically equal just because the various members of the Christian faith would have it that way. More realistically, members of the human race must prove their capacity to compete and to want to be part of the community.

FIGHT's only local outlet was WBBF, which Kodak people called "the Voice of FIGHT." This station presented FIGHT's publicity releases as news copy and made no attempt at giving Kodak's viewpoint to the listeners.

In my opinion, the local news media failed in their duty to inform accurately. By feeding their readers and listeners the news they wanted to hear, the local news media—whether supporters of Kodak or of FIGHT—further reinforced prejudices, making real communication and trust between the warring groups more difficult if not impossible.

The National News Media

The coverage by the wire services—especially the Associated Press—and the nationally prominent newspapers, like the *New York Times*, was quite extensive. Most other newspapers in the leading metropolitan areas in the United States reported the conflict at its various high points: Saul Alinsky's visit to Rochester to organize FIGHT as well as his visits to other towns to drum up support for FIGHT; Kodak's repudiation of the agreement of December 20; Stokely Carmichael's visit to Rochester; the announcement by various national church organizations of withholding their proxies from Kodak management; Kodak's annual stockholders' meeting; FIGHT's annual conventions; the setting up of Rochester Jobs Inc., and Rochester Business Opportunities Corporation; Kodak president Eilers' announcement of a reconciliation with FIGHT; and the setting up of Fighton, a joint FIGHT-Xerox operation. Most of the newspapers used the wire services as their source of information.

The biggest coverage by the press, radio, and television was accorded the stockholders' meeting. The proceedings of the meeting, the demonstrations outside the auditorium where the meeting was held, and the pronouncements of the spokesmen for Kodak and FIGHT were reported by all of the national television networks, radio stations, and newspapers across the country. The only other occasion when network television cameras visited the scene was to record Stokely Carmichael's visit to Rochester in January 1967.[4]

The role of television seems to have been crucial to Minister Florence's strategy. To some extent he was able to use television networks to escalate the issue to national prominence because he believed that only then could he pressure Kodak into conceding FIGHT's demands. Although television cannot be blamed for unwittingly serving Minister Florence's purpose while reporting items which it considered newsworthy, there is no question in my mind that, but for this coverage, Florence would have been hard put to keep the issue alive for such a long period or to draw national attention.

In order to get a better idea of the emphasis given to the Kodak-FIGHT controversy, it is necessary that we make a detailed analysis of the nature and extent of coverage accorded the incident by various news media.

The *New York Times*, which is perhaps the most influential newspaper in the country, was constantly on the scene. Starting with the first FIGHT convention in June 1966, the paper continuously reported the story as it developed. Immediately after Kodak's repudiation of the agreement of December 20, the newspaper published a long article, followed by four more related articles in January 1967 (three in the first week alone), two in February, nine in April, and three in May. The coverage thereafter declined in quantity, but was adequate for reporting all the relevant news.

A close reading of the coverage given the controversy by the *New York Times* reveals certain interesting points. First, the reporting was carefully balanced and was very "objective" in the sense that this term was used in the first part of this chapter. John Kifner, who did most of the reporting, as well as Edward Fiske and M. J. Rossaut, presented the viewpoints of the opposing groups in every story. The captions for different articles were either neutral or balanced to give equal billing to different parties. Nevertheless, one is struck by the complete lack of any interpretive articles or in-depth analyses that are generally associated with this paper. Not a single editorial was written on the controversy which had vast social implications and had received so much national attention. Moreover, the reporting appeared to this author as somewhat indifferent, in that it was confined to merely quoting the utterances of the spokesmen for Kodak and FIGHT. (As we will see in a subsequent section, it was the *Wall Street Journal* which did the best investigative job of reporting on the controversy, although it printed fewer stories than the *Times*.)

The *Washington Post* presented the other extreme. Nicholas Van Hoffman made no secret of where his sympathies lay. In a long article on January 9, 1967, entitled "Picture's Fuzzy as Kodak Fights FIGHT," he blamed Kodak for a large part of the conflict. In colorful language he suggested that Kodak management was "out of focus" and hinted darkly that if the situation did not improve soon, "Negroes may again be out on the streets shooting, and not with Brownie Instamatic!" [67]

Among the national news magazines and general periodicals which covered the story at various times were *Time, Newsweek*, and *U.S. News and World Report*. Of the three, *Newsweek's* coverage appeared more extensive, with sufficient interpretive material to enable readers to see the conflict in its proper perspective. However, there was no expressed opinion by any of the magazines.

In contrast, the national magazines with liberal leanings were full of interpretive articles by well-known writers. The *New Republic* published two articles by James Ridgeway, "Attack on Kodak" and "Saul Alinsky in Smugtown." The *Reporter* had two articles, one by Barbara Carter entitled "The FIGHT against Kodak" and the other by Jules Witcover entitled

"Rochester Braces for Another July." The *Atlantic* had an article by William C. Martin entitled "Shepherds vs. Flocks, Ministers vs. Negro Militancy." While most of these articles listed the contributions made by Kodak to Rochester's civic causes, they minimized their real value in the light of changing social conditions. These authors also faithfully reported Kodak's position in the conflict but berated the company's rationale and were generally pro-FIGHT in their writings.

The conservative magazine *National Review*, in an article entitled "The FIGHT-Kodak Fight" by Dorothy Livadas, took a strongly pro-Kodak position and largely blamed "the starry-eyed churchmen," Saul Alinsky, and Florence for aggravating racial tension in Rochester. The article implied that most Rochester blacks wanted "no part of FIGHT" and suggested that Saul Alinsky was a man who "capitalized on the plight of the downtrodden and made a 'hero' of himself while exploiting their misery." [98]

In an interview with the author, a Kodak public-relations executive expressed the conviction that the company's position in the controversy was not fairly reported in the national press:

It always makes good copy for David to be throwing a stone at Goliath. If Minister Florence were anywhere in the vicinity, the reporters would go after him to say something and he would take full advantage of this opportunity . . . .

The problem was primarily local in nature until the stockholders' meeting when, despite the 116 newspaper people present, the national press reported the thing so poorly that most people who read the account that appeared in a local paper hadn't the slightest idea what it was all about except that Kodak was having some trouble with Negroes.

According to an article by Raymond Schroth in the magazine *America*,

Kodak officials are still smarting from stories by James Ridgeway in the *New Republic* (January 21, 1967) and by Nicholas Van Hoffman in the *Washington Post* (January 9, 1967), in which Kodak claims to be misquoted. [156]

In an interview with the author, Kodak spokesmen again repeated this charge.

The Business News Media

The Kodak-FIGHT controversy was of special interest to the business community, as businessmen all over the country asked themselves: "Will this happen to my corporation?" Alinsky himself saw Kodak as just the beginning of a pattern of attacks by racial minorities against outmoded corporate behavior.

The business news media covered the controversy extensively as news, provided their readers with in-depth analysis and interpretive articles, and also wrote policy editorials. The opinions of most business magazines ran from sympathy for Kodak to extreme hostility toward FIGHT—both in terms of its objectives and tactics.

The news coverage by the *Wall Street Journal* was perhaps by far the best of any newspaper in the country. For example, it was the *only* newspaper to report the fact that after Kodak repudiated the agreement of December 20, Minister Florence and his associates offered to allow Kodak officials to amend the agreement in any manner acceptable to Kodak or even to scrap the agreement if Kodak officials would jointly announce with Minister Florence on television their willingness to cooperate with FIGHT "to get more jobs for Negroes." [55] This was indeed an important concession by FIGHT, asking Kodak to do only what the company had said all along that it was willing to do. Yet Kodak officials turned down FIGHT's offer.

One wonders why FIGHT did not choose to publicize Kodak's refusal at that time. Minister Florence was desperate after Kodak's repudiation and was probably willing to go to great lengths to salvage at least something out of the situation. There might also have been a realization on his part of FIGHT's lack of staying power in a long-drawn-out contest. However, when Kodak turned down his offer, it was in Minister Florence's interest to keep this incident quiet, for fear that it would appear as a "sellout" to his followers and would show lack of courage and militancy on his part. Kodak was also not interested in publicizing the event because it would make the company look stubborn and unreasonable and refute all the pro-cooperation propaganda it had been making in public.

However, the fact that neither the *New York Times*, the wire services, nor other news media reported this news of vital importance reflects on the somewhat indifferent reporting job done by the mass media. It is my belief that had this information been given the publicity it deserved at that time, it would have brought enough public pressure on Kodak and FIGHT, and might have resulted in an amicable and constructive settlement of the dispute.

An analysis of the coverage provided by the business news media reveals some interesting points:

The business news media presented the news to their audience in such a manner that Kodak was always presented in the most favorable light possible. For example, given below are some of the captions used by different magazines in their coverage of the controversy.

Wall Street Journal: "Eastman Kodak Accuses Rochester Rights Groups of Pushing for Power" [35], "Kodak Refuses to Restore Negro Job Pact; Rights Group Vows 'War' against Concern" [91], "Eastman Kodak and Negro Group Reach Compact to Work in Harmony" [38], "Kodak's Ordeal: How a Firm That Meant Well Won a Bad Name for Its Race Relations" [55], "Kodak Announces Plan to Help Slum Dwellers Start Own Business" [83].

Business Week: "The Fight That Swirls around Eastman Kodak" [47], "Kodak and FIGHT Agree to Agree" [87], "What the Kodak Fracas Means" [171].

Fortune: "And Kodak Will Ask, 'How High?' " (a reference to Stokely Carmichael's inflammatory statement in his press conference of January 19, 1967, in Rochester) [3].

Factory: "There's a FIGHT in Kodak's Future" [165].

Barron's National Business and Financial Weekly: "Who's Out of Focus? A Note on the Harassment of Eastman Kodak" (an attack on FIGHT and the church organizations supporting FIGHT) [174].

A major failure of the business news media in covering this controversy lay in their looking at the issues from a narrow viewpoint of analyzing the role of business organizations and established institutions as having an adequate and socially acceptable response to their external environment, and looking at FIGHT as a threat to the Establishment. Thus the business media regarded the behavior of business as inherently right. The changes when suggested were more of a peripheral nature calling for a readjustment of corporate response—for doing a little bit more of what was already being done—and did not call for any major rethinking on the part of the corporations of their social role in society. Their criticism of Kodak was confined to questions of strategy alone. By failing to suggest that minority groups in particular and society in general might have some genuine reasons for dissatisfaction with the functioning and performance of business corporations, the business news media failed in their task of educating their audience and making it aware of the changes which were taking place in the external social environment and the expectations of the society from the business institutions. These media viewed the impact of various events strictly from the business viewpoint. They accepted Kodak's explanation for repudiating the agreement as the only "logical" and "right" thing to do, without questioning it or analyzing the effect of such repudiation on the relationship between Kodak and the minority group and on the peace in the community except in terms of the public posture of large corporations. No substantive criticism was offered on Kodak's position, the criticism of Kodak being confined to questions of mechanics in terms of poor logic and bad strategy.

Reviewing Kodak's handling of the situation, *Business Week* [47] commented that after the second meeting, "Kodak was admittedly sidestepping FIGHT's demands . . . . [N]o major company could remain union free in New York State, as has Kodak, without considerable skill at evasive tactics." On Kodak's repudiation of the agreement, *Business Week* said: "While the agreement clearly ran counter to what Kodak had insisted all along, disavowing it weakened the company's position." Further, quoting one executive, the same periodical stated: "At least one executive thinks Kodak's lack of labor negotiating experience explains some of its clumsiness. 'Union negotiating teaches you when your name is on something, you have got an agreement.' "

Fortune [3], on the other hand, confined itself to quoting Kodak spokesmen and wrote:

Two days later, Kodak declared that the agreement was "unauthorized" and unacceptable. Chairman William S. Vaughn subsequently issued a statement saying that Mulder . . . had acted "through an overzealous desire to resolve the controversy."

Barron's National Business and Financial Weekly [174] presented the extreme end of the continuum on anti-FIGHT opinion. In an article on May 1, 1967, it stated: "Legally and morally, however, the company could not make the commitment demanded by FIGHT." *Barron's* thought Kodak had a lot to learn about labor relations: "If anything, it has taken not too hard a line, as its radical critics aver, but too soft. The presence on the payroll of an executive who failed to grasp the elementary principles cited above suggests as much."

Although some of the business magazines recognized the need for change in corporate behavior and suggested more positive action in the

area of assistance to minorities, most of them were editorially critical of
FIGHT and its supporters. *Business Week's* policy of giving business what
it likes to hear was typical of most of the editorial comment by the
business news media. In an editorial entitled "What the Kodak Fracas
Means," *Business Week* [171] called the Kodak-FIGHT conflict the fore-
runner of similar conflicts. The editorial further stated:

The demand that Kodak simply put to work whatever Negroes FIGHT produces is
preposterous. . . . It is not the business of any corporate management to run a public
welfare establishment. Efficient production of goods and services is the name of the
business game. Personnel policies that are violently inconsistent with profitability
violate one of the private corporation's cardinal rules. Management must retain its
rights to hire, fire, promote, and assign work in ways that serve business objectives.

The editorial urged business to understand and appreciate the objectives
of civil-rights groups in Rochester—the main objective being more jobs for
blacks—but said that "hiring unskilled Negroes cuts into profits, at least in
the short run," and argued that "business must be paid for undertaking
what is in the end a public responsibility." It exhorted civil-rights groups
to abandon their militancy and warned them that like the Wobblies and
the Knights of Labor,

they will get nowhere unless they avoid inflicting serious injury on the effective
operation of private business in this country. . . . Black Power won't work any better
than did labor power, when directed at radical objectives.

In another article *Business Week* [47] commented:

Alinsky—and FIGHT—are intent on using Kodak to press their conviction that corporations must assume more responsibility for the poor in their communities than
business customarily takes on. Says Alinsky: "American industry had better recognize—and some do—that they have a special obligation . . . . [T]he Kodak situation
dramatically reveals that today's ghettobound, militant urban Negro may generate
even more problems for business than the civil rights struggle in the South created."
    No business would find it easy to keep pace with Alinsky's fast-moving, bare-
knuckles style of civil rights campaign . . . .
    Kodak's dealings with FIGHT, in fact, starkly dramatize the clash of modern,
radical Negro tactics with well-meaning but traditionalist business attitudes.

An editorial in *Fortune* [3] described FIGHT's action at the stockholders' meeting as a harassment and described the Kodak-FIGHT situation so
that businessmen would understand "what the battle is really about." The
editorial agreed that

Many U.S. industrial corporations are failing to move fast enough to help Negro
applicants qualify for employment. No company can be expected to "create instamatic jobs," as Minister Florence has said Kodak should. But in one way or another,
industry should try to help unskilled and uneducated Negroes who want jobs to
qualify for jobs. What makes FIGHT's "war" against Kodak appalling is that Kodak
has recognized its obligations here. It is hard to imagine a worse way for Negro
organizations to try to beat down employers.
    [As far as the clergy was concerned, their] desire to support better job opportuni-
ties was good but [*Fortune*] questioned their use of stock voting proxies to achieve
these objectives. However in the specific case at hand, a proxy for FIGHT is not a
vote for Negroes but a vote for giving FIGHT power. "And that cause imposes no
moral claim upon churchmen or businessmen or anybody else."

In its article [174], *Barron's* rebuked Kodak for its softheadedness in dealing with FIGHT and questioned the logic of the concept of social responsibility for corporations:

The time has also come to do a little soul-searching with respect to corporate responsibility. Companies want to be good citizens, and, by providing jobs, paying taxes and the like, they generally succeed. However, management is the steward of other people's property. It can never afford to forget where its primary obligations lie.

... [T]he company policy as outlined in a 1966 Management Letter ... speaks of going beyond selection of the best qualified person, to seeking "to help the individual who lacks the necessary qualifications to become qualified."

... [M]ore suited to a sociology text than a corporate manual, the Letter adds: "Industry must look less critically at the individual's school record and work experience and more at his potential." Throughout the protracted dispute with FIGHT, Kodak's executives have chosen to ignore repeated provocations, insults and lies, an excessive forebearance which has merely incited their tormentors. In the corporate realm, as in any other, appeasement is a losing game. For Kodak and the rest of U.S. industry, it's time to stop turning the other cheek.

... The clergy is in bad company. In taking issue with the employment policies of Eastman Kodak, moreover, the churchmen stand on very shaky ground.

The Religious Press

The religious press not only actively participated in the process of informing its audience about the Kodak-FIGHT conflict but also contributed to molding the opinion of the clergy nationwide through editorials and interpretive articles. By and large, the religious press supported the stand taken by national church organizations in assisting FIGHT and also supported FIGHT's demands against Kodak.

In an editorial entitled "Economic Leverage of the Churches" [40], *America*, the national Catholic weekly, supported the stand taken by Protestant groups in withholding their proxies from the management of Eastman Kodak and further asserted:

Anyone who believes that it is morally reprehensible to buy the products of a firm that discriminates against colored workers must hold that passive, uncritical ownership of the firm's securities is also wrong.

It must be admitted, however, that in many cases it simply has not occurred to managers of church funds or purchasing agents to use their economic power for moral goals. Like other investors, they have single-mindedly sought security and a satisfactory rate of return. Similarly, purchasing agents have felt that they discharged their duties when they obtained goods and services at a favorable price.

All this leads one to wonder why a theology of consumption and investment for modern market societies has not been more intensively cultivated. The humbling fact is that before the civil rights movement challenged God-fearing people to practice what they preach, most of us in transacting business performed as economic men. Or, which is nearly as bad, we absent-mindedly followed the rule attributed to the late Henry Ford: "Whatever is good business is also good morals."

The *Episcopalian* [22] echoed similar views. The same tone was present in an article entitled "Rare Days in Any Month" in the *United Church Herald* [137], which commented on the involvement of the churches in the Kodak-FIGHT conflict:

Nor will the role of the churches in these developments go unnoticed. The Christian community often has been called the conscience of America but seldom has its voice been heard so clearly. Such a role is bound to be controversial—especially when the church challenges the intentions of its own members. But in a nation where the structures of power are increasing rapidly in size and influence, the corporate body of Christ must speak its convictions and may occasionally need to flex its muscles.

Chronicles and Documents [21], in an editorial entitled "The Church and Capitalism," commented on the economic wealth of the church and its possible uses:

But, have the Church administrators always been aware of the duties imposed by the possession of this wealth? In countries where the economy rests greatly on private initiative, shouldn't it be necessary that the Church herself show some initiative, and set an example wherever the possession of certain resources gives her the right to be present? The Kodak case shows very clearly the positive role that the ecclesiastic structures could play in a business concern.

The religious press, however, was not unanimous in support of church involvement in racial problems and issues of job discrimination in general and in support of FIGHT in particular.

The *Christian Century* for one did not agree with either FIGHT or its church supporters. As reported in the *New York Times* [81], an editorial entitled "Alinsky Denounces Reconciliation" stated:

But one wing of the clergy—greatly and properly concerned and determined to do something, even if it is the wrong thing—gulp and swallow what in the opinion of many of us is a highly dubious nostrum. Moreover, this minority is enraged by those of us who, having studied the Alinsky method closely and for a long time, resolutely refuse to gulp and swallow. What amazes and puzzles us is not Alinsky—he declares himself most forthrightly—but the hypnotic effect he has on some members of the clergy.

In another editorial, entitled "Episcopal Editor Denounces Saul Alinsky," the *Christian Century* concurred with the opinion of another Alinsky critic, Carroll E. Simcox, editor of the *Living Church*. As reported in the *New York Times* [134], the editorial remarked:

And Simcox, with whom we are not always in agreement, said a great deal more to which we found ourselves tapping our feet, including his statement: "I don't want one nickel of my church offering ever to find its way to anything that this man Alinsky administers or even comes near, and if I learn in advance that it has an Alinsky-related destination I won't offer it."

The editorial policy of *Christianity Today* also did not concur with the actions of those clergy who supported FIGHT. In an editorial entitled "Church Leaders Put the Squeeze on Kodak" [23], the paper cautioned:

Members of denominations backing FIGHT must consider whether their churches should be so deeply involved in big business, and whether their stock voting power should be used to harass responsible private enterprise. . . .
Every Christian must be committed to equal-employment opportunities for men of all races. But race is not the only issue in the Rochester controversy. The basic issue in all agitation aroused by the Saul Alinsky forces centers on changing the economic structure of our nation. Church members should repudiate and withhold financial support from leaders who back such rabble-rousing causes. All Christians should become involved in the Church's foremost enterprise: sharing with men poor in spirit the unsearchable riches of Christ.

In another editorial, entitled "A Fight Church Officials May Regret" [44], *Christianity Today* said:

Denominational officials are rendering a great disservice to the cause of Christ and the betterment of the Negro's status in American life by supporting the Saul Alinsky FIGHT organization in its calculated controversy with the Eastman Kodak company .... In its zeal to aid the Negro, the Church must exercise care that it does not promote organizations that sow disruption and seek political power while professing to help the less fortunate.

The *Presbyterian Journal* was perhaps the most vocal and vociferous in its attack against those clergy who sympathized with FIGHT or supported their churches' involvement in seeking economic justice for the poor. In a strange indictment of FIGHT supporters [138], it said:

Notice that the people on whose behalf the Church was called to picket were not necessarily Christians. No. The Church merely considered that its mission was to decide between two contending factions in a business dispute, and join the picket lines across the nation against one faction. [Emphasis added.]

Dr. L. Nelson Bell, in an article entitled "Church Activists Have Gone Wild" in the *Presbyterian Journal* [11], stated his views of the blacks which sounded like an echo of the apologetics of the segregationists of a (hopefully) bygone era. Among other things, he stated:

Perhaps the Eastman Kodak Co. has been too slow in making use of all available labor. On the other hand, some may be demanding "rights" for which they are not equipped. We do believe the Church in its eagerness to promote civil rights may have omitted an even greater duty–the promotion of a sense of responsibility which can only be attained by hard work.

The Black Press

The Kodak-FIGHT conflict was covered for the black press by the Negro Press International whose reporting was quite sparse compared to other special-purpose media and was confined to reporting the statements made by the spokesmen for FIGHT and Kodak on different occasions during the dispute. The only black paper of national repute, the *Chicago Daily Defender* (National Edition), carried a total of eight stories on the dispute, only three of which related the background in any detail. The paper also carried an editorial entitled "Economic Justice." [39] However, this editorial was devoid of any statement of position or philosophy by the editors or publisher of the newspaper and was just a brief summary of events.

Crisis, the official organ of the NAACP, published only one article on the problems of Rochester, Arthur L. Whitaker's "Anatomy of a Riot" [173], and carried two short news items ("NAACP Hits Rioters" and "Rochester NAACP Aids in Bringing Peace to Riot-Torn City") in the news section under the caption "Along the NAACP Battlefront." [2] The news items appeared in the August-September 1964 issue. Mr. Whitaker's article appeared in the January 1965 issue and preceded the Kodak-FIGHT conflict by at least six months.

Footnotes for Chapter 6

1. Leslie R. Colitt, in an article entitled "The Mask of Objectivity" [29], gave an example of so-called objective reporting in the *New York Times* of November 10, 1967. The reporter gave the views of the CIA on the undesirability of building bridges between the East and West as supported by the State Department. His emphasis on the CIA's views clearly indicated his own preferences. The reporter also failed to indicate that the State Department did not propose lessening any vigilance activities and that there was progressive improvement in relations between East and West despite espionage activities by both parties.

2. The accounts of coverage by local television and radio stations reported in this section were obtained indirectly through newspaper reports and magazine articles.

3. Gannett Co., Inc., is a chain of newspapers and radio and television stations located in small and medium-size cities primarily in the Northeastern states. The group's headquarters is in Rochester, New York. It has 30 newspapers (29 owned and 1 affiliated) with circulation ranging from 6,550 to 218,600. In addition, Gannett owns AM radio and VHF television outlets in Rochester and Binghamton, New York, AM-FM radio outlets in Danville, Illinois, and Cocoa, Florida, and a VHF television outlet in Rockford, Illinois. Of the two Rochester newspapers, the *Democrat & Chronicle* is published mornings and Sundays (circulation 142,794 and 218,586 respectively), and the *Times-Union* is an evening paper (circulation 143,855). [5, 17, 41]

4. The account of coverage by network radio and television described here was gathered only indirectly through a study of the press reports.

CHAPTER 7

Conclusions and Implications

Reason without passion is sterile, but passion without reason is hysterical. I have always supposed that reason and passion must be united in any effective form of public action. – Arthur Schlesinger, Jr.

Most of the confrontations, accusations, and demonstrations involving Kodak and FIGHT have subsided as of this writing, January 1969. Rochester has had a relatively peaceful period of about 18 months.[1] New relationships, as yet unexplained and undefined, have evolved between various groups. Some understanding and even progress have taken place in attacking problems of the hard-core unemployed, in providing housing and jobs for the poor, and in obtaining dignity and equality for the blacks. Kodak has gone ahead with the inner-city business plans without FIGHT. FIGHT no longer meets with Kodak except through the auspices of Rochester Jobs Inc. It has gone on to bigger and better things than Kodak was willing to give.[2]

Where Are We Now?

However, many questions remain unanswered. Why did all this happen, and could it have been avoided? Notwithstanding the basic structural problems which were of national character, one feature that came out of this study was the inability of the parties to communicate. Neither side could agree to the basic assumptions and rights of the other group. Each group was fighting for recognition from the larger community. The best-intended plans were foiled by poor communication and distrust of both the channels of communications and the beliefs and prejudices of the negotiating personalities. The minority groups were ignorant of the ways of modern business and understandably distrustful of Rochester's Establishment.

I think it is more than hindsight to say that FIGHT would have been satisfied with a program that met only a few of the criteria the group initially proposed. The ambiguity of the agreement of December 20 and Minister Florence's subsequent willingness to let Kodak officials amend it in any manner and even scrap it, provided Kodak publicly agree to work with FIGHT, showed that. The problem was that Kodak was unwilling to communicate with FIGHT in a meaningful way, for that would have meant dealing with FIGHT spokesmen as equals—a proposition, it seems to me, more unacceptable to the company than even accepting FIGHT's demands. From the early stages of the conflict, company officials made a pretense of listening to FIGHT's demands—and then proceeded to tell FIGHT about their program for developing black potential. The controversy and bitterness that followed could have been all but predicted beforehand by any astute observer given the environmental conditions and bargaining stance taken by the opposing parties.

There is also some doubt—if one may believe the *Rochester Democrat & Chronicle*—that the man on the street in Rochester has become any more aware of the problems of the poor in his community or that his understanding of the real issues involved has increased as a result of the

Kodak-FIGHT conflict. In a private poll taken by the newspaper in July 1967, it was revealed that the extent of involvement by the local citizenry was at best superficial.

Asked whether Alinsky (FIGHT) had improved the situation of blacks living in the Rochester area, made it worse, or not affected it, 61.5 per cent of those polled said worse; 14.5 per cent found no effect; and 13.5 per cent didn't know. To the question of whether FIGHT had helped or harmed relations between blacks and whites, an overwhelming majority —69 per cent—said "harmed." Of the rest, 14.5 per cent didn't know and 8 per cent felt it had done neither.[3] [98]

Where Do We Go from Here?

The controversy is far from over. The FIGHT-Kodak conflict was not an isolated incident, but only a point in a chain of events which is likely to continue not only in Rochester but all over the country. And the dissatisfaction against the business corporations is not confined to black minority groups alone, but is equally widespread among students, consumers at large, conservationists, and many other groups of well-meaning and concerned citizens who believe that they must fight business corporations if they are to protect their existing rights and achieve what they consider to be their proper share of this country's endowments. It seems, therefore, appropriate that we place the Kodak-FIGHT conflict in a broader perspective and see if any generalizations can be drawn which may be useful in averting similar incidents in the future and also make at least a start toward finding long-term solutions for some of our problems.

The reason for the dissatisfaction with big business seems to me to be twofold. One, the corporation is a manifestation of the structural injustices and inequities in our society—regardless of whether or not these injustices were inflicted by the parties immediately involved—and the dissatisfaction is likely to persist until these inequities are effectively eliminated. Minister Florence may have been right when he said that the civil-rights movement of the early 1960's was dead and that there would be other FIGHTs, other Kodaks, other Rochesters—and new alliances and new forms of action which would take their place. [18]

The second part of the reason is more fundamental, subtle, and complex than the first. Even if the obvious, measurable inequities in our society are substantially eliminated, there is no guarantee that the discontent and frustration that now pervade our social system will decline. The have-nots of today not only are seeking redress against inequities which are based on the existing value system and performance-reward ratios, but also are questioning the very value system on which the present reward system is based. The three most fundamental elements of this value system which are being critically examined and criticized are (1) the power and authority to dispense rewards, (2) the basic rights of the members of a social system, and (3) the definition of property and its relationship to power and other human rights.

Presumably, all parties concerned in the Rochester dispute wanted to "solve the problem" and create more jobs, but they disagreed on how to do it. They disagreed on how much power they should acquire (or keep) and how much they should relinquish. In Rochester, the struggle for the answer was a "contest of wills" over the allocation of power in the community: who has the right to allocate society's wealth in the form of jobs and hence dignity for the down and out. This reluctance to give up power is frequently labeled as conservatism or adherence to the status quo. Within this framework the corporations have sought answers to current problems in ways which do not upset the orthodox criteria of corporate performance or question management's prerogatives in managing corporate assets and distributing profits. To management, "reasonable" means least painful and, by implication, gradual, small, and conservative. Perhaps one reason Kodak was reluctant to consider FIGHT's plan was that the magnitude of change it represented, in the division of power among various groups and in the new social role of business, was far bolder than Kodak management was willing to accept.

The business institutions must change if they are to survive in an environment which is continuously evolving. These changes not only will have to come in the operating strategies but must extend to the basic values and premises of the business subsystem. However, changes by business institutions alone will not be sufficient in revitalizing our society. Other social institutions, including the present antagonists of the business institutions, must also change if a uniformity of approach and a program for concerted action are to emerge. Needless to say, the changes required of business institutions will be by far the biggest and most far-reaching for the simple reason that ours is a society where the means of production and, therefore, the resources necessary for economic and social change are concentrated in private hands.

In the following sections, I attempt to outline a positive program which business institutions, minority groups, and other concerned groups can consider as a framework within which necessary changes in a social system can be effected. There will also be suggestions as to avoiding violent and often destructive disruption of an economic system which, in its own way, has been quite successful in providing this country with the means which can now be used to tackle the problems of the minority groups.

What Business Institutions Are Doing

A necessary prerequisite for developing mutual trust and cooperation is the willingness on the part of various groups to see and understand an issue from the opposing group's viewpoint. Too often businessmen and other members of the Establishment have complained of the blacks' impatience and lack of understanding of the efforts being made to bring them into the mainstream of American economic life. The businessmen cite statistics to show the rate of progress, assert that a faster rate cannot be achieved because human training and development take time, and because the smooth functioning of the economy would be disrupted if greater sums were to be diverted to "social-welfare programs." They pat themselves on the back for the progress made through their efforts, and they denounce those militants who are bent on destroying the system.

The source of dissension, however, is not based on the fact that the progress has not been made but on who is measuring the rate of progress and against what criterion it is being measured. While the Establishment is comparing progress with what conditions were earlier, the black man is measuring it in terms of how far he still has to go. The black man does not want to wait for the economic and social convenience of the white man to grant him what has been his right by law but has been denied him by custom and tradition.

This disparity in outlook and approach between the business institutions and the blacks becomes apparent when one views a given set of data from the eyes of both the Establishment and the poor minorities. For example, in January 1968, a *Fortune* editorial [170] stated:

Negroes' incomes, jobs, housing and education have been getting significantly better in recent years—and Negroes in general know it. They have a strong sense that they are more respected—i.e., by whites—than they were a few years ago.

However, one year later, on January 12, 1969, the *New York Times* was headlining an article "Negro Is Found Lagging Despite 8 Years of Gains." The *Times* article [65] quoted Kenneth Clark, author of a Brookings Institution publication entitled *Agenda for the Nation*:

The homicide rate and delinquency rate for the Negro ghettos, which are higher than in most other areas of the Northern cities, have not decreased. The ugliness of the ghetto has not been abolished. The overcrowding has increased. Most Negroes are still restricted to ghettos by income and white resistance.

The statistical data mean different things to different people. The white Establishment may quote with satisfaction figures of the Bureau of Census that the median family income for blacks in 1967 was $4,939 which was 59 per cent of white income of $8,319 and compared well with 1965, when it was only 54 per cent. However, from the viewpoint of the blacks, their median income was still 41 per cent less than that of whites, so that a narrowing of the gap between the median incomes of whites and blacks by 5 percentage points over a two-year period was wholly unsatisfactory. Again, in 1967 only 34 per cent of the blacks were below the poverty line, compared to 55 per cent in 1960. But, for the blacks the relevant figure was that only 10 per cent of the whites were below the poverty line in 1967, indicating that they still had a long way to go. In 1967, only 27 per cent of the blacks earned more than $8,000, compared to 53 per cent of whites, and the unemployment rate in 1968 among nonwhites, most of whom are blacks, remained twice as high at 6.7 per cent compared to that among whites, which was 3.6 per cent.

Not only is there a disparity in income and rate of employment, but also there is an effective exclusion of blacks from various jobs of economic influence and power by both trade unions and employers. In a special issue of *Fortune* on business and the urban crisis [123], Thomas O'Hanlon reported some estimates made by Arthur M. Ross, Commissioner of the Bureau of Labor Statistics. Ross had analyzed a number of major building trades in an attempt to determine statistically how many of those jobs ought to be held by blacks. He concluded that

if the percentage of the Negro work force employed was proportionate to white employment Negroes would hold 37,000 more jobs as carpenters, 45,000 more as construction workers, 97,000 more as mechanics, 82,000 more as metal craftsmen, and 112,000 more as construction foremen.

From these figures it seems reasonable to conclude that the higher one goes in job specialty or wages, the lower is the likelihood that blacks will be proportionately represented. One wonders why *Fortune* did not commission a study to find out if a similar phenomenon existed for nonunion supervisory and managerial jobs in business corporations from office managers onward to corporate presidents. The absence of blacks in the corporate corridors of power is perhaps too obvious a fact to need further confirmation.

That the black man's distrust of the white man's Establishment has not diminished significantly in 1967 compared to what it was 3-5 years ago was revealed in a study of Negro attitudes conducted for *Fortune* by Daniel Yankelovich, Inc., a New York firm specializing in social-science research [172]. While a majority of the respondents felt that there had been an over-all improvement, their feelings about the whites and their trust in the white Establishment were in sharp contrast to the trend of their other responses. The data from this study are reproduced in Table 1.

The thrust of the argument in this section is not to deny that progress has been made in improving the lot of the black people in this country, but to emphasize that the desirable rate of progress cannot be determined on one dimension only, that dimension being the past—what the blacks' lot *was*—because it is the most comfortable from the viewpoint of the white Establishment. To be acceptable to all concerned, the desirable rate of progress must be measured on two additional dimensions, that is, forward or what it ought to be, and lateral or what other groups in the society have achieved.

Another area where rethinking by the business institutions is needed is that of the goals of business as a subsystem. As was stated in Chapter 1, the American society has long identified its goals with those of the business subsystem. Consequently, production of goods and services has become the foremost priority of the nation. This objective makes sense at a time when the bare necessities of life of a country's population are not being fulfilled. However, once basic needs have been achieved, the production of goods and services in ever increasing quantities must be considered only after taking into account other social costs involved, such as pollution of the physical environment, inequalities in income distribution, and production of goods for public consumption as against private consumption.

By perpetuating the myth of consumer sovereignty, business institutions have tried to avoid reevaluating their goals. Since business corporations produce only according to the wishes of the consumers in the marketplace, so the argument goes, they do not impose their goals on the society but instead perform a useful social function by efficiently producing only those goods which the consumers desire. However, if this were so, business institutions should not object to curtailing their freedom of production and "persuasion of consumers," should the consumers collectively decide either through their duly elected governments or other voluntary associations that they want to restrict the choices available to business in what it produces or how.

Economic facts of life cannot be isolated from social values since it is the assumptions of the latter on which economic institutions are based. Therefore, social values must determine the character and direction of business institutions. In determining their objectives, business institutions will be making a serious mistake if they ignore those factors which affect the direction of a society's order of priorities. Moreover, if business institutions insist on defining over-all social goals in terms best suited to their own interests, then they must accord a similar right to other subsystems. It is not difficult to see that such a course could lead to some difficult problems for society as a whole as well as for business institutions. The ascendancy to power by different subsystems would require radical readjustments in the goals of the over-all social system and a rearrangement of power relationships among various subsystems. As Commons [30] pointed out,

Neither the rights of individuals nor of corporations are inalienable—they are vested by operation of law and they take effect only on occasion of operative facts recog-

TABLE 1. FEELINGS ABOUT CONDITIONS NOW VERSUS 3-5 YEARS AGO

How Negroes Feel about Whites		Better	Worse	About Same
	Total	37%	33%	30%
16 to 25 years		34	34	32
26 years and over		39	31	30
Non-South		31	42	27
South[1]		50	15	15
	n = 300			

Whether Negroes Can Get What They Want under the U.S. System[2]		Yes	No	Maybe-Not Sure
	Total	53%	43%	4%
16 to 25 years		53	45	2
26 years and over		53	42	5
Income under $100 a week		60	39	1
Income $100 or more a week		45	48	7
Non-South		46	51	3
South[1]		67	27	6
	n = 300			

[1] Due to the small size of the sample in the South, these figures are shown only as indicators of trends that diverge markedly from those in the North.

[2] The replies to this question indicate that many respondents interpreted, "the way this country is set up and run" to mean the white man's "establishment." Although their answers were often ambivalent, the thrust of their replies seemed sufficiently striking to warrant inclusion.

Source: "What Negroes Think," *Fortune* (January 1968), p. 148. Courtesy of Fortune Magazine and Daniel Yankelovich, Inc.

nized by courts, and they are held only on condition, or to the extent, that certain reciprocal duties are lived up to.

Moreover, economic performance as a paramount corporate and even national goal makes little sense to the poor when they observe that the increasing abundance of material goods in one segment of society is persistently matched by poverty for their own members. It is not surprising that they refuse to play the game by the rules set by those who have most to lose. They see their salvation not in learning to play the game well but in acquiring that power by which they may have a say in setting the rules of the game in the first place.

Business institutions must recognize that above all they are social institutions having social power; therefore, like all other social institutions, their objectives must be secondary to those of the over-all system. The danger to society is not merely that business institutions insist on equating their goals with those of the over-all system, although that is great enough, but that business institutions may come to believe in this parity of goals. As Sylvia and Benjamin Selekman pointed out in their book *Power and Morality in a Business Society* [158],

Not until businessmen recognize that they are the administrators of power systems can they face realistically the task of how to discharge morally the power they wield. In this day and age, social and moral imperatives carry with them not the giving up of material things but the giving up of absolute, unilateral power.

The moral involvement of power calls, in other words, for a new look at management and its authority. It means doing things with people as equals, not *for* them as inferiors. It means indeed, that other power systems must be recognized and accepted—whether they be the power systems of labor, the state, the farmer, or other interest groups. And it means that businessmen must learn how to negotiate *with* others as equals, rather than dictate *to* them as subordinates.

But at the same time businessmen must hold on to power so as to safeguard the efficiency of their establishments; for without power it is impossible to operate effectively. And so a dilemma constantly faces businessmen as custodians and organizers of power and negotiators with other power systems.

The question remains as to what should be the response of business corporations to groups seeking power—often at the expense of the corporations. The nature and effect of corporate power over individuals and things are quite different from the nature of individual power similarly placed. In the case of individuals, such power is dictatorial, socially abhorred, and effectively curbed in democratic societies. But corporate power is subtle, often disguised, and so entangled with the problem of the efficiency of performance that any attempt to curb power is seen as an attempt to reduce productive efficiency and is immediately decried. The performance criterion of economic efficiency is, therefore, used to sidestep the more basic issue of power.

Another element of corporate power is that an increase in it is not associated with increased discretion for its use, except in the maintenance of the status quo. Being the repository of power, the corporation also becomes the object of pressure by various groups who depend on its largess. Any distribution of gains is therefore subject to various compromises. This element also indicates that power helps develop a kind of maturity in its use, though not necessarily a willingness to change the application of power when conditions change.

One of the ways in which new groups can really be brought into the mainstream of society is to recognize their legitimate claims, to help them through their period of growth, and when they have matured, to share power with them. While everybody may agree with this basic premise, implementation is not easy. First, a generalized interest lacks focus and commitment. Since the amount of sacrifice required of various established groups is not equal, the groups that stand to lose most mount the most vigorous campaign against changes, and invariably these groups win out against the lukewarm support of people at large. Second, the emerging groups lack unity and do not present issues in a manner cohesive enough for their supporters to rally around their cause. In the very nature of things, institutions and value systems in their embryonic stages lack central direction and crystallized goals. They may even seem destructive, at least in the short run, since they are tied together only in their opposition to an existing institution. Lacking this central purpose, they are not likely initially to offer constructive alternatives or effective leadership. As the rewards of success loom phenomenal when measured from the originally meager power base, it is no wonder that the leaders of such groups often resort to extremist and sometimes even bizarre techniques to achieve their immediate objectives. It does corporation and community no good to mobilize their resources for the destruction of these emerging institutions before they have a chance to develop. By doing so, corporations will not eliminate the discontent but simply prepare the ground for breeding more militant and from the corporation's standpoint more antisocial and destructive institutions.

Another area where business institutions will have to alter their traditional approach is that of communication with the emerging groups. As we noted in the case of Kodak and FIGHT, the basic problems of more jobs for the poor and greater power in determining their own future were considerably complicated by poor communication between the two.

One reason for this communication gap is that corporate managements have tended to set the new pressures in the old environmental framework and have tried to deal with them through traditional channels. They have expected, by reading reports prepared by their staff experts, to come up with several alternative solutions, of which one would be selected for implementation. What management has failed to see is that discontent—whether of a minority group or of the community at large—is not organized enough to articulate its objectives in a form amenable to the development of a list of priorities. For that matter, an approach based on priorities may not be feasible because the problems have been accumulating for so long that all of them have reached desperate proportions. Furthermore, an organization geared to maintaining efficient operations develops rigid structures for information flow and decision making, at the expense of a certain flexibility which might be needed to accommodate unusual situations. According to Kenneth Boulding [15], one of the two major weaknesses of large organizations is the breakdown of the internal communications system (the other weakness is a tendency for disloyalty among executives):

The communications breakdown is particularly likely to take place in a time of crisis and difficulty, when environments are changing fast and rapid adjustments have to be made to them. Then the normal channels of communications between the ranks of hierarchy "jam" hopelessly, and it becomes virtually impossible for those at the top to find out what is really happening.

This phenomenon incidentally illustrates an important proposition in the theory of organization—that playfulness, informal communications, and even extravagance and wastefulness in "normal" times give an organization survival value in times of crisis, for they develop and keep open spare channels of communication and reserves of energy which can be drawn upon for "serious" purposes in time of crisis. The greatest threat to survival can easily be efficiency.

To remedy this situation, corporation managements will have to investigate new procedures for decision making.[4] There may have to be units for making policy on behalf of the corporation as well as for making policy on behalf of the public. Or there may be a restructuring of channels of communication to allow for emotion and compassion as well as for financial cost data. These channels must indeed communicate social costs. Once such channels are established, militant leaders will no longer fear the bureaucracy of middle management and perhaps will not take up so much of the time of top corporate officials. The introduction of flexibility in the corporations is necessary in order that problem solving can cut across traditional departmental lines; that is, money-profit groupings of an organization may not be social-profit groupings.

How Can Business Corporations Help?

Let us assume that business institutions can and will undertake the above-mentioned changes in their attitudes and beliefs, that is, looking at the problem from the black man's point of view in addition to their own, modifying their goals to bring them in better conformity with social expectations, and establishing better communication channels with the outside groups and revamping their internal decision-making structure to make their organizations more sensitive and responsive to changes in the external social environment.

The next question that needs answering concerns the kinds of policies business corporations must pursue to translate into action the objective of making ours a qualitatively better society. Although the suggestions made in subsequent sections of this chapter may be adaptable to the solution of other social problems involving business institutions, the analysis here will be limited to only those problems which relate to the minority groups.

There seems to be a general consensus among both whites and blacks that private business will have to play an important role if any progress is to be made in tackling the problems of minority groups. The programs undertaken so far by business corporations, government agencies, foundations, church organizations, and minority groups cover the entire spectrum of possibilities. However, on the basis of general philosophy, these programs can be combined into two categories: black capitalism, and the integration of blacks into the present white Establishment. It may be contended that many of the techniques employed to assist the members of minority groups are similar under the two categories and that the ultimate objectives of the two approaches are also similar in that they aim to bring the black man to the level of his white brethren. Notwithstanding, there are some basic differences in the two approaches, and because the differences have important social implications, the approaches warrant separate consideration.

Is Black Capitalism the Answer?

The concept of black captialism has had a fascination for the black bourgeoisie since the days of Booker T. Washington, and has recently found new adherents among the followers of widely different ideologies like black militants and white conservatives. Even President Nixon subscribes to this philosophy and "has made it a central point in his program for dealing with racial inequality." [70]

Black capitalism has generally been defined as giving the blacks control over their own economic institutions. It appeals to conservatives with its flavor of self-reliance, entrepreneurship, and individual initiative—concepts which have always been glorified in American folklore. Black separatists favor it because, rejecting the idea of integration, they believe that a separate black economy can be created and viably sustained based on the black population alone.

It is my belief that black capitalism is a myth and doomed to failure. No amount of "boy wonder" success stories like that of John Johnson, publisher of *Ebony* magazine, or similar others on a more modest scale, can hide the fact that an all-embracing black capitalism cannot survive within the economic and social realities of life in the United States. If pursued to its ultimate end, it will permanently relegate the black community to an inferior status and condemn the blacks to live in what Kenneth Clark calls "gilded ghettos" which will be "little better than the ghettos of today." [70] The very fact that black capitalism finds its supporters among such strange bedfellows as extremists of the right and of the left should make one consider twice before endorsing it. Neither small businesses employing 10-15 people of the type suggested by Kodak to give the black "dignity and pride of ownership" nor comparatively larger units employing 100-200 people like Fighton (the joint FIGHT-Xerox-RBOC venture)—if they are to depend for their managerial talent, manpower sources, and markets for selling products *solely on the black community*— can survive. Let us briefly examine some facts to see the progress made by black capitalism so far and evaluate its chances of future success given the current and potential economic sources of the black community.

An article in *Time* magazine [13], after reviewing the available evidence, stated that there was widespread agreement between well-informed whites and blacks that

Negroes are not really part of the mainstream of American enterprise.... [B]eyond doubt, black capitalism today is meager. Though Negroes constitute 12 percent of the country's population, they own scarcely one percent (about 50,000) of the country's 5,000,000 private business firms. One out of every forty white Americans is a proprietor, but only one Negro in 1,000 is.... Almost all black businesses are mom-and-pop operations, catering to a ghetto clientele and providing a slim income for their owners and a few jobs for others.

Very few of these small number of firms employ more than 100 workers. [125] In New York City, with a black population of more than 1 million, only about a dozen black-owned or black-managed firms employ as many as 10 workers. [183] Even in the retail field, where black businesses are concentrated, their representation varies inversely to the importance of the type of business in the economy and its growth potential. Thus in 1960, blacks operated 2.6 per cent of all retail establishments, but 5.6 per cent of the eating and drinking outlets, and less than 1 per cent of retail firms selling hardware, furniture, and apparel. [32]

Let us now turn our attention to the black insurance companies—the pride demonstration pieces of black capitalism. In 1956 the black insurance companies had in force less than 0.4 per cent of the insurance in the United States. [69] North Carolina Mutual Life Insurance Company, the largest black-owned company in the United States, has assets of only $94 million [125], compared to the $25 billion in assets of Prudential Life, the largest white-owned insurance company. [13] According to *Fortune*, the number of substantial black-owned enterprises in manufacturing and construction "can almost be counted on one hand." [69]

Moreover, the story of black capitalism is more the history of decline than of growth. Between 1950 and 1960 the total number of black businessmen declined by more than one-fifth. During the same period the number of self-employed black bankers shrank from 90 to 41. [32] The number of blacks in the South classified as farm proprietors and managers dropped from 492,000 to 167,000 during the decade 1950-1960, and according to one estimate if this trend continues there will be almost none remaining by 1975. [8]

It is futile to compare the black minority with other ethnic minorities who worked and raised their social and economic standards through self-help. The reasons are manifold. First, the Jews, the Italians, and other minority groups brought a business-oriented cultural background with them—something which was not allowed to develop and was, in fact, ruthlessly suppressed by the white bosses among their slaves on the plantations. Second, these ethnic minorities did not develop their economic base solely by catering to their own people but by offering products and services to the rest of the community. Third, the nature of industrialization in the late 1890's was still relatively simple, so that individual entrepreneurs could carve out a niche for themselves without depending on the Establishment, at least in the initial stages of their growth.

In contrast, not only does the black suffer from the lack of a cultural tradition, but also he has a host of other problems. Today's economy is more technically sophisticated, with relatively large industrial units requiring greater initial investments. However, even under today's industrial conditions small businesses can exist and grow according to what Kenneth Boulding [15] calls "the principle of interstices":

In a pile of large stones, especially if these are fairly regular and round in shape, there will be interstices—holes which can be occupied by stones of smaller sizes, right down to grains of dust. It is a striking fact in the biological world that the development of larger organizations does not lead to the disappearance of smaller; in the great equilibrium of the ecological system there seems to be room for organizations of all sizes.

The black community cannot take advantage of the opportunity to fill these interstices because of several lacks: technical education among its youth; cooperation of the white community in providing financial help and other supporting services; and the means of attracting superior, trained, and qualified white employees. [119]

Despite all the rhetoric, the economic and human resources of the black community are just not big enough to provide growth-oriented business opportunities for the blacks to either service their own people or compete with other white businesses to provide specialized services to large industrial enterprises as subcontractors or component suppliers. According to *Fortune* estimates [43], with 11 per cent of the country's population,

TABLE 2. NEGRO REPRESENTATION IN DIFFERENT JOB CATEGORIES

	Occupation	1940	1956	1961	1966
HIGHER STATUS	Professional and Technical	3.7%	3.7%	4.1%	5.9%
	Managers, Officials, Proprietors	1.7	2.2	2.4	2.8
	Clerical		3.8	5.4	6.3
	Sales	1.2	1.8	2.5	3.1
	Craftsmen and Foremen	2.7	4.2	4.9	6.3
LOWER STATUS	Semiskilled	5.8	11.3	11.9	12.9
	Laborers	21.0	26.8	25.7	25.3
	Household Service	22.4	46.6	43.4	41.8
	Other Service Workers	11.8	21.3	20.1	21.0
	Farmers and Farm Managers	15.2	8.5	7.4	6.1
	Farm Laborers and Foremen	17.5	22.9	24.8	20.2

Source: Edmund K. Faltermayer, "More Dollars and More Diplomas," *Fortune* (January 1968), p. 142. Maurice Berson. Courtesy of Fortune Magazine.

blacks still have only 6-7 per cent of the aggregate money income, as shown in Table 2. Despite recent gains, Negroes are still heavily underrepresented in the higher-paid and higher-status jobs:

Negro gains look most discouraging when they are matched against whites' gains .... Negroes are still a long way from occupational parity.... If they were represented in all occupations in proportion to their share of the population, they would today have one-ninth of the jobs in each category....

Most of the gains [for the Negroes] in white collar employment has been confined to government jobs.... Barriers in the private sector are beginning to drop, but Negro representation in the business world is still relatively small. And it is virtually non-existent so far as the top jobs are concerned.

Perhaps more disturbing is the scarcity of companies owned and operated by Negro entrepreneurs. In 1966, Negroes still represented only 2.8 percent of the country's "managers, officials and proprietors," and a good many of them were working in government or for white controlled companies. [43]

Black Integration into the White Economy

Having discarded the notion that the black community can be revitalized through the black ownership of business enterprises which either cater to blacks alone or act as suppliers to the white industrial Establishment, we now turn our attention to the second approach, that of integrating the black community through better jobs in the existing large industrial enterprises. This is not to say that the former approach is not likely to yield any dividends. However, it is the contention here that—given the highly complex and technological nature of the American industrial system, the trend toward larger-sized organization units in the private sector and the resulting concentration of economic power in fewer hands, the narrow economic base of the black community, and the lack of technical education among the black people—black capitalism will not effect economic growth in the black community at a rate fast enough to raise hopes that full economic equality will take place in the foreseeable future, if at all.

The integration of black Americans into the industrial system and economy on the basis of full equality in opportunity and rewards can succeed *only* if an attack on the present inequities against the black man and his competitive disadvantage is made *at both ends of the spectrum, that is, at the highest and at the lowest level of job categories.*

At the upper level, business corporations should seriously consider appointing to their boards of directors such responsible and moderate black leaders who can bring to these corporations a real understanding of the needs of the black community, and who can familiarize the businesses of opportunities which, properly explored and cultivated, could be beneficial both to the business corporations involved and to the concerned communities. Such a suggestion is not as radical as it appears on first consideration. Business corporations do appoint outside directors—from banks, academic institutions, the scientific community, and the legal profession—on the presumption that persons from these fields have an expertise which is relevant to the operations of the business. Once we accept the premise that business corporations have a vital stake in the problems of the community and of ethnic minorities, the justification for appointing such people on the boards is not hard to find.

Such an approach may not open many job opportunities for the black man; it may even expose the corporations to a charge of tokenism. However, such a move can speed up the process of constructive change by bringing the problem closer to the seat of power, where economic decisions of far-reaching impact are made in the American system. One might also argue that giving black people positions on corporation boards may open these corporations to pressures by other interest groups, thereby rendering these boards ineffective as the policy-making units in corporations. However, I believe that such fears are likely to be unfounded. Once the black community has achieved its rightful place in the American economy, its members will no longer need special consideration because the problem of the black community will no longer be a special problem. Unfortunately, the business community has not shown any enthusiasm for such a course of action. As noted earlier, the number of black people in the higher-paid executive jobs in the private sector is almost nonexistent.

Much of the effort of the private sector has so far been directed toward training and hiring minority-group members for entry-level positions. The reason is that the rate of unemployment is twice as high among blacks than among whites. Furthermore, the provision of jobs with accompanying dignity and pride will ensure greater incentive for self-improvement among the black people. However, in this area as well, business corporations have been very long on promises and very short on delivery. Newspapers have been full of announcements of the formation of businessmen's councils, like National Businessmen's Alliance, New Detroit Committee, and Urban Coalition to find jobs for the hard-core unemployed and for ghetto youth. Moreover, every large corporation worth its name has some sort of training program, at least on paper, for the minority groups.

What has business done so far? On March 1967, the Secretary of Labor announced the Concentrated Employment Program to provide from 25,000 to 40,000 new private-sector jobs in six months and from 100,000 to 150,000 during the fiscal year through federal-corporate cooperation. Nine months later, only 6,900 people had jobs; an additional 6,600 had completed training but had not found any employment. According to various reports in the *Wall Street Journal*, the number of men employed by industry in Pittsburgh was 7, Oakland 8, and New York none. With tremendous fanfare it was announced in October 1968 that Westinghouse, AVCO, IBM, and Control Data had built plants in the ghettos with federal help creating 870 jobs. Westinghouse made a big publicity splash when it opened a new installation in Pittsburgh's slums hiring 75 workers, but kept quiet about its $65,000,000 installation in Charlotte that will employ 1,000 people. The National Alliance of Business was supposed to have come up with 200,000 summer jobs; it located fewer than 60,000. [60] The situation was best summed up by Clifford L. Alexander, Jr., chairman of the Equal Employment Opportunity Commission, at a United Negro College Fund Symposium in Washington [121]:

Things are changing, say the executives in the conference room, the officials in the union hall; soon there will be numbers of [blacks] who are qualified, and when that happens we will accept them on an equal basis. The publicity campaign is impressive, but the real facts are less than encouraging—are indeed shocking to all those who have believed education is in truth the key to equality for black people.

... the disparity of income between black and white actually increases with the level of education attained. There is a closer approximation of equality in earnings among people with elementary school education than there is among college graduates. ...

Too many companies are giving only lip service to hiring graduates of black universities. ... They want a black man in order to put him in a special slot. Something like "director of Equal Opportunity Programs" is always a good one; there is just one to a company.

Industry must prove to the black community that its programs are genuine. This it can do by offering programs which are meaningful, jobs which are not dead ends, and plans which are correlated positively with implementation. Otherwise, industry will simply increase the cynicism and disillusionment of the black community and further widen the gap between whites and blacks in terms of trust in one another.

A Caution and a Plea

To conclude this analysis, I believe a word of caution is necessary to the black militants. Thomas Pettigrew and other scholars have warned us that black militancy will continue to grow while gains are being made by the blacks because the relative affluence among whites is increasing at a faster rate, thereby increasing the black people's sense of relative deprivation and their feeling of frustration. It must also be admitted that black militancy has indeed been instrumental in waking up self-pride among the black people and a desire to fight for their rights. Even *Fortune* magazine conceded that at least some of the activity by business corporations in training and hiring black people has been spurred by black militancy. However, black militants will make a fatal mistake if they became obsessed with their own rhetoric and confuse means with ends. The fear of unrestricted, senseless, and limitless militancy may very well stir the forces of white racism, bigotry, and fascism, thereby plunging the whole of society into bloodshed. As Saunders Redding [140] put it,

Chauvinism is as impractical for the Negro in America as it is fundamentally dangerous for any people anywhere. Even if Negroes could duplicate the social and economic machinery—and I doubt that they could—the material resources on which their racial island must then depend would have to come from somewhere outside. In a constantly shrinking world, complete independence and isolation are impossible. And even if they were not impossible for the Negro in America, would not the achieving of them result in permanent relegation to a secondary status? The very numbers involved—that is, the popular ratio—would assure it. I cannot imagine the white majority saying, "Sure, come on and set up your self-sustaining household in a corner of my house."

Finally, I would close this study with the observation that the business corporations have a golden opportunity to utilize their immense resources in helping the country to alleviate the misery of her black citizens—and with the plea that they do so. We have seen that on moral, social, and economic grounds the black man is only asking what is his due and what his white brothers have, that is, an equal chance to prove that he is a man. How can we do less and still call ourselves decent men?

Footnotes for Chapter 7

1. On July 24, 1967 (three years after the first summer riots), violence again erupted in two of Rochester's ghetto areas and was accompanied by widespread rioting and looting. In the melee, "two Negroes were shot to death, one the driver of a car which tried to crash through a police blockade." [150]

2. See Chapter 2, pp. 00ff.

3. In interpreting the figures from this poll, the reader should bear in mind the newspaper's anti-FIGHT stand. Further, even the *Rochester Democrat & Chronicle* did not claim that the poll was scientific. We do not know how many of the respondents were nonwhites. We also do not know what the Rochester citizenry in general and the blacks in particular thought of Kodak's stand in relation to FIGHT or of the efforts made by local businesses and city government in alleviating the problems of the local poor.

4. It might be noted here that Kodak has since moved in this direction. In September 1968, the company announced the formation of a new administrative division entitled "Corporate Relations." The division was to combine the activities formerly assigned to four departments: personnel, industrial relations, public relations, and community relations. According to the company announcement, "The pres-

ent environment, particularly at the community level, is such that industrial and public relations activities are so interrelated that they must be planned as a unified, corporate program." It is also interesting to note here that the man selected by the company to supervise this division was formerly in charge of the administration of the company's over-all marketing operations; he did not come from either the personnel or the industrial-relations department.

APPENDIX A

Chronology of the Kodak-FIGHT Controversy

June 1962—Kodak becomes one of first 100 corporations to participate in President's Committee on Equal Employment Opportunity's "Plans for Progress."

July 23-26, 1964—Rochester riots.

December 1964—Funds raised by Council of Churches' Board for Urban Ministry to bring Alinsky and Industrial Areas Foundation to Rochester.

April 1965—FIGHT is organized.

June 18, 1965—FIGHT holds first convention, adopts a constitution, and elects Florence temporary chairman (later to become president).

April 25, 1966—Kodak management letter announces plans for six special Kodak training programs in summer of 1966.

June 19, 1966—FIGHT holds second convention, Florence survives sharp challenge for second year as president. FIGHT singles out Kodak for "special investigation."

September 2, 1966—First Kodak-FIGHT meeting (Florence, Vaughn, Eilers, and Chapman at Kodak).

September 14, 1966—Second Kodak-FIGHT meeting (Vaughn and Florence at Kodak).

September 15, 1966—Kenneth Howard (Kodak director of industrial relations) and other Kodak officials meet with Florence and other FIGHT members.

September 19, 1966—Kenneth Howard and other Kodak officials meet with Florence at FIGHT headquarters.

September 22-October 22, 1966—FIGHT and Kodak hold no meetings, but exchange letters.

October 22, 1966—Retainer of Board for Fundamental Education by Kodak.

November 17, 1966—Kodak announces changes in top management effective January 1, 1967. Retiring Chairman of the Board Chapman to be replaced by President Vaughn, and Executive Vice President Eilers to become president.

December 16, 1966—Further Kodak-FIGHT meetings approved, John Mulder and Marvin Chandler to be chief representatives.

December 19, 1966—Kodak-FIGHT meeting at which Florence acts as chief FIGHT representative.

December 20, 1966—Agreement signed.

December 21, 1966—Kodak executive committee votes to disavow agreement.

December 22, 1966—Kodak board of directors approves executive committee's vote of December 21.

January 3, 1967—Catholic Bishop Sheen appoints Reverend Finks as Episcopal Vicar of Urban Ministry.

January 3, 1967—Representatives of National Council of Churches' Commission on Religion and Race, Board of National Missions of United

Presbyterian Church, and Board for Homeland Ministries of Church of Christ visit Rochester and express support for FIGHT.

January 6, 1967—At press conference Eilers accuses FIGHT of "a power drive in this community."

January 6, 1967—At news conference Florence shows duplicates of 45 job applications sent to Kodak by FIGHT-sponsored blacks.

January 7-9, 1967—Two cold meetings between Florence and Eilers.

January 10, 1967—At third Kodak-FIGHT meeting Florence discovers Kodak discussions have been delegated to industrial-relations department. Florence, angered, walks out of meeting, refusing to talk to "janitors."

January 10, 1967—United Auto Workers' Citizens' Crusade Against Poverty votes to support FIGHT.

January 19, 1967—Stokely Carmichael rally and announcement of national boycott of Eastman Kodak products.

First week of February 1967—Kodak announces 158 job openings. Four days later Florence brings 87 people to Kodak employment offices.

February 14, 1967 (Valentine's Day)—Protests and picketing of Kodak plants in Atlanta, Chicago, Detroit, and San Francisco.

Late February 1967—Kodak letter to FIGHT states Kodak not interested in any more "meetings about meetings." FIGHT responds with "long, hot summer" telegram.

February 27, 1967—Xerox announces plans to hire 150 disadvantaged blacks and other minority members within the year in cooperation with FIGHT referrals.

March 1967—FIGHT purchases 10 shares of Kodak stock.

April 6, 1967—St. Louis: Episcopal and United Church of Christ groups announce withholding of Kodak stock proxies from management.

April 7, 1967—Board of Missions of Methodist Church votes to withhold Kodak stock proxies from management.

April 11, 1967—Rochester Jobs Inc., is officially incorporated.

April 12, 1967—United Presbyterian Church's Commission on Ecumenical Missions and Relations votes to withhold Kodak stock proxies from management.

April 17, 1967—Announcement by 21 private investors of intention to withhold Kodak stock proxies from management.

April 24, 1967—Boston: YWCA national board votes to withhold Kodak stock proxies from management.

April 25, 1967—Kodak annual stockholders' meeting.

April 27, 1967—Kodak announces hiring of black public-relations firm, Uptown Associates.

May 18, 1967—Kodak board of directors' meeting. John Mulder loses title of assistant vice president.

May 19, 1967—Xerox annual meeting. FIGHT praises company programs, but is rebuffed for criticism of Kodak.

June 23, 1967—Third annual FIGHT convention. FIGHT endorses Kodak telegram recognizing FIGHT as "broad-based community organization." Convention elects DeLeon McEwen as new FIGHT president.

Summer 1967—More Kodak-FIGHT meetings.

Fall 1967—Kodak-FIGHT discussion on inner-city businesses.

November 18, 1967—*New York Times* mistakenly announces Kodak will join FIGHT "in developing a microfilming factory that will hire and train 400 to 500 unskilled Negroes." Kodak-FIGHT talks soon break up.

December 5, 1967—Kodak announces plans to continue initiating independent small businesses in black slums without FIGHT.

January 1968—Rochester Business Opportunities Corporation is officially incorporated.

April 1, 1968—Kodak announces special training programs to enroll 200 new employees in 1968.

April 30, 1968—Kodak annual meeting.

June 15, 1968—FIGHT holds fourth annual convention. Florence is elected president.

June 20, 1968—FIGHT and Xerox announce formation of Fighton in cooperation with U.S. Department of Labor and Rochester Business Opportunities Corporation.

APPENDIX B

Communications between Kodak and FIGHT

B.1—Letter from FIGHT to Kodak, September 14, 1966

Kodak's Position

Kodak Management Letter dated April 25, 1966, stated "Previously, our policy had been simply to try to employ the person best fitted to do the work available without regard for his or her background. We have moved actively beyond that position. We now seek to help the individual who lacks the necessary qualifications *to become qualified*. In other words, we are contributing to the training of the individual so that he or she can qualify for employment."

"Overall, it appears that industry must look less critically at the individual's school record and work experience and more at his potential. Frustration and unfavorable circumstances in early life often result in a school record far below the person's actual potential."

Because of the encouraging and enlightened words FIGHT offers the following proposal.

FIGHT's Position

The FIGHT organization, an affiliation of over 100 neighborhood groups, church, social and fraternal clubs in the 3rd, 11th, 5th and 7th and 16th Wards is the only mass based organization of poor people and near poor people in Rochester. The biggest untapped labor market in Rochester resides in the wards.

The Board of Education figures for 1966-67 will show that nearly 1/3 of all students in the Rochester school system are Negroes. This figure will continue to grow as whites flee the city. Industries that plan to stay in Rochester need a solid economic and social base in order to enjoy continued growth and prosperity. Major industry must carry the major share of this responsibility.

FIGHT has contact and a working relationship with the future labor market. We can begin to address ourselves to the poor and near poor today—or wait for a series of explosions that are rocking cities across the country.

Kodak dominates Rochester. If Kodak leads, others will follow.

Proposal

A project to help unemployed and underemployed members of the Rochester community to meet Kodak employment standards. It would be geared to individuals with limited education and skills and would make employment opportunities more broadly available for them.

Kodak would train over an 18-month period between 500 and 600 persons so that they qualify for entry level positions across the board.

FIGHT would recruit and counsel trainees and offer advice, consultation, and assistance in the project.

Areas to be worked out would include:

a) Selection criteria
b) Recruitment
c) Training needs
d) Programs should include:
1. Remedial reading and arithmetic
2. Industrial orientation and training to afford a basic understanding of industrial processes, tools, machinery, and work rules
3. Basic skills training like materials handling, blueprint reading, and mechanical principles
4. Others

Length of programs would vary according to requirements and skills needed. Proper division of classroom and actual work would have to be worked out. Trainees would be paid benefits. Upon completion of training and meeting regular selection standards, the trainees would be promoted to the entry level position and become regular employees.

This kind of program would help close the gap between a major industry employing over 40,000 people with around only 2% Negro employees.

B.2—Statement by Kodak to FIGHT Representatives, September 14, 1966

Eastman Kodak Company believes in the principle of Equal Employment Opportunity, and in line with its belief has previously inaugurated a number of special programs aimed at creating employment opportunities for members of minority groups and others lacking the required skills. It has benefited from the assistance of various organizations such as the State Employment Service, the Urban League, and the Monroe County Human Relations Commission, in recruiting people for these special programs and for regular employment. The Company has been attempting to broaden the number and type of training activities it sponsors and welcomes referrals of prospective applicants from all organizations dedicated to the principle of equal employment opportunity.

Because of the technical nature of Kodak's operations, many jobs require considerable education and training. However, in the interest of promoting employment possibilities for those who do not have such education and training, Kodak does accept a number of applicants for special training. This training aims to give people additional skills which will enable them to meet minimum job requirements.

Among the important factors which have to be considered by the Company in selecting people for these special training openings are:

1) The potential to further develop their basic skills such as reading and writing, etc.

2) The desire to improve themselves so that they will be sufficiently motivated to take advantage of training and to adjust to the requirements of an industrial organization.

People may be selected for one of several different training opportunities as follows:

1) A trades trainee program which may qualify a person to become a skilled trades apprentice or a skilled trades helper.

2) Laboratory training which may qualify a person to become an assistant in one of Kodak's several chemical laboratories.

3) Machine operator training which prepares a person to operate screw machines, punch presses, plastic molding machines, and similar equipment.

4) On-the-job training for production and other types of jobs. The emphasis here is on gaining experience on a particular job under close instruction and supervision.

5) Clerical training which gives people an opportunity to upgrade clerical skills by a concentrated course at Rochester Business Institute.

All of these arrangements couple actual work experience with classroom training as may be required to provide the individual with the basic skills which he will need on the job.

Recognizing that even these special programs are not fully adapted to the needs of some persons seeking employment, Kodak now plans to undertake an expanded concept of on-the-job training under which people will be employed to gain experience on the job during part of the day, with the remainder of the day being devoted to basic education. The Company hopes to benefit from suggestions which FIGHT may offer, as it has in the past been helped by the advice of a number of organizations on these matters. FIGHT and other interested organizations are invited to refer possible applicants for all these programs.

Continued employment, of course, depends on the amount of progress which the individual is able to make and on general employment conditions.

These special training programs are in addition to the normal employment of minority group people who are qualified for regular jobs and skilled trades apprenticeships.

In meeting its commitments as an Equal Opportunity Employer, the Company must, of course, take full account not only of its legal obligation to avoid discrimination but also of its responsibilities to Kodak customers, employees, stockholders, other applicants for employment, and the community. Therefore, the Company's efforts to create employment opportunities for members of minority groups must be consistent with the principle of fairness to all.

B.3—Letter from Kodak President Vaughn to FIGHT President Florence, September 19, 1966

I understand from Mr. Howard that you and he had a meeting on Thursday afternoon, September 15, to discuss further the matters we had discussed in our earlier meetings. He also tells me that apparently you did not understand the purpose of that meeting in the same way that we did. In order to avoid any misunderstanding, I want to review the situation as we see it.

On Friday, September 2, we met with you and some of your associates at your request, to hear your presentation of the need, as you see it, to provide job opportunities for certain unemployed and underemployed members of minority groups.

On Wednesday, September 14, we met again, at which time we presented to you and your associates a statement outlining a plan for expanded programs, which we at Kodak would undertake, aimed at developing and providing employment opportunities for members of minority groups and others lacking required skills. We told you at the September 14 meeting that we were prepared to proceed to implement this plan. A copy of this statement is enclosed for your further reference.

This statement invited FIGHT to cooperate in the implementation of these special programs, and, along with other interested organizations, to refer to us possible applicants both for the special programs and also for regular employment.

We asked Mr. Kenneth Howard to represent the Company in discussing with you specific and practical ways in which the FIGHT organization might cooperate with us in implementing our planned programs, and the meeting held on September 15 was arranged for that purpose.

Mr. Howard tells me that little if any progress was made in the September 15 meeting toward working out ways and means of realizing the plans and objectives outlined in our statement of September 14—more specifically, that you and your associates were not prepared to discuss specific practical ways of referring to us applicants for the special programs we had offered to undertake. This came as quite a surprise to us, in view of the urgency of the need as previously outlined by you, and in view of FIGHT's expressed anxiety to seek remedies.

May I just repeat that if you and your associates in FIGHT are prepared to work with us in seeking means of implementing the plan presented in our September 14 statement, Mr. Howard is ready to carry on discussions with you. If you do not wish to cooperate on this basis, we will plan to proceed with the implementation of our plans as rapidly as we can on a sound basis.

I hope this will help to reaffirm and clarify our position, and we trust we may hear that you are ready and willing to renew discussions on the basis set forth in this letter.

B.4—Letter from Kodak President Vaughn to FIGHT President Florence, September 28, 1966

I have your letter of September 26 from which I note that apparently considerable misunderstanding still exists as to what we tried to convey to you and your associates in FIGHT at our meeting on September 14.

In the first place, Kodak's programs and plans described at that meeting, in response to your verbal proposal of September 2, were *not* simply "a repeat of your limited special training programs," as you state in your letter. If you will reread, closely and carefully, the second paragraph on page 2 of the statement handed to you at our meeting on September 14 you will see that we are talking of "an *expanded* concept of on-the-job training," which we go on to describe in general terms. We went on to say that we hoped "to benefit from suggestions which FIGHT may offer," as well as from those of other organizations interested in these matters.

Since the goals of "the FIGHT proposal" seemed to be so close to the aims of our programs, we assumed that you wanted to cooperate in making our efforts more successful.

We have indicated to you on several occasions that we cannot accept your "proposal," which is, quoting from your September 14 memorandum, as follows: "Kodak would train over an 18-month period between 500 and 600 persons so that they qualify for entry level positions across the board. FIGHT would recruit and counsel trainees and offer advice, consultation, and assistance in the project." Your memorandum also states that the project ". . . would be geared to individuals with limited education and skills . . ." and that ". . . areas to be worked out would include selection criteria, recruitment, training needs . . ." and that "programs should include remedial reading and arithmetic; industrial orientation and training to afford a basic understanding of industrial processes, tools, machinery, and work rules; basic skills training like material handling, blueprint reading, and mechanical principle; others." In addition, you have indicated that you expected this company to undertake all this exclusively in cooperation with FIGHT.

We have tried to make clear to you why we cannot accept the "FIGHT proposal." Apparently, it is necessary at this time for me to restate our position.

1. In light of the company's legal obligations and its responsibilities to Kodak customers, employees, stockholders, other applicants for employment, and the community, the company obviously cannot discriminate by granting any one organization an exclusive or monopolistic position in the recruitment, selection, or training of Kodak people.

2. We are not in a position to establish any statistical objective or quota for any special training programs which we undertake. Our ability to hire a person at Kodak depends first on the existence of a job opening and, second, on the availability of a person qualified to fill that opening.

During the last several months, we have hired a good many people, among whom were many Negroes. We hope we can continue to provide additional job opportunities in the future. But it is impossible for us to say how many, if any, such opportunities will be available at Kodak six months, a year, or 18 months hence. It would be an inexcusable deception on our part to promise something we cannot be sure of honoring.

You are quoted in this morning's paper as having said last evening, "I hate to believe a company of this stature would misguide poor people." We have no intention of misguiding anyone and it is precisely for this reason we cannot promise a given number of jobs at some future date when we do not control the economic and other factors which create the job opportunities.

I think both you and we are concerned with a problem to which no one has yet found a satisfactory solution—that is, how to motivate people to prepare themselves for job openings, and how to train people for industrial jobs who are lacking in such fundamental skills as reading, writing, and arithmetic. Certainly it would be dishonest and unfair to the people involved if we were to suggest that we have the knowledge or manpower to take on such a complete job where, so far as I know, no others have succeeded. However, as we have told you, we are planning to expand our special training efforts to see what further we can do. We are naturally anxious that any program we undertake have some reasonable chance of success.

What we are trying to do is to see what we can accomplish, by special training programs, to upgrade persons who are willing to try to improve themselves so they can qualify for the kinds of jobs we have. In doing this, we will seek the assistance of interested organizations which are willing to cooperate in constructive ways.

If FIGHT is interested in cooperating on this basis by making suggestions for the programs or referring applicants for them, I would again suggest that you resume discussions with Mr. Howard. If, on the other hand, your interest is solely in talking further about "the FIGHT proposal," I doubt that anything very useful could come from just going over the same ground that has been covered in the several talks that have already taken place.

B.5—Letter from FIGHT President Florence to Kodak President Vaughn, October 7, 1966

I have your letter of September 28 and offer at this time the following observations.

An American economy which is in the first stages of inflation and which has shown an accompanying rising employment rate finds itself threatened by an alarming increase in unemployment among Negroes. The last figure issued by our government pointed out that 8.3 per cent of all employable Negroes were unemployed. It is clear to all students and observers of economic conditions among the Negroes of America that the unemployment rates in the various ghettos from Harlem to Watts are substantially higher. This dangerous condition not only for the Negro population but the general American public becomes particularly ominous since it follows on the heels of civil rights legislation, extensive job retraining programs, and a convergence of public opinion and government pressure upon private industry and organized labor to drop their discriminatory hiring practices and to open jobs for Negro fellow Americans. So, we are confronted with the strange and frightening anomaly of increasing employment for whites occurring simultaneously with decreasing employment for Negroes.

There are a number of reasons for this kind of economic sickness and one of the major ones is the fact that large industries such as Eastman Kodak persist in employing the same testing procedures for hiring eligibility to Negro applicants as they do with white applicants. The pursuit of this practice indicates an extraordinary insensitivity to the social and educational circumstances which have prevailed in our country for many years: circumstances of limited opportunities, economy-wise, education-wise, and in almost every other sector of our life which all Americans today are fully cognizant of and are moving toward their correction. It is clear that a Negro of the same age as that of a white has not had the academic opportunities to qualify for the same test. It is clear that if there is to be an intelligent approach to this issue that those factors must be taken into consideration in terms of equity as well as the practical politics of keeping a healthy American way for all people.

The obvious remedy lies in avoidance of the trap of this discriminatory test and hiring of Negroes for jobs where they will not only receive on-the-job training, but also special educational programs to bring them up to the point where they could then qualify under the test. Any employer who would regard this as discrimination in reverse would be guilty of an extraordinary short-sightedness and unawareness of the general situation prevailing in our nation today.

This has been the issue in our approach to Eastman Kodak. With it has gone our own feelings that if private industry does not meet this challenge that we will of necessity have to assume that there is no other recourse but massive governmental public projects and we have nowhere else to turn except to our government. Paradoxically, major industries in America, including Eastman Kodak, have always expressed concern for the ever-expanding encroachment by government in various areas of our life. They have regarded this with a great deal of alarm. Some of the most conservative of them have denounced it as creeping socialism. We, ourselves, believe that the democratic way of life would hold to most problems being met and resolved on a local community basis and that there is that kind of free initiative in various sectors of our society: that government should not move in unless local communities are obviously unable, incapable, or unwilling, to meet their own problems. Eastman Kodak has the opportunity to make a significant contribution by cooperating with FIGHT's proposal. But, if FIGHT continues to be stalled and politely rejected as it has been to this date, then we must conclude that while industry talks about government encroaching upon all spheres of the American scene that, in fact, it is just talk and that it is coming because industry refuses to act. We, like all other Americans, prefer to be employed by our government, to have our dignity, to have a job and to have an economic future rather than to have a basket full of empty generalities and unemployment by private industry which is immobilized by its own straightjacket by antiquated definitions of discrimination and by an astounding blindness to their own self-interest.

Use of terms like "exclusively," "monopolistic," "arbitrary demands," etc., in reference to the FIGHT Proposal does an injustice to the careful thought and consideration that has gone into our suggestions. We have not even had the opportunity to discuss the details of our approach with Eastman Kodak.

B.6—Letter from Kodak President Vaughn to FIGHT President Florence, October 21, 1966

I am sorry for the delay in replying to your letter of October 7, which reached my office on October 10, a delay occasioned in large part by my being out of the city for a number of days recently.

I am, of course, conscious of the degree of unemployment which exists in this country in a period of general prosperity. We are all aware of the many problems related to the relatively high rate of unemployment among non-whites, and that the rate of unemployment among this group appears to have increased in recent months. It is somewhat encouraging to note that figures from the same source also show that non-white *employment* in this country has increased during the same period, although not sufficiently to diminish the rate of unemployment. We in our company are concerned, as you rightly are, with the situation we find in our own community of Rochester, and we both want to do something about it.

It is because of our concern that we have conducted, are conducting, and will continue to conduct special training efforts to help disadvantaged people qualify for jobs in our company, whether they be whites or non-whites. We have said to you and your associates in FIGHT, and to other organizations, that we are searching for ways and methods of expanding and improving such training efforts. We have also made it clear that we welcome suggestions from FIGHT or any other groups or individuals who can help in practical and realistic ways to alleviate the local unemployment situation.

The so-called "FIGHT proposal," which you first submitted to us in mid-September, contained as one of its principal features the suggestion that we at Kodak agree to train, within an 18-month period, up to 600 people with "limited education and skills" who would be selected by FIGHT. At the time of our meeting with you and a number of your associates on September 14, and in subsequent correspondence, we have tried to explain as clearly as we know how that we cannot agree in advance to train and subsequently employ any specific number of people during any specific period of time. The number of people we can employ during any period of time depends on the jobs we have available and the number of people available to fill those jobs. May I suggest that you read again my letter of September 28, which clearly explains our position in this respect and further emphasizes our desire and intention to engage in special training programs in an effort to help people qualify for the kinds of job openings we have, or may have in future. We have solicited the cooperation of FIGHT and many other willing organizations to help us in recruiting candidates for these training programs.

In view of this record of expressed intention and sincere endeavor on our part, it is somewhat surprising to read the following statement in your letter of October 7: "We have not even had the opportunity to discuss the details of our approach with Eastman Kodak." As you will recall, we talked about this matter at some length at our meeting on September 14 and, by agreement at that time, qualified representatives of our employment and industrial relations department called upon you and some of your associates on two occasions thereafter with the idea of seeking ways to implement the proposal we had made to you on September 14. Up to this time FIGHT has not seen fit to cooperate on that basis. Meanwhile, you and other members of FIGHT might be interested in knowing that while these discussions and subsequent correspondence have been going on, the Kodak Company has continued to employ a substantial number of people in this community, including many Negroes.

There is much work to do in this area in this community. We at Kodak are serious about our desire to be helpful, constructive, and imaginative, in any way we reasonably can. We admit that we have much to learn in the field of training disadvantaged people and, hopefully, bringing them up to the level where they could qualify for jobs with our company. We are seeking in other ways, to sharpen our techniques and abilities in this unfamiliar territory. But, we have to learn to walk before we can run, and that is what we are trying to do now. We certainly plan to give it a good try, and I am hopeful that our accomplishments will prove rewarding and gratifying to all concerned.

In this spirit of seeking to find answers to this perplexing community problem, may I earnestly request once again that FIGHT follow the example of other organizations with whom we have worked successfully, by referring to us the kind of people who need the kind of training we are already putting into effect. I hope that you and your associates will be willing to cooperate in this way, and a phone call to Mr. Kenneth Howard that you wish to resume discussions on that basis will find us responsive.

B.7—Telegram from Kodak President Eilers to FIGHT President Florence, June 23, 1967

Recently representatives of FIGHT and of Kodak have held a number of conversations seeking a common ground for cooperative action on community problems. This telegram is intended to recognize the merit of these discussions and to review some of the ways in which Kodak and FIGHT can work together.

As a result of these meetings, there now appears to be an opportunity to create better understanding and to work in mutual respect. Kodak recognizes that FIGHT, as a broad-based community organization, speaks in behalf of the basic needs and aspirations of the Negro poor in the Rochester area. Kodak, too, desires to help create a better community.

During the past several months FIGHT and Kodak, along with others, have joined in the community effort that brought about Rochester Jobs Incorporated. Both FIGHT and Kodak support RJI which promises to be an effective way of providing job opportunities for the hard-core unemployed. Certainly the work of RJI will be made easier and more effective if the relationships among the member companies and organizations are harmonious. The matters covered in this telegram are within the spirit of our commitment to RJI.

A number of ideas have been expressed in the recent discussions. They include:

1. A mutual concern as to how hard-core unemployed Negroes can be motivated and prepared to take advantage of job opportunities as they become available.

It was suggested that FIGHT and Kodak establish a relationship under which Kodak would send employment interviewers into selected places in inner-city neighborhoods in cooperation with FIGHT.

It was also suggested that it may be helpful to the people referred by FIGHT and employed by Kodak to have special guidance and advice from your organization, particularly during the early stages of their employment.

2. FIGHT representatives could help Kodak interviewers working in the inner-city by informing them of the special problems and perspectives of

hard-core unemployed persons and others who, because of a lack of opportunity, are at a disadvantage in getting jobs.

3. The desirability of continuing dialogue between FIGHT and Kodak. These discussions, it was suggested, would cover various areas bearing on the economic needs and the aspirations of the Negro community. There would be periodic meetings between FIGHT representatives and those people at Kodak most closely concerned with the subjects to be considered.

4. Discussion of Kodak's proposal to develop a slide presentation or movie which would be useful in motivating the hard-core unemployed, in letting them know the kinds of job and training opportunities which are available, and in helping to prepare them to seek these opportunities. Kodak and FIGHT will submit this as a project for RJI.

We feel that all of these approaches are constructive and workable. As the result of our discussions, it is my understanding that we are both willing to work together to put these ideas into effect. Neither FIGHT nor Kodak considers any of these arrangements to be exclusive.

The recent meetings have demonstrated that, with an atmosphere of cooperation, it is possible for us to work together constructively. We are sure you will agree that a continuation of this atmosphere is essential if any future efforts are to be successful.

New leadership for FIGHT is to be elected shortly. We want to assure these new leaders that Kodak will be pleased to work with them in the same constructive climate that made possible the progress accomplished in the recent meetings.

APPENDIX C

Internal Communications at Kodak

C.1—Management Letter Issued by Industrial-Relations Department, April 25, 1966

You may recall that a Management Letter, dated June 28, 1962, dealt with the matter of non-discrimination in employment and announced Kodak's adoption of a Plan for Progress. This Plan formed the basis for our voluntary cooperation with the President's Committee on Equal Employment Opportunity. Kodak was among the first 100 companies to participate in the Plan for Progress program. The same Management Letter also took account of the New York State Law Against Discrimination and Federal Executive Orders which established legal prohibitions against discrimination.

A Management Letter of July 9, 1965, reviewed the enactment of the Federal Civil Rights Act of 1964.

These various laws and Executive Orders mean that, in addition to our moral responsibility to avoid discrimination, which we have always taken seriously, there is now a legal obligation as well. While these developments did not, in any real sense, change our traditional policies and principles governing relationships with applicants or with Kodak people, they did afford an opportunity to review and restate long-standing Company policies in this area. These legal developments have served to re-emphasize our responsibilities, and they have opened our performance to review and appraisal by various agencies of government.

Since formulating our Plan for Progress, we have sought in many ways to meet our commitments. Thanks to a generally favorable atmosphere throughout the Company, the co-operation of our personnel people, and the diligence and understanding of supervision, we have taken *affirmative action* to insure truly equal opportunities for employment.

A copy of the Company's Plan for Progress which was signed in 1962 by then Vice President of the United States, Lyndon B. Johnson, and by Kodak's President, William S. Vaughn, is attached as a helpful reference. (If this were being written today, it would also take note of the prohibition against discrimination on account of sex which was included in the Civil Rights Act of 1964.)

Since the adoption of the Plan for Progress, the number of people from minority groups employed by Kodak through its *normal* recruitment and selection procedures has continued to increase. The purpose of this letter is to bring you up to date regarding some *special* efforts which are being made to further implement the principles outlined in the Plan and with which you may not be familiar.

A Change in Emphasis

In reviewing this report, you will recognize that our efforts to provide equal employment opportunities are increasingly more positive and far-

152

reaching than in past years. Previously, our policy had been simply to try to employ the person best fitted to do the work available without regard for his or her background. We have moved actively beyond that position. We now seek to help the individual who lacks the necessary qualifications *to become qualified.* In other words, we are contributing to the training of the individual so that he or she can qualify for employment. Various measures for this purpose are described below.

Members of minority groups are usually considered to be most in need of assistance to qualify for industrial work, but help may be equally needed by others. It is essential that we bring out the full potential of every person employed or being trained at Kodak, whatever his or her background.

Skilled Trades Trainee Program

As provided in the Plan for Progress, the Company has long sought applicants from minority groups for its Apprenticeship Training Programs. However, experience has shown that there are a number of young people who have the potential ability but lack the education and training to enter into a skilled trades apprenticeship.

In order to give these people an opportunity to enter the program, Kodak Park established an arrangement two years ago designed to assist young people who, but for this assistance, could not qualify.

Under this arrangement, the person devotes part of his time to work and on-the-job training in the shops and field departments and part of his time attending classes in the Apprenticeship School and the Training Department. At the end of one year, if then qualified, he enters a regular apprenticeship.

About 15 people are enrolled each year, approximately half being members of minority groups. Based on our experience to date, it appears that this will be a successful and continuing effort.

Laboratory Trainee Program

At the present time, we are engaged in the development of another special program to train young people to become laboratory assistants. Representatives of technical divisions and members of the Kodak Park Training Department are developing course material now, and it is expected that about 12 persons will start their laboratory training in June, 1966.

Similar to the Skilled Trades Trainee Program, this effort will include part-time work and on-the-job training in a laboratory under supervision, and part-time classroom instruction in subjects related to laboratory work. In this way, opportunities are provided for young people who, but for this training, would not qualify in this field.

Clerical Training Program

The Rochester Urban League is now developing a program with the Rochester Business Institute to upgrade the skills of people who have had some clerical training but whose inexperience prevents their qualifying for clerical positions. Kodak is financing this special course and will provide part-time employment opportunities where this is appropriate. It is hoped that up to 20 people will participate this spring and summer. Several people have already started their training at R.B.I.

High School Co-operative Students

In addition, we are currently working with the Rochester Board of Education to help students relate their studies to industrial requirements by working part time while they are in school. Special benefits should accrue to those young people who for cultural, family, or other reasons might otherwise fail to complete high school. Twelve young men and women are currently employed on this part-time basis at Kodak Park, and it is hoped that their exposure to the industrial environment under supervision will encourage them to continue their academic studies and thereby improve their opportunities for employment upon graduation. The other divisions are also working on similar projects.

Machine Operator Training

A&O [Apparatus and Optical] Division is providing special training for machine operators in punch press, screw machine, plastic molding and optics work. This involves classroom assignments in certain fundamental skills and on-the-job training in the operation of a variety of machines.

People are selected for this training on the basis of their capacity for learning and job potential. Because no prior experience is required, a number of people, including members of minority groups, are gaining new skills through this experience.

On-the-Job Training Program

With federal assistance, the Rochester Urban League is helping to place unemployed and underemployed people in industry to receive on-the-job training. In some instances, these people will already have taken part in government-sponsored training and development activities. The employer is expected to provide specific job training. Some of these people may require more than normal help until they become acclimated to an industrial environment.

Kodak has an agreement with the Urban League to employ a number of men and women for this on-the-job instruction. How many are to be taken on will depend on the number of available applicants as well as job opportunities within the Company. Several people have already been employed at A&OD and at Kodak Park.

College Recruitment

The Company has traditionally recruited college students without regard to race, color, creed, or national origin. We have recently added a number of predominantly Negro colleges to the list of those regularly visited by our representatives. In this way, opportunities have been increased for recruiting Negro students with regular and advanced degrees.

Individual Responsibility

Employers have a responsibility to open job opportunities for people of all races and creeds even though some may initially have certain limitations. But once given the opportunity, the individual is himself responsible for taking advantage of that opportunity. It is hoped that many such people will benefit from the Company's training activities and especially that those who can will participate in the Tuition Aid Plan in the interest of their own development. Here, much depends on the encouragement of supervision.

Help from Outside

Helping the unemployed and underemployed required both our own efforts and the co-operation of educational and social welfare groups outside the Company.

Valuable help has come from the Urban League, the Monroe County Human Relations Commission, local school officials and others. The assistance of these groups in designing special training programs and in referring people for training and employment is contributing much to our success. Both the Company and the people involved stand to gain by these cooperative efforts.

Employment Considerations

Overall, it appears that industry must look less critically at the individual's school record and work experience and more at his potential. Frustration and unfavorable circumstances in early life often result in a school record far below the person's actual potential.

If our Plan for Progress is truly to provide equal employment opportunities, as we intend that it shall, our approach to the problem of those with limited education must be flexible. In a very real sense, we are trying to help certain of our trainees and employees to overcome the handicaps of misfortune. To do this, the supervisor himself must play a sensitive role.

He is in the best position to understand the problems of each individual and to encourage him to his best efforts. Providing this kind of leadership demands a great deal of understanding of people and their daily problems and the obstacles they encounter in their work. Patient attention to each person striving to overcome temporary handicaps of inexperience, uncertainty, and educational limitations is essential to helping him realize his full potential.

Another requirement is constant attention to our promotion-from-within policy which aims to advance Kodak people to more responsible jobs in line with their ability and available opportunities. All divisions are, of course, regularly concerned with the implementation of this policy. The Apparatus and Optical Division has now developed a special plan to look for promotional opportunities and systematically search out people within the organization who have the potential to fill them. Wherever a person is upgraded, a place is made for a less experienced man or woman.

The success of our Plan for Progress requires the continual and constructive attention of each of us. It is hoped that this report will be helpful in furthering our efforts.

C.1 Enclosure—Kodak Plan for Progress, June 1962

Preamble

Eastman Kodak Company has for many years followed a policy of employment and promotion based on ability to perform the job in question. It has tried to live within the letter and spirit of the Fair Employment Practice legislation wherever it has operations.

The Company is volunteering to cooperate with the President's Committee on Equal Employment Opportunity which has restated a national policy that all persons are entitled to equal employment opportunities without regard to race, creed, color or national origin.

Recognizing that, on a national basis, much is being accomplished in this area, the Company welcomes this opportunity to review its practices and to re-emphasize the importance of its long-standing policy.

The Company does not include race, creed, color or national origin in its personnel records since these are not pertinent to the employment relationship. By the same token, the Company will not establish any targets or quotas for employment of minority groups or other groups. Any statistical information provided will be estimates based on general observation.

In this spirit, the Company is formalizing a positive program to further assure that it is providing fair employment opportunities without regard to race, creed, color or national origin. This program is outlined in the following Plan for Progress.

Plan for Progress

1. The Company will distribute a Management Letter to all of its supervisory people restating the Company's policy on equal employment opportunity, and reminding each supervisor of his responsibility in the implementation of this policy. A copy of the Plan for Progress will be enclosed with the Management Letter.

2. The Company will hold a series of meetings throughout the Company in which management people will discuss with those supervisory people reporting to them the Company's policy, its meaning, and its implementation. Thus, all supervisory people will be reminded of the seriousness with which the Company views its obligations to fulfill its policy. Such meetings will also afford an opportunity to exchange ideas among supervisors and with their superiors as to what additional steps can be taken to realize the national and Company goal of employment based on merit.

3. We are including in our Code of Industrial Relations in the "Handbook for Kodak Men and Women" a statement to the effect that hiring and promotions are made without regard to race, creed, color or national origin.

4. We will continue to make available to applicants for employment a leaflet entitled "How Kodak People are Selected." This describes the Company's policy as follows:

"For any particular job, the person is chosen who appears best fitted to do that job. That is an especially important point because it means that such things as race, creed, color or national origin neither help nor hinder in getting a job at Kodak."

5. We will from time to time hold discussions with the employment interviewers in the various divisions to remind them of the Company's policy and their role in its implementation, and to obtain their suggestions as to any further steps the Company can take to enhance employment opportunities for all people on the basis of ability.

6. Our employment people will continue to work with guidance counselors in schools in our major employment areas to let them know of our anticipated employment needs. This gives them the opportunity to counsel students to obtain the type of training and develop the kind of skills that will prepare them for available jobs in the Company.

7. The Company will continue to consider all qualified applicants for employment without regard to race, creed, color or national origin. Furthermore, it will continue to make known to schools, colleges, and interested community organizations and agencies its employment policy so that they will know of the opportunities which are available.

8. All of the Company's training programs are available without regard to race, creed, color or national origin. This policy will be continued. Furthermore, the Company will encourage qualified applicants of any race, creed, color or national origin for its apprenticeship training program. From time to time, the Company will review its progress in finding qualified applicants who are members of minority groups for its training programs.

9. Practically all employee facilities are desegregated. In a few areas where segregated facilities are required by local social custom, desegregation has not been completely accomplished. We will work toward the desegregation of these facilities.

10. Wages, salaries and employee benefit plans will, as in the past, be administered without regard to race, creed, color or national origin.

11. The control and implementation of this policy will be the responsibility of the Company's Industrial Relations Committee, consisting of the Directors of Industrial Relations for the Company and each of its major divisons. Periodically, this Committee will review the Company practices to see that the policy is complied with in practice. Each Director of Industrial Relations will make a report to his Division Manager and to the Company Director of Industrial Relations every six months. The Company Director of Industrial Relations will in turn make a report concerning the program to the President of the Company every six months. It will include a report on any difficulties being encountered in the implementation of the policy with suggested steps for eliminating the difficulties. In addition, the Company will submit an initial status report and subsequent written progress reports to the President's Committee on a periodic (at least annual) basis.

C.1 Enclosure–Undertakings by the President's Committee on Equal Employment Opportunity, June 1962

I. Recruiting

The Committee will:

A. Continue to work with the United States Department of Labor's employment specialists to cooperate with the appropriate State Employment services in reviewing efforts to obtain qualified applicants for referral to Eastman Kodak Company without regard to race, creed, color or national origin.

B. Upon request, solicit the support of appropriate specialized community agencies to assist recruiting efforts under this Plan for Progress.

II. Training

The Committee will work with the U.S. Department of Health, Education and Welfare in reviewing, encouraging and strengthening counseling and guidance services in school systems where Eastman Kodak Company has major operations. That Department has assigned personnel to encourage participation of persons in minority groups in its vocational education programs. In addition, new programs are being developed aimed at the encouragement of cooperative efforts between educational facilities, community agencies and employers as to this program.

III. Contracting Agencies

The Committee will work with the appropriate contracting agencies to assist Eastman Kodak Company and the Committee in coordination and follow-through on their undertakings under this Plan for Progress.

IV. General

Eastman Kodak Company officials should feel free to report to the Committee any difficulties encountered in achieving this Plan for Progress in those instances where it is reasonably believed services of the Committee can be materially constructive in overcoming them.

C.2—Letter to Kodak Supervisors Issued by Industrial-Relations Department, November 15, 1966

You have undoubtedly read or heard about recent discussions between Eastman Kodak and FIGHT. As a member of Kodak management, it is important that you be well informed about the company's position on this matter.

Perhaps the best way to gain a clear understanding of what has occurred is to read the correspondence which has passed between Kodak and FIGHT. A complete set of this correspondence, as well as some related material, is reproduced herewith. While the package speaks for itself, there is some background which you should have in mind as you read it.

On September 2, FIGHT proposed that they recruit and that Kodak train 600 undereducated persons over an 18-month period for entry-level jobs.

We felt there were two major objections to the FIGHT proposal:

1) We could not enter into an arrangement exclusively with any organization to recruit candidates for employment and still be fair to the thousands of people who apply on their own initiative or are referred by others.

2) We could not agree to a program which would commit Kodak to hire and train a specific and substantial number of people in a period which would extend so far into the future. Obviously, our employment needs

depend on the demand for our products, which is affected by economic conditions and many other factors.

Nevertheless, it seemed to us that the goals of this proposal had much in common with Kodak's own expressed concern and existing programs in this field. So we responded by telling FIGHT that we would expand and broaden certain special training activities, and we expressed the hope that they would refer candidates to us. FIGHT indicated that it was not interested in these programs.

We have been sincere in our discussions with FIGHT. We have repeatedly made it clear that we would welcome their cooperation in working toward what should be largely common goals. At the same time, we have affirmed that we cannot delegate decisions on recruitment, selection, and training for Kodak jobs to any outside group. Other organizations with whom we have worked readily understand this.

At the risk of stating the obvious, we should remind ourselves that Kodak is a business organization. The company must operate within the limits of sound business practice and legal requirements. If we are to meet our obligations to Kodak people, to our customers, to our shareholders, and to the community, we must act responsibly from all points of view.

This doesn't mean that the company should disregard important social problems; and it hasn't. For a long time Kodak has been endeavoring to employ more members of minority groups. However, we have become increasingly aware that we need to go still further—to take even more aggressive measures—if we are to help sizable numbers of untrained persons to find useful employment in a technically oriented business like ours. To this end, we have done and are doing a number of things, while preserving the sound hiring policies developed and proven over years of experience. For example:

—We have been reviewing our employment standards to make sure they are realistic, especially as they affect untrained and undereducated persons.

—We have sought and received help from several outside agencies in recruiting members of minority groups.

—We have established new training activities and expanded others.

—We have announced an experimental arrangement with the Board for Fundamental Education (BFE) to provide education in reading, writing, and arithmetic for 60 people hired especially for our Laboratory Trainee and Trades Trainee programs.

—In an allied project, we have arranged for BFE to conduct a similar educational program, outside working hours, for some 40 persons who already hold regular entry-level jobs. We hope that such training will make it possible to promote some of these persons into better jobs. If so, new openings will be created in the entry-level positions which then could be filled by untrained and undereducated people. These people, in turn, would be given an opportunity to participate in BFE training which might qualify them also for promotion. This approach recognizes the needs and interests of people who are already Kodak employees. It also should create additional employment opportunities for undereducated people.

Considerable progress has already been made. Hundreds of members of minority groups have been hired by Kodak units in Rochester during the past twelve months alone.

It is our hope that the special programs will prove successful; if so, we expect to extend them—depending, of course, on our future employment needs. But it should be emphasized that some of these programs are experimental, their effectiveness is yet to be proved. All we can say now is that, in venturing into areas that are new to us, we mean to make an honest and serious effort.

We shall continue to solicit constructive suggestions from people both within and outside the company—indeed, we welcome their assistance, counsel, and cooperation.

We urge you to read the attached material carefully so you can factually answer questions raised by Kodak people, as well as by friends in the community.

APPENDIX D

Saul Alinsky and the Industrial Areas Foundation

. . . I do know one simple thing—regardless of what the situation is, people will not be able to do anything constructive, anything in the true democratic spirit for themselves, unless they have the power to cope with the situation whatever it may be and whenever it occurs. So I'm just holding that point. Just build the organization and cross each bridge as we come to it.

If man has opportunity and the power to use that opportunity, then I'll bet on him to cross any bridge, no matter how tough or seemingly hopeless it may look. As a matter of fact, I've already bet my life on it.—Saul Alinsky [153]

Many of the events in the Kodak-FIGHT controversy can be explained in the light of local circumstances and growing black militancy. But some of the events, FIGHT's actions in particular, represent the best of a number of tactics time-tested in forty other communities by Saul David Alinsky, who has spent the greater part of his career organizing poor, slum communities. According to Charles Silberman, no other man in America "has proposed a course of action or a philosophy better calculated to rescue Negro or white slum dwellers from their poverty and their degradation." [161] Other observers are as vehement in their criticisms as Silberman is enthusiastic in his praise.

Alinsky's Career

Alinsky was born in 1909 of Russian Jewish immigrant parents in "one of the worst slums in Chicago." [4] His parents were divorced when he was a teenager and his father moved to California. Alinsky entered the University of Chicago in 1926, majoring in archaeology though taking many courses in sociology as well. [152]

He graduated in 1930 and, to his surprise, won a fellowship in criminology. As a graduate student he became an observer inside the Capone gang (they were perfectly aware that he was studying them). Due to the interrelationships between the gang and the city government, Alinsky sarcastically recalls, "I came to see the Capone gang as a huge quasi-public utility servicing the population of Chicago." [152]

Following his second year of graduate school, Alinsky took a job with the State Division of Criminology, hoping to return eventually to graduate school (he never did). Later he became a criminologist at the state prison in Joliet, Illinois, and during this period he became involved in political and social controversies in his free time. "Wherever you turned you saw injustice," Alinsky said. And so he got himself involved in fighting for public housing and against evictions of poor city people from their homes (this was during the depression) and raising money for a host of groups: the Spanish Civil War's International Brigade, Southern sharecroppers, and the Newspaper Guild. After three years at Joliet he was offered a high-paying job as the head of probation and parole for the city of Philadelphia.

The offer was a turning point in his life, for Alinsky felt the comforts of the Philadelphia job might lure him away from the social battlefield. [152]

Thus in 1939, without any financing, Alinsky began his organizing career in Chicago's "Back of the Yards" slum district. The Union Stockyards slum had been made famous by Upton Sinclair's book *The Jungle*. Marion K. Sanders, writing in *Harper's* magazine [152], says of the Back of the Yards Neighborhood Council:

[It was] an effective coalition of Catholic priests, left-wing labor leaders, local businessmen, and the stockyard workers. The catalyst of this mass movement was shared anger. The common enemies were the meatpackers, slum landlords, a City Hall dominated by a callous political machine and bankers who turned their backs on small homeowners in need of mortgages, and on small merchants seeking credit. The tools were picket lines and boycotts, mass meetings, rent strikes, demonstrations, and sit downs. Conservative Americans were dismayed by these aggressive tactics. They also caused consternation in "liberal" circles, dedicated to benign, orderly social-welfare programs. As a result the Back of the Yards movement and its originator became objects of bitter controversy.

According to several observers, the Back of the Yards organization turned the area into a model working-class neighborhood. [74, 161] The tactics used in the neighborhood were patterned after John L. Lewis's union-organizing strategies. (Alinsky's second book was *John L. Lewis: A Biography*, published in 1949.)

I learned a lot about organizing tactics watching him and working with him in the early days of the CIO. Many things that happen during an organization drive are utterly unplanned and the biggest job of a leader is to develop a rationale, a moral basis for these spontaneous actions. [152]

While Alinsky was involved with the Back of the Yards Neighborhood Council, a liberal Catholic clergyman, Bishop Bernard J. Shiel, introduced him to the millionaire Marshall Field. Field was impressed with Alinsky's work and set up the Industrial Areas Foundation (IAF) with a grant of $15,000, one half of which was for Alinsky's salary and travel expenses. Alinsky had been somewhat dubious about the foundation idea at first, but was finally persuaded that the IAF would not hamper his independence. [152]

On one of his first jobs, in a midwestern city, Alinsky was frequently harassed by the police and, although never booked, often found himself arrested and put into jail. It was in jail that he wrote his first book, *Reveille for Radicals*, in 1946.

[This book] blueprinted his design for militant "people's organizations" which would translate the despair born of frustration, hopelessness, and apathy into fruitful action. [152]

In the 1940's and 1950's Alinsky concentrated his efforts primarily on Mexican-American slums (some thirty of them), New York City's Chelsea section, and slums in Detroit and Chicago. However, it was not until The Woodlawn Organization (TWO) was founded that Alinsky achieved national recognition. [4]

Alinsky's efforts with TWO were of course controversial. According to Charles Silberman, TWO "represents the first instance in which a large, broadly representative organization has come into existence in any Negro district in any large American city." Chicago urban planner Julian Levi, on the other hand, has said that Alinsky's tactics have "been proved in practice in the assembling of lynch mobs." [161] Regardless of these opinions, the Alinsky pattern in the founding of TWO provides a useful comparison to the FIGHT controversy.

The Woodlawn Area of Chicago

The Woodlawn area of the southern part of Chicago is an "oblong slum running south of the University of Chicago campus" and is populated with from 80,000 to 150,000 people, according to how the area is defined. Prior to the depression it was a desirable residential area, but the community showed a decline during the 1940's. In the early 1950's a small, later to become large, migration of Southern blacks began. In 1960, despite the fact that 25 per cent of the area's residents were recipients of money from one welfare program or another, rents were about $10 per month higher than the city's average. The high birthrate in the area soon resulted in overcrowded schools. According to one observer [161],

there is a flourishing traffic in gambling, narcotics, and prostitution. . . . [T]he commercial business district is active but declining, with large numbers of stores vacant. [Woodlawn is the type of community] social workers and city planners assume can never help itself.

An early Alinsky memo said:

The daily lives of Woodlawn people leave them with little energy or enthusiasm for realizing principles from which they themselves will derive little practical benefit. They know that with their education and economic handicaps they will be exceptional indeed if they can struggle into a middle-class neighborhood or a white-collar job. [161]

The Alinsky Pattern of Organization

Alinsky's organizing approach is to appeal to a community's self-interest, resentment, and distrust of outsiders. His aim is to develop indigenous leadership although, at first, full-time IAF organizers are necessary to repair the disunity in the community. They enter an area only after being "invited by something like a cross-section of the population," and insist that the community itself assume full financial responsibility within 3-5 years. From the moment the organization is founded, IAF men steadily phase themselves out of the organization's activities, to be replaced by paid, full-time local people. [161]

The IAF's step-by-step preorganization approach is, first, to send organizers into the community to listen and discover the residents' grievances; second, to find the indigenous leaders; third, to get the leaders together; and finally, to stage a series of demonstrations (rent strikes, for example) which show how effectively community power can be used. In this final stage, the emphasis is on *action*. [161]

The Founding of TWO

The impetus for TWO's founding came from three Protestant ministers and a Catholic priest who were concerned with the "spiraling decline of their neighborhood and the indifference of both the city and the University of Chicago." These men felt that the decline of the community could be checked only if the residents directed their own efforts toward that end. When they first invited Alinsky, he refused, saying he "would not come into Woodlawn until a representative committee had extended the invitation." The invitation was finally extended by the Greater Woodlawn Pastors Alliance, and TWO was founded in the spring-summer of 1960—some 18 months after the four clergymen first invited Alinsky. Financing for the project came from the Catholic Archdiocese of Chicago, the Presbyterian Church of Chicago, and the Schwarzhaupt Foundation, which had supported previous IAF work. [161]

TWO is actually a federation of 85-90 smaller groups allegedly representing some 30,000 Woodlawn residents. These smaller groups include the area's most influential churches, three businessmen's associations, block clubs, neighborhood associations, and social groups. As the IAF staff members began phasing themselves out of the action, the grass-roots nature of the organization came to fruition. In 1963, for example, many of the more active members of TWO's education committee were mothers receiving Aid to Dependent Children. [161] By 1966, TWO was completely under local administration. [4]

Early TWO Activities

The IAF's chief organizer in the Woodlawn area was Nicholas Van Hoffman (who now writes for the *Washington Post* and bitterly attacked Kodak's stance against FIGHT in a column in that newspaper). Hoffman found that two of the chief complaints of many Woodlawnites were high interest rates of credit purchasing and alleged short weights and overcharges in food markets. To gain support for their organization, IAF men brought together a group of honest businessmen and consumers to establish a "Code of Business Ethics," which they publicized with a parade and a "weigh-in." The latter was held at a local Catholic church where residents could come and check the weights and charges on their cash-register slips. The names of the offending merchants were publicized, and "most of the offending merchants quickly agreed to comply with this 'Square Deal' agreement. To bring recalcitrant merchants to terms, leaflets were distributed through the community accusing them of cheating and urging residents to stay away." The Square Deal campaign brought a great deal of publicity to TWO's efforts, "eliminated a considerable amount of exploitation," and brought home the realization that through organization Woodlawnites could improve the circumstances surrounding their lives. [161]

With the momentum of the Square Deal still high, TWO embarrassed landlords who did not keep their property in good repair by picketing the *landlords'* neighborhoods with signs reading "Your neighbor is a slum lord." This tactic frequently brought success within a matter of hours, as landlords quickly called TWO offices agreeing to make repairs. TWO also put pressure on the board of education in connection with overcrowded schools. Soon after TWO members sat outside the school-board chairman's office at Inland Steel (calling him a segregationist), he resigned "because of the pressure of company business." When the superintendent of schools said that overcrowding could not be reduced by transferring black students to all-white schools, TWO sent "truth squads" of mothers into neighboring white schools to photograph empty and half-empty classrooms. Pressure on the board was effective, for by the spring of 1963 the double shift of school attendence was dropped and "over-crowding substantially reduced." [161]

Silberman has written [161]:

The basic characteristic of the slum—its "life style" so to speak—is apathy; no organization can be created unless this apathy can be overcome. But slum residents will not stir unless they see a reasonable chance of winning, unless there is some evidence that they can change things for the better.

The organizers' activities can be compared to war: "the only way to build an army is by winning a few victories," and to gain victories without an army requires guerrilla warfare—concentration on hit-and-run tactics against the enemy's weak spots to insure early victories. Once this guerrilla warfare begins, the best organizing help of all frequently comes from "the enemy"—the established institutions who feel themselves threatened by the new organization. [161] In TWO's case, the established institution was the University of Chicago.

TWO and the University of Chicago

In July 1960, the University of Chicago announced plans to annex a small amount of Woodlawn territory to its campus. The land itself was not going to be missed by many Woodlawnites, but there was a fear that "the annexation of this strip was simply the prelude to bulldozing a large part of Woodlawn itself for middle- and upper-income apartment and town houses." The university had previously driven out blacks from other areas close to its boundaries through "urban renewal," and

unless they [TWO] acted quickly to establish the principle that no plan be adopted for Woodlawn without active participation by Woodlawn residents in the planning process itself, the community might be faced with a *fait accompli.* [161]

TWO reacted to the university's announcement by demanding that the city meet with Woodlawn leaders and discuss a long-range plan for Woodlawn before the university be allowed to expand. If not, "Woodlawnites would lie down in front of the bulldozers and wrecking equipment to prevent them from moving in." Some 300 TWO members overwhelmed a hearing of the City Plan Commission and "succeeded in blocking the quick approval the University had expected." The university responded by attacking "the evil forces" of Alinsky as a church-supported hate group. [161]

Finally, in March 1962, the City Plan Commission did present a comprehensive plan for Woodlawn—"urban renewal clearance, conservation, and rehabilitation, a massive investigation of illiteracy, ill-health, crime and unemployment; a pilot attack on these problems to be financed by large government and foundation grants." However, when asked if the commission had consulted community opinion in its plans, the Coordinating Consultant of the committee said, "There is nobody to speak for the community. A community does not exist in Woodlawn." [161]

TWO responded to these new plans by joining with the Businessmen's

Association and hiring its own city-planning firm to criticize the city's plans and propose alternative actions. The critique found "glaring contradictions" between the city's evaluation of Woodlawn in 1962 when it was mostly black and in 1946 when it was all-white. TWO's planners noticed that

the city's program would demolish a substantial number of attractive, well-kept homes in an area of relatively high owner-occupancy, but left untouched the bulk of the area classified as the most blighted.

TWO also attacked the commission's "social planning" as adamantly as urban renewal planning. At its 1962 convention the organization said that

the best programs are the ones that *we* develop, pay for and direct ourselves . . . opposing all notions of "social planning" by either government or private groups. We will not be planned for as though we were children. [161]

TWO's actions only angered the planners and University of Chicago sociologists who had tried to ignore TWO's existence. TWO found that it did have *political* muscle, however, for Mayor Daley pressured the university's chancellor to meet with TWO representatives. An agreement was reached which, for the first time in the history of urban renewal in the United States, "called for construction of low-income housing on vacant land *before* any existing buildings were torn down." The plan specified that "only houses beyond salvage will be torn down; units to be rehabilitated will be repaired without evicting tenants." City officials also agreed to give TWO majority representation on the citizens' planning committee which would draw up further plans and supervise their execution. [161]

Other TWO Activities

Besides its conflicts with the board of education and the University of Chicago, TWO has persuaded Chicago businesses to open up jobs for blacks, has "stimulated a number of block organizations to clean up and maintain their neighborhoods," and has "forced landlords to repair their property." [161]

TWO's attack on "the silent six" Negro aldermen of the Dawson machine has forced an unaccustomed militancy on them, and thereby changed the whole complexion of Chicago politics. In the process, TWO's president, Rev. Arthur M. Brazier, has become the principal spokesman on civil rights for Chicago Negroes. [161]

Silberman sees the significance of TWO in its having given the members a sense of accomplishment and purpose.

TWO hasn't made Woodlawn a "model community"; it still remains a slum, and an enormous amount of help is needed to reverse the decline of the community. "TWO's greatest contribution, therefore, is its most subtle: it gives Woodlawn residents the sense of dignity that makes it possible for them to accept help." [161]

Alinsky's Philosophy

Alinsky sincerely believes in what he is doing and although, like everyone else, he suffers "that ever-gnawing inner doubt" as to whether he is right, he feels that no one else has a monopoly on "truth." [152]

I've never treated anyone with reverence. . . . I believe irreverence should be part of the democratic faith because in a free society everyone should be questioning and challenging. [153]

Alinsky rarely replies to critics, for, he says, once a person becomes concerned about criticism, it will affect his actions, at least subconsciously:

I told Silberman when he first came in to write about us in *Fortune*, "I don't care what you write. It isn't going to make a bit of difference. Who reads *Fortune* in Woodlawn anyway?"

Alinsky feels that the most significant change in the organizing he has done over the years has been the increasing role of the churches. The churches have taken over the position of the labor unions in supporting his community organizations. [153]

He states that the civil-rights movement falls far short of his organizing techniques in the good it accomplishes for the poor. Whereas Alinsky effectively builds coalitions of people with different goals, civil-rights movements are built on one issue, thus limiting the number of people attracted to the movement. Alinsky appeals to immediate problems; civil-rights groups appeal to distant, abstract goals. In his view,

Civil-rights groups have repeatedly found themselves compelled to demonstrate, not so much because a particular situation demanded action but because action, *any action*, was essential to keep the organization alive. [153]

Some civil-rights leaders are more interested in publicity than in helping people, Alinsky thinks. Demonstrations come, create white backlash, then go—leaving the poor in a worse situation than they were beforehand. [4]

The Achilles' Heel of the civil-rights movement is the fact that it has not developed into a stable, disciplined, mass-based power organization. Many of the significant victories that have been won in civil rights were not the result of mass power strategy. They were caused by the impact of world political pressures, the incredibly stupid blunders of the status quo in the South and elsewhere, and the supporting climate created particularly by the churches. Without the ministers, priests, rabbis, and nuns I wonder who would have been in the Selma march. The tragedy is that the gains that have been made have given many civil-rights spokesmen the illusion that they have the kind of organization and power they need. . . . [T]he truth is that . . . [those] organizations are miniscule in actual size and power. Periodic mass euphoria around a charismatic leader is not an organization. It's just the initial stages of agitation. [153]

Interestingly enough, Alinsky does not "glorify" the poor:

I do not think that people are specially just or charitable or noble because they're unemployed and live in crummy housing and see their kids without any kind of future. . . . Too often I've seen the have-nots turn into haves and become just as crummy as the haves they used to envy. [153]

Alinsky would just as soon organize Mexican-Americans or Indians as blacks. "We're not trying to lead anything," he says. "We're just technicians trying to organize people."

Because Alinsky believes in political participation by the poor, he feels that the government's antipoverty program is turning into a pork barrel for the "welfare industry," a "prize piece of political pornography." [153] Accordingly, accepting money from the local Establishment will not really help the poor, for then class conflicts are ignored and there is no progress without conflict. [74]

Alinsky is often accused of being an outside agitator who "rubs resentments raw." In answer to the "outside agitator" accusation, he responds that the invitation issued by slum dwellers to the IAF is something no other agency allegedly "helping" the poor can claim. [153] As for the "resentments" charge, Alinsky says that he does not need to tell blacks they are being discriminated against. "Don't you think they have resentments to begin with, and how much rawer can I rub them?" [152]

The Industrial Areas Foundation

At this writing, the IAF has a 12-man staff based in Chicago. Over the years Marshall Field's $15,000 grant has been augmented by churches, philanthropists, and foundations to the point where the organization has an annual budget of $250,000. [4, 74] For the most part Alinsky stays in the background, communicates daily with his organizers by telephone, and makes visits to the various communities every few months to "rally his forces." Alinsky draws an annual salary of $25,000, and his organizers earn between $10,000 and $15,000 each. The scope of IAF operations is limited by the difficulties in obtaining good organizers; there is a three-year training period and the turnover is very high. Some of Alinsky's best organizers have gone out on their own, as did Cesar Chavez who is now leading a boycott of California table grapes in support of nonunionized grape pickers. Alinsky eventually hopes to start a permanent training institute for organizers in the New York or San Francisco area. [4] In the middle 1960's Alinsky and the IAF were working with communities in Rochester, Buffalo, Kansas City, Detroit, and were considering St. Louis and Los Angeles. [74]

References

[1] "Alinsky Defends Black Power." *Rochester Times-Union*, October 24, 1966.

[2] "Along the NAACP Battlefront." *Crisis*, August-September 1964, p. 470.

[3] "And Kodak Will Ask, 'How High?' " *Fortune*, June 1, 1967, p. 78.

[4] Anderson, Patrick. "Making Trouble Is Alinsky's Business." *New York Times Magazine*, October 9, 1966, pp. 28ff.

[5] *Ayer Directory of Newspapers and Periodicals, 1967*. Philadelphia: N. W. Ayer and Son, 1968.

[6] Baker, Sam Sinclair. *The Permissible Lie: The Inside Truth about Advertising*. Cleveland: World Publishing, 1968.

[7] Bannon, Anthony. "Alinsky Groups Link Up for 'Big Black' Power." *National Catholic Reporter*, May 10, 1967.

[8] Beardwood, Roger. "The Southern Roots of the Urban Crisis." *Fortune*, August 1968, p. 84.

[9] Bell, Daniel. "Notes on the Post-Industrial Society, I." *Public Interest*, Winter 1967, pp. 24-35.

[10] ———. "Notes on the Post-Industrial Society, II." *Public Interest*, Spring 1967, pp. 102-118.

[11] Bell, L. Nelson. "Church Activists Have Gone Wild." *Presbyterian Journal*, March 8, 1967.

[12] Bennis, Warren G. *Changing Organizations*. New York: McGraw-Hill, 1966.

[13] "Birth Pangs of Black Capitalism, The." *Time*, October 18, 1968, p. 98.

[14] Boller, Chuck. "Priest Backs FIGHT." *Rochester Democrat & Chronicle*, February 2, 1967.

[15] Boulding, Kenneth E. "The Jungle of Hugeness." *Saturday Review*, March 1, 1958, pp. 11ff.

[16] Brady, Fred. "New Way to Deal with Dropouts." *Boston Sunday Advertiser*, October 15, 1967, p. 32.

[17] *Broadcasting Year Book, 1968*. Washington, D.C.: Broadcasting Publications, 1968, p. A-112.

[18] Carter, Barbara. "The Fight against Kodak." *Reporter*, January 21, 1967, pp. 28-31.

[19] Catell, Jacques. *The Physical and Biological Sciences, F-K*, Vol. II: *American Men of Science*, 10th edition. Tempe, Ariz.: Jacques Catell Press, 1960.

[20] Chamberlain, Neil W. *Business and Environment: The Firm in Time and Place*. New York: McGraw-Hill, 1968, pp. 104-105, 112, 120, 141.

[21] "Church and Capitalism, The," in *Chronicles and Documents*. Brussels: Auxiliare de la Presse, S.A. Bureau voor Persknipsels, N.V., 1967.

[22] "Church vs. Kodak: The Big Picture." *Episcopalian*, June 1967, pp. 43-44.

[23] "Church Leaders Put the Squeeze on Kodak." *Christianity Today*, April 28, 1967, p. 1.

[24] Churchman, C. West. *Challenge to Reason*. New York: McGraw-Hill, 1968.

[25] Clark, Kenneth B. *Dark Ghetto: Dilemmas of Social Power*. New York: Harper & Row, 1965.

[26] ———. "No Gimmicks, Please, Whitey." *Training*, November 1968, pp. 27-30.

[27] Cloward, Richard A., and Frances Fox Piven. "Migration, Politics, and Welfare." *Saturday Review*, November 18, 1968, pp. 31-35.

[28] Cohen, Oscar. "The Responsibility of American Business," in Eli Ginzberg, ed., *The Negro Challenge to the Business Community*. New York: McGraw-Hill, 1964, pp. 100-103.

[29] Colitt, Leslie R. "The Mask of Objectivity." *Nation*, June 17, 1968, pp. 789-791.

[30] Commons, John R. *Legal Foundations of Capitalism*. Madison: University of Wisconsin Press, 1959, pp. 144-145.

[31] "Council's Defense." *Rochester Democrat & Chronicle*, June 16, 1967.

[32] Davis, John P., ed. *The American Negro Reference Book*. Englewood Cliffs, N.J.: Prentice-Hall, 1966, p. 293.

[33] Diesing, Paul. *Reason in Society*. Urbana: University of Illinois Press, 1962, p. 246.

[34] Dworsky, David. "Kodak, Olin and Burroughs Shift Top Management." *New York Times*, November 18, 1966, p. 63.

[35] "Eastman Kodak Accuses Rochester Rights Group of Pushing for Power." *Wall Street Journal*, January 9, 1967, p. 10.

[36] "Eastman Kodak Company Annual Report for 1965." Rochester, N.Y.: Eastman Kodak Company, 1966.

[37] "Eastman Kodak Company Annual Report for 1966." Rochester, N.Y.: Eastman Kodak Company, 1967.

[38] "Eastman Kodak and Negro Group Reach Compact to Work in Harmony." *Wall Street Journal*, June 26, 1967, p. 9.

[39] "Economic Justice." Editorial, *Chicago Daily Defender*, National Edition, May 20-26, 1967, p. 10.

[40] "Economic Leverage of the Churches." *America*, May 13, 1967, p. 714.

[41] *Editor & Publisher International Year Book, 1968*. New York: Editor & Publisher Co., 1968, p. 312.

[42] "Equal Employment Opportunity. Eastman Kodak Company's Positive Program." Rochester, N.Y.: Public Relations Department, Eastman Kodak Company, 1967.

[43] Faltermayer, Edmund K. "More Dollars and More Diplomas." *Fortune*, January 1968, pp. 140ff.

[44] "Fight Church Officials May Regret, A." *Christianity Today*, May 12, 1967.

[45] "Fight at Kodak." *Newsweek*, May 8, 1967, pp. 81ff.

[46] "FIGHT vs. Kodak." *Facts on File*, May 4-10, 1967, pp. 154-155.

[47] "Fight That Swirls around Eastman Kodak, The." *Business Week*, April 29, 1967, pp. 38-41.

[48] "FIGHT Vows New Push for Kodak Jobs." *Rochester Democrat & Chronicle*, October 26, 1966.

[49] Flynn, Patrick J. "In Defense of Eastman Kodak." Letter to the editors of *America*, June 10, 1967, p. 823.

[50] Friedman, Milton. *Capitalism and Freedom*. Chicago: University of Chicago Press, 1962.

[51] Galbraith, John Kenneth. *The Affluent Society*. Boston: Houghton Mifflin, 1958.

[52] ———. *The New Industrial State*. Boston: Houghton Mifflin, 1967.

[53] Gassler, Lee S. "How Companies Are Helping the Undereducated Worker." *Personnel*, July-August 1967, pp. 47-55.

[54] "GM Apologizes for Harassment of Critic." *New York Times*, March 23, 1966, p. 1.

[55] Gottschalk, Earl C., Jr. "Kodak's Ordeal: How a Firm That Meant Well Won a Bad Name for Its Race Relations." *Wall Street Journal*, June 30, 1967, pp. 1ff.

[56] Graham, Gene S. "History in the (Deliberate) Making: A Challenge to Modern Journalism." *Nieman Reports*, September 1966, pp. 3-7.

[57] ———. "The Responsibilities of the Doubly Damned." *Quill*, February 1968, pp. 8-12.

[58] "Handicraft Plan Offered by Kodak." *New York Times*, December 16, 1967, p. 37.

[59] Harrington, Michael. *The Other America*. New York: Macmillan, 1962.

[60] ———. "The Urgent Case for Social Investment." *Saturday Review*, November 23, 1968, pp. 32-38.

[61] Hayden, Karl. "The Business Corporation as a Creator of Values," in Sidney Hook, ed., *Human Values and Economic Policy*. New York: New York University Press, 1967.

[62] Hayek, Friedrich A. *Road to Serfdom*. Chicago: University of Chicago Press, 1944.

[63] Heilbroner, Robert. *The Future of Capitalism*. New York: Macmillan, 1967.

[64] Henderson, Hazel. "Should Business Tackle Society's Problems?" *Harvard Business Review*, July-August 1968, pp. 77-85.

[65] Herbers, John. "Negro Is Found Lagging Despite 8 Years of Gains." *New York Times*, January 12, 1969, pp. 1ff.

[66] Hodgson, James, and Marshall H. Brenner. "Successful Experience: Training Hard-Core Unemployed." *Harvard Business Review*, September-October 1968, pp. 148-156.

[67] Hoffman, Nicholas Van. "Picture's Fuzzy as Kodak Fights FIGHT." *Washington Post*, January 9, 1967.

[68] Hoover, Paul R. "Social Pressures and Church Policy." *Christianity Today*, July 21, 1967, pp. 12-14.

[69] Hughes, Emmet John. "The Negro's New Economic Life." *Fortune*, September 1956, p. 254.

[70] "Is Black Capitalism the Answer?" *Business Week*, August 3, 1968, p. 60.

[71] "Is the Press Biased?" *Newsweek*, September 16, 1968, pp. 66-67.

[72] Jones, Vincent S. "How Rochester Reacted." *Nieman Reports*, June 1965, pp. 16-17.

[73] Key, V. O., Jr. *Public Opinion and American Democracy*. New York: Knopf, 1961, p. 515.

[74] Kifner, John. "Critics Assailed by Head of Kodak: He Accuses Negro Group of Power Drive Upstate." *New York Times*, January 7, 1967, p. 25.

[75] ———. "Kodak Holds Its Meeting amid Racial Protests." *New York Times*, April 26, 1967, p. 49.

[76] ———. "Methodists to Withhold Proxies to Question Kodak on Rights." *New York Times*, April 8, 1967, p. 16.

[77] ———. "Negro Ad Agency Hired by Kodak." *New York Times*, April 28, 1967, p. 46.

[78] ———. "Negro Federation Points to Advances in Its First Year in Rochester." *New York Times*, June 20, 1966, p. 26.

[79] ———. "Negroes to Set Up Company Upstate." *New York Times*, June 21, 1968, p. 24.

[80] ———. "Sheen to Help Rochester 'Inner City.' " *New York Times*, January 6, 1967, p. 23.

[81] ———. "21 Kodak Investors Withhold Proxies." *New York Times*, April 17, 1967, p. 25.

[82] ———. "2 Churches Withhold Proxies to Fight Kodak Rights Policies." *New York Times*, April 7, 1967, p. 1.

[83] "Kodak Announces Plan to Help Slum Dwellers Start Own Business." *Wall Street Journal*, November 20, 1967, p. 15.

[84] "Kodak to Continue Training Program." *New York Times*, April 2, 1968, p. 18.

[85] "Kodak Defended by Xerox on Jobs." *New York Times*, May 20, 1967, p. 16.

[86] "Kodak-FIGHT Accord." *Facts on File*, September 7-13, pp. 377-378.

[87] "Kodak and FIGHT Agree to Agree." *Business Week*, July 1, 1967, p. 22.

[88] "Kodak Job Plan Rejected." *New York Times*, January 11, 1967, p. 19.

[89] "Kodak Officials to Meet Rochester Rights Group Today on Disputed Pact." *Wall Street Journal*, December 12, 1966, p. 4.

[90] "Kodak Questions FIGHT Job Demands." *Rochester Democrat & Chronicle*, September 8, 1966.

[91] "Kodak Refuses to Restore Negro Job Pact; Rights Group Vows 'War' against Concern." *Wall Street Journal*, April 26, 1967, p. 7.

[92] "Kodak Reviews Record on Job Talks with FIGHT." *Rochester Times-Union*, September 21, 1966.

[93] "Kodak Will Train Negroes for Jobs." *New York Times*, November 18, 1967, p. 34.

[94] Kuhn, J. W., and Ivar Berg. *Values in a Business Society*. New York: Harcourt, Brace & World, 1968, pp. 150-153, 262-268.

[95] Lees, Hannah. "The Not-Buying Power of Philadelphia's Negroes." *Reporter*, May 11, 1961, pp. 33-35.

[96] Leonard, Richard. "Role of the Press in the Urban Crisis." *Quill*, May 1968, pp. 8-11.

[97] Lewin, Kurt. *Resolving Social Conflicts*. New York: Harper & Row, 1948, pp. 195-196.

[98] Livadas, Dorothy. "The FIGHT-Kodak Fight." *National Review*, June 27, 1967, p. 683.

[99] Loh, Jules. Associated Press feature story for Sunday A.M. papers, April 23, 1967.

[100] Lyford, Joseph P. "Business and the Negro Community," in Eli Ginzberg, ed., *The Negro Challenge to the Business Community*. New York: McGraw-Hill, 1964, pp. 96-100.

[101] MacIver, R. M. *Community: A Sociological Study*. London: Macmillan, 1928, as reproduced in Clarence Walton and Richard Eells, eds., *The Business System*, Vol. II. New York: Macmillan, 1967, pp. 1144-1148.

[102] McConnell, Grant. *Private Power and American Democracy*. New York: Knopf, 1966, pp. 119-154.

[103] McKersie, Robert B. "Vitalize Black Enterprise." *Harvard Business Review*, September-October 1968, pp. 88-99.

[104] Mallon, Paul W. "But and Rebut." Letters to the editors of *America*, May 6, 1967, pp. 664-665.

[105] Martin, William C. "Shepherds vs. Flocks, Ministers vs. Negro Militancy." *Atlantic*, December 1967, pp. 53-59.

[106] "Meet Ralph Nader, Everyman's Lobbyist, and His Consumer Crusade." *Newsweek*, January 22, 1968, pp. 65-73.

[107] "Meeting of Minds." *Forbes*, October 1, 1965, pp. 37-38.

[108] Mises, Ludwig Von. *Human Action*. New Haven: Yale University Press, 1949.

[109] "Moral of the Story." *Newsweek*, November 11, 1968, p. 80.

[110] National Council of Churches of Christ in the United States of America. "Background Paper of Information Relating to Resolution on the Use of Economic Pressure in Racial Tensions." Prepared by Department of Church and Economic Life, in consultation with Department of Cultural Relations of Division of Christian Life and Work, June 9, 1963, p. 5.

[111] ———. "Christian Influence toward the Development and Use of All Labor Resources without Regard to Race, Color and Religion or National Origin." Resolution adopted by General Assembly, December 9, 1960.

[112]   ———. "Christian Principles and Assumptions for Economic Life."
Resolution adopted by General Board, September 15, 1954.

[113]   ———. "The Church as Purchaser of Goods and Services." Policy
statement adopted by General Board, September 12, 1968.

[114]   ———. "The Churches' Concern for Housing." Resolution adopted
by General Board, November 18, 1953.

[115]   ———. "The Churches and Segregation." Resolution adopted by
General Board, June 11, 1952.

[116]   ———. "Resolution on the Sit-in Demonstrations." Adopted by
General Board, June 2, 1960.

[117]   ———. "Statement on the Decision of the U.S. Supreme Court on
Segregation in the Public Schools." Adopted by General Board, May
19, 1954.

[118]   ———. "The Use of Economic Pressure in Racial Tensions." Resolution adopted by General Board, June 8, 1963.

[119]   "Negro Business Feels Stresses." *Business Week*, April 9, 1966, pp.
70-74.

[120]   Nisbet, Robert A. *The Quest for Community*. New York: Oxford
University Press, 1953, as reproduced in Clarence Walton and Richard
Eells, eds., *The Business System*, Vol. II. New York: Macmillan, 1967,
pp. 1149-1154.

[121]   "Notable and Quotable." *Wall Street Journal*, January 15, 1969, p.
7.

[122]   "Of Many Things." *America*, July 8, 1967, p. 2.

[123]   O'Hanlon, Thomas. "The Case against the Unions." *Fortune*, January 1968, pp. 170ff.

[124]   "One Man's Meet." *Newsweek*, December 4, 1967, pp. 29-30.

[125]   "Ordeal of the Black Businessman, The." *Newsweek*, March 4,
1968, p. 34.

[126]   "Our Readers Write Their Views." *Rochester Democrat & Chronicle*, January 23, 1967.

[127]   Packard, Vance. *The Hidden Persuaders*. New York: David McKay
Co., 1957.

[128]   ———. *The Waste Makers*. New York: David McKay Co., 1960.

[129]   "Pastors Refer to FIGHT Case." *Rochester Times-Union*, January
23, 1967.

[130]   Peterson, William J. "J. Irwin Miller: The Revolutionary Role of
Business." *Saturday Review*, January 13, 1968, pp. 62-72.

[131]   Pettigrew, Thomas. "White-Negro Confrontations," in Eli Ginzberg, ed., *The Negro Challenge to the Business Community*. New York:
McGraw-Hill, 1964, pp. 39-55.

[132]   *Plan for Establishing Independently Owned and Operated Business
in Inner-City Areas, A*. Rochester, N.Y.: Eastman Kodak Company,
November 1967.

[133]   Polanyi, Karl. *The Great Transformation*. Boston: Beacon Press,
1957, p. 46.

[134]   "Presbyterian Unit Bars Kodak Proxies." *New York Times*, April
13, 1967, p. 52.

[135] Purcell, Theodore V. "Break Down Your Employment Barriers." *Harvard Business Review*, July-August 1968, pp. 65-76.

[136] "Pushing Harder for Ghetto Jobs." *Business Week*, January 20, 1968, pp. 123-126.

[137] "Rare Days in Any Month." *United Church Herald*, August 1967, p. 23.

[138] "Re: Church Strikes and Boycotts." Editorial, *Presbyterian Journal*, March 8, 1967.

[139] Reagan, Michael D. *The Managed Economy*. New York: Oxford University Press, 1967.

[140] Redding, Saunders. "The Methods," in John Hope Franklin and Isidore Starr, eds., *The Negro in America*. New York: Vintage Books, 1967, pp. 113-116.

[141] *Register of Corporations, Directors, and Executives, 1968*. New York: Standard and Poor's, 1968.

[142] *Report of the National Advisory Commission on Civil Disorders*. New York: Bantam Books, 1968, pp. 362-388, 558-569.

[143] "Reporters Are Subpoenaed for Hearing on ABC-ITT." *Wall Street Journal*, April 20, 1967, p. 19.

[144] Ridgeway, James. "Attack on Kodak." *New Republic*, January 21, 1967, pp. 11-13.

[145] ———. "Saul Alinsky in Smugtown." *New Republic*, June 26, 1965, pp. 15-17.

[146] "Rochester Gets Training Program." *New York Times*, March 31, 1968, p. 17

[147] "Rochester Honors Dr. King." *New York Times*, April 18, 1968, p. 95.

[148] "Rochester Slums May Get Factory." *New York Times*, November 4, 1967, p. 38.

[149] *Rochester Times-Union*, October 24, 1962.

[150] "Rochester's Second Riot Played under 2-Col. Head." *Editor & Publisher*, July 29, 1967, p. 12.

[151] Rostow, Eugene V. "To Whom and For What Ends Is Corporate Management Responsible?" in Edward S. Mason, ed., *The Corporation in a Modern Society*. New York: Atheneum, 1966, pp. 46-71.

[152] Sanders, Marion K. "The Professional Radical. Conversations with Saul Alinsky, Part I." *Harper's*, June 1965, pp. 37-47.

[153] ———. "A Professional Radical Moves in on Rochester. Conversations with Saul Alinsky, Part II." *Harper's*, July 1965, pp. 52-59.

[154] Schaertel, Elmer G. "A Pastor Speaks Up for Kodak." *Rochester Democrat & Chronicle*, January 15, 1967.

[155] Schroth, Raymond A. "Return to Rochester—One Year After . . ." *America*, August 14, 1965, pp. 163-164.

[156] ———. "Self-Doubt and Black Pride." *America*, April 1, 1967, p. 502.

[157] Schwartz, Louis B. "Institutional Size and Individual Liberty: Authoritarian Aspects of Bigness." *Northwestern University Law Review*, March-April 1960, pp. 4-20.

[158] Selekman, Sylvia K., and Benjamin M. Selekman. *Power and Morality in a Business Society*. New York: McGraw-Hill, 1956.

[159] Sethi, S. Prakash, and Dow Votaw. "Do We Need a New Corporate Response to a Changing Social Environment? Part II." *California Management Review*, Fall 1969.

[160] "Sheen Appoints a Vicar for Poor." *New York Times*, January 4, 1967, p. 4.

[161] Silberman, Charles. *Crisis in Black and White*. New York: Random House, 1964, pp. 142-144, 153-155, 312-313.

[162] Smith, Richard A. *Corporations in Crisis*. Garden City, N.Y.: Doubleday, 1964, p. 19.

[163] Tannenbaum, Frank. "Institutional Rivalry in Society." *Political Science Quarterly*, December 1946, pp. 481-504.

[164] "Target: Negro Jobs." *Newsweek*, July 1, 1968, pp. 21-30.

[165] "There's a FIGHT in Kodak's Future." *Factory*, June 1967, p. 69.

[166] "TV's Credibility Gap." *Newsweek*, January 6, 1969, pp. 42-43.

[167] Votaw, Dow, and S. Prakash Sethi. "Do We Need a New Corporate Response to a Changing Social Environment? Part I," *California Management Review*, Fall 1969.

[168] Walton, Clarence C. *Corporate Social Responsibilities*. Belmont, Calif.: Wadsworth, 1967, pp. 70, 73-75.

[169] ———, and Richard Eells, eds. *The Business System*, Vol. II, New York: Macmillan, 1967, p. 1141.

[170] "What Business Can Do for the Cities." Editorial, *Fortune*, January 1968, pp. 127-128.

[171] "What the Kodak Fracas Means." Editorial, *Business Week*, May 6, 1967.

[172] "What Negroes Think." *Fortune*, January 1968, pp. 140ff.

[173] Whitaker, Arthur L. "Anatomy of a Riot." *Crisis*, January 1965, pp. 20-25.

[174] "Who's Out of Focus? A Note on the Harassment of Eastman Kodak." *Barron's National Business and Financial Weekly*, May 1, 1967, p. 1.

[175] Whyte, William H., Jr., and the Editors of Fortune Magazine. *Is Anybody Listening?* New York: Simon and Schuster, 1952.

[176] "Widening of Anti-Semitism Seen in 'Black Revolt.' " *New York Times*, December 29, 1968, p. 36.

[177] Williams, Robin M., Jr. *The Reduction of Intergroup Tensions*. New York: Social Science Research Council, 1947, p. 61.

[178] Witcover, Jules. "Rochester Braces for Another July." *Reporter*, July 15, 1965, pp. 33-35.

[179] *World Almanac, 1968, The*. Cleveland: Newspaper Enterprise Association, 1967.

[180] Wright, Robert A. "Kodak Meeting Keeps Cool on Rights Issue." *New York Times*, May 1, 1968, p. 63.

[181] "Xerox Will Assist Rochester Negroes." *New York Times*, June 16, 1968, p. 35.

[182] *Yearbook of American Churches.* New York: National Council of Churches of Christ in the United States of America, 1965.

[183] Zeidman, Philip F. "The Negro Businessman, the Need for Help." *Vital Speeches,* January 15, 1968, p. 210.

[184] Ziegler, Harmon. *Interest Groups in American Society.* Englewood Cliffs, N.J.: Prentice-Hall, 1964, pp. 210-213, 221-226, 233-243.

Index